B1 Ref

D0302188

Pressure Groups and British Politics

X

METROPOLITAN BOROUGH OF WIRRAL

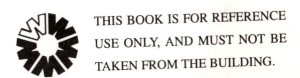

THIS BOOK IS FOR REFERENCE
USE ONLY, AND MUST NOT BE
TAKEN FROM THE BUILDING.

LEISURE SERVICES & TOURISM DEPARTMENT
LIBRARIES AND ARTS.

Contemporary Political Studies

Series Editor: John Benyon, *University of Leicester*

Pressure Groups
and British Politics

Wyn Grant

First published in Great Britain 2000 by
MACMILLAN PRESS LTD
Houndmills, Basingstoke, Hampshire RG21 6XS and London
Companies and representatives throughout the world

A catalogue record for this book is available from the British Library.

ISBN 0–333–74484–5 hardcover
ISBN 0–333–74485–3 paperback

First published in the United States of America 2000 by
ST. MARTIN'S PRESS, INC.,
Scholarly and Reference Division,
175 Fifth Avenue, New York, N.Y. 10010

ISBN 0–312–22648–9

Library of Congress Cataloging-in-Publication Data
Grant, Wyn.
Pressure groups and British politics / Wyn Grant.
p. cm.
Includes bibliographical references and index.
ISBN 0–312–22648–9 (cloth)
1. Pressure groups–Great Britain.   I. Title.
JN329.P7G69   1999
324'.4'0941—dc21   99–23758
                                                    CIP

This book is printed on paper suitable for recycling and made from fully managed and sustained forest sources.

10 9 8 7 6 5 4 3 2 1
09 08 07 06 05 04 03 02 01 00

Printed in Hong Kong

Contents

Abbreviations

AA	Automobile Association
ALF	Animal Liberation Front
ASA	Advertising Standards Authority
ASAG	Advisory and Support Group
ATL	Association of Teachers and Lecturers
BMA	British Medical Association
BSE	Bovine Spongiform Encephalopathy
CAP	Common Agricultural Policy
CBI	Confederation of British Industry
CEEP	European Centre for Publc Enterprises
CEFIC	European Chemical Industry Council
CFI	Court of First Instance
CIA	Chemical Industries Association
CJD	Creutzfeld Jakob Disease
CNE	Climate Network Europe
COGECA	Comité Genéral de la Coopération Agricole des Pays de la Communauté
COPA	Comité des Organizations Professionelles Agricoles
COREPER	Committee of Permanent Representatives
CPAG	Child Poverty Action Group
CPRE	Council for the Protection of Rural England
DTI	Department of Trade and Industry
EAIC	European-American Industrial Council
EATP	European Association of Textile Polyolefins
ECJ	European Court of Justice
EEB	European Environmental Bureau
EEO	European Express Organization
EMU	Economic and Monetary Union
EP	European Parliament
ERT	European Round Table
ESC	Economic and Social Committee
ETUC	European Trade Union Confederation

EUROPMI Independent	European Committee for Small and Medium-Sized Companies
HDTV	High Density Television
IEA	Institute of Economic Affairs
IECC	International Express Carriers Conference
IGC	InterGovernmental Conference
IMUSA	Independent Manchester United Supporters' Association
LEA	local education authority
LMS	local management of schools
MAFF	Ministry of Agriculture, Fisheries and Food
MAG	Motor Cycle Action Group
NATFHE	National Association of Teachers in Further and Higher Education
NEDC	National Economic Development Council
NFU	National Farmers' Union
NFOAPA	National Federation of Old Age Pensioners' Associations
NFRPA	National Federation of Retirement Pensions Associations
NGQs	non-governmental organizations
NUT	National Union of Teachers
QMV	qualified majority voting
RSPB	Royal Society for the Protection of Birds
RSPCA	Royal Society for the Prevention of Cruelty to Animals
SME	small and medium sized enterprise
SOS	Save Our Solsbury
TUC	Trades Union Congress
UEAPME	European Association of Craft, Small and Medium-Sized Enterprises
UNICE	Union of Industrial and Employers' Confederations

List of Tables, Boxes and Figures

Preface

This book seeks to provide a general review of the role of pressure groups in British democracy. While some material is reproduced from the book published in two editions as *Pressure Groups, Politics and Democracy in Britain*, so much has been added and revised as to justify publication as a new book. Reflecting the upsurge of work on pressure groups at the EU level, the sections dealing with this topic have been expanded and substantially rewritten. A considerable amount of new material is included on direct action politics and also on the role of the media. There is a new chapter on the politics of production and collective consumption which attempts to reflect on some of the shifts in pressure group politics in the context of changes in society as a whole. The typology of insider and outsider groups is revisited and defended against some of its critics. Other parts of the book have been rewritten to take account of new literature and developments.

While this book was prepared, Mancur Olson Jnr, a leading theorist of pressure groups, sadly died. I had the opportunity of meeting him on a number of occasions. While I do not find myself in agreement with all his arguments, I have always found his work stimulating. Not all academics who have accomplished so much were as open or approachable, or as willing to discuss their work with anyone, whatever their standing.

I would like to thank two younger members of the political science profession for permission to quote from their research theses: Eva Gronbech and Nicholas Robinson. I also benefited from reading the final draft of Annabel Kiernan's thesis on policy networks when I was completing the book. Professor Edward Page of the University of Hull permitted me to quote from and make use of an as yet unpublished critique of the insider–outsider distinction. Carsten Daugbjerg of the University of Aarhus allowed me to reproduce a table from his book on policy networks.

This book is dedicated to the memory of my uncle, Sidney Field, who sadly died before publication of the first edition.

Conversations I heard as a child in his newsagent's shop in Plumstead SE18 helped to stimulate my interest in politics, and gave me my first lessons in looking for the story behind the story in the day's newspapers. One writer quoted in the first version of the book wrote to point out to me that we had been fellow pupils at St.Margaret's Church of England Primary School and other former pupils have contacted me via the Internet. Alternatively, anyone can find me in the Rose of Denmark before Charlton home games.

I would like to express special thanks to my publisher, Steven Kennedy, with whom I have now worked for many years. This has been a very fruitful relationship and I am grateful for his suggestions for editorial improvements.

As always, special thanks are due to my wife, Maggie, who was writing up an updated version of her own work on pressure groups at the same time as I was working on this book.

Leamington   WYN GRANT

1
Introduction: the Key Characteristics of Pressure Groups

Pressure groups lie at the heart of the political process in Britain. The largest pressure group with one million members, just under a thousand staff and an income of nearly £35 million in 1997 is the Royal Society for the Protection of Birds (RSPB). Two-and-half times more people are members of the RSPB than of the Labour Party.

The freedom to associate is at the heart of liberal democracy and the presence of a vast array of political associations in Britain could be seen as a sign of a healthy civil society. There is, however, a less sanguine view of pressure groups. Some see 'vested interests' such as big business, farmers or doctors distorting the political process through the resources of finance and influence they are able to mobilize. Other commentators are worried about the rise of 'single issue' pressure groups which they see as putting pressure on politicians to respond to their particular demands without any regard to the other policy options that have to be given up in terms of public spending or the impact on other groups in society.

Much of this book will be concerned with explaining how pressure groups set about seeking to influence political decisions. Which are the principal pressure groups and how are they organized? What is the structure of the policy process they are trying to influence and what are the strategies and tactics that they use? To what extent are they effective? However, an attempt will also be made to tackle broader issues about the role of pressure groups in a democracy. Does the existence of such groups enhance the democratic process, or undermine it? Do the activities of pressure groups tend to reinforce existing distributions of power in society, or can they bring about fundamental changes?

Continuity and Change in the Role of Pressure Groups

The second half of the twentieth century might be regarded as the era of pressure groups in British politics. The postwar settlement created a 'Keynesian welfare state' which increased government intervention in the economy and in the social sphere. Pressure groups were created or revitalized in response to this more interventionist climate, both because their members needed government representation and because government required their expert advice and informed consent. The trade unions were established as a major and legitimate political interest and the importance of business associations was enhanced. A number of other interests acquired a new importance as they were drawn into a closer relationship with government, for example, the medical profession and local government.

The basic pattern of relationships established during the war and in the immediate postwar period persisted throughout the 1950s and the 1960s. The main development was an even closer relationship between government, business and the unions, exemplified by the formation of the tripartite National Economic Development Council in 1962. With some prompting from the Labour Government, business reorganized into one peak association, the Confederation of British Industry (CBI) in 1965 to facilitate a more effective dialogue with government. It says much of the temper of the times that the Labour prime minister, Harold Wilson, could talk of the arrangements for 'negotiations on broad policy with the CBI and the TUC' (Wilson, 1974, pp.287–8).

This tripartite relationship with the CBI and TUC was intensified by the Heath Government once it moved away from its original intention to pursue less interventionist policies. The cooperation of the CBI and the TUC was seen as crucial to obtain price restraint on the one hand and wage restraint on the other. This even closer relationship with the main economic interests came to be characterized, somewhat inaccurately, as corporatism.

The two defeats of the Conservatives in the 1974 elections sounded the death knell of Heath's tripartite approach within the Conservative Party. The new Labour Government continued to operate very much on tripartite lines. The unions were able to obtain a number of important legislative concessions, while the employers were able substantially to modify or kill off policies of which they disapproved, such as state intervention in industry or industrial democracy. The importance of the leading pressure groups was emphasized in major statements of government policy such as the 1978 Queen's Speech which contained the declaration, 'My Ministers will co-operate closely with the Trades Union Congress and the Confederation of British Industry'. The tripartite embrace was even extended to new organizations such as the Retail Consortium which was involved in a 'red triangle' scheme to limit increases in the prices of basic foodstuffs. Interests which found themselves outside these arrangements, such as small businesses and local taxpayers, formed new and more militant organizations (King and Nugent, 1979).

The election of Mrs Thatcher heralded a new approach to pressure group relationships. The CBI and the TUC found themselves sidelined, with a greater welcome being given to organizations like the Institute of Directors which were more in tune with government thinking. Mrs Thatcher made clear her opposition to established interests, stating in a television interview in June 1984, 'I can give you a check list now of the way in which we have tackled vested interest'. Some of the weaker professions such as opticians certainly did lose their protected position, as did teachers and, to a lesser extent, the medical profession, although farmers emerged relatively unscathed. It should be emphasized, however, that many of the routine relationships between government and pressure groups at departmental level continued largely unaltered and from the viewpoint of many pressure groups, these were the relationships that mattered in terms of obtaining concessions for their members.

Although the Major Government was more inclined to moderate the style of its approach, the retreat of many established interests tended to continue. As some of the long established interests found themselves unwillingly giving ground, the vacuum they left was filled to some extent by a new set of groups with very different agendas. What had happened since the 1970s was the development of a considerable number of new cause groups, particularly in the areas of the environment and animal protection. Excluding the rather special case of the National Trust, membership of environmental organizations in Britain has quadrupled since 1971 (Hall, 1998, p.3). Unlike long established cause groups such as the Council for the Protection of Rural England (CPRE) or the Howard League for Penal Reform, which counted many of 'the great and the good' among their members and relied on tactics of quiet persuasion and a 'word in the right ear', many of these new cause groups were less respectful of established procedures and more reliant on forms of direct action.

With its sometimes almost suffocating inclusiveness, the Blair Government was prepared to enter into a dialogue with a wide range of groups. Closer relationships were re-established with big business and, to a much lesser extent, with the trade unions. However, there was no reversion to the old-style corporatism of the 1970s. One would not find the Blair Government referring to the CBI or the TUC in the Queen's Speech. The CBI once occupied fifteen floors of Centre Point in Tottenham Court Road, but its smaller staff can now be accommodated on just two floors. Organizations like the teaching unions continued to find themselves marginalized in terms of their influence on policy. A politics of production had been replaced by a politics of collective consumption, a shift largely endorsed by the Blair Government in its attempt to define a 'Third Way' which could be seen as representing a compromise between Thatcherite neo-liberalism and traditional social democracy.

The Range and Significance of Pressure Group Activity

It is difficult to say how many pressure groups there are in Britain, as many voluntary organizations intervene only sporadically in the political process when their interests are threatened. What is clear is that a tremendous diversity of interests and causes is represented from small businesses to sexual minorities and from the elderly to motor cyclists. Some of the largest organizations in terms of income and staff resources continue to represent long established sectional interests. For example, the British Medical Association (BMA) had a staff of 635 and 114 000 members in 1998 and the National Farmers' Union (NFU) employed 808 staff to look after its 121 454 members (although many of its local staff spend much of their time selling insurance to farmers) (figures from *Trade Association Forum, 1998*). Table 1.1 below provides a snapshot of the range of pressure groups and their relative resources, selecting one leading group from each of a number of categories.

Some of the most important associations are not necessarily the most visible. The associations representing local government have enjoyed a close relationship with government throughout the postwar period, given that their members are responsible for implementing much government legislation. Compared 'with other major pressure groups such as the CBI and TUC, the [local government] associations could be described as fairly affluent' (Rhodes, 1986, p.95). They were, however, always weakened by conflicts between the associations representing different types of authority. These were overcome by the formation of a single

Local Government Association in 1997 which can be expected to enjoy a close working relationship with government. It quickly became involved in as many as fifty different policy areas and claimed some early policy successes.

The associations which represent business interests, organized labour and the professions are flanked by a wide range of cause groups covering a range of issues from penal reform to third world aid. The groups with the largest membership are, however, to be found in the areas of the environment and animal protection. Their membership has expanded rapidly over the last twenty-five years at a time when the membership of political parties has been declining.

For the ordinary citizen, apart from voting, participation in pressure group activity is one of the most commonly experienced forms of political activity. In the British Political Participation Study, 14.6 per cent of respondents had attended a protest meeting, 13.8 per cent had engaged in informal group activity and 11.2 per cent in an organized group. In contrast, 8.6 per cent had attended a party meeting and 3.5 per cent had canvassed for a political party (Parry, Moyser and Day, 1992, p.44). Politics is a minority activity (although the composition of the minority is constantly changing), but for those who do participate, pressure groups offer what may be seen as one of the more accessible means of influencing decision-makers.

Pressure groups exert influence on the policy process in Britain and at the EU level in a wide variety of ways from direct action protests to discussions with ministers. To a large extent, however, the way in which they exert influence is substantially affected by the structure of the policy process. Pressure groups tend to cluster where the power is which in Britain and Europe is principally in the executive branch of government (see Chapters 4 and 6). The extent to which they are effective is a complex methodological problem which is explored in depth in Chapter 10, but the case study in Chapter 4 of the attempt to form a Food Standards Agency shows how groups may be effective, while examples at the European level are provided in Chapter 6.

Before starting to examine how pressure groups exert influence, and the extent to which they are effective, it is necessary to explore what is meant by a pressure group. A number of problems have to be resolved before a definition can be attempted.

Table 1.1   The range of pressure groups

Category and group	Members (individuals)	Staff	Income range
Business:			
CBI	250 000 (firms)	220	B
Organized labour			
TUC	69 (unions)	200	B
Agriculture:			
NFU	121 000	808	A
Professions:			
British Medical Assn.	114 000	635	A
Local government:			
Local Government Assn.	480 (local authorities)	200	A
Elderly:			
Age Concern	N/A	575	A
Consumers:			
Consumers' Assn.	781 000	521	A
Women's organizations:			
National Federation of Women's Institutes	296 000	41	C
Animal protection:			
Royal Society for Protection of Birds	1,000,000	923	A
Environment:			
Friends of the Earth	200 000	110	B
Amenity organizations:			
Ramblers Association	126 000	35/40	B
Conservation and biodiversity:			
World Wide Fund for Nature	245 000	203	A
Poverty:			
Child Poverty Action Group	N/A	27	B
Mental health:			
Mind	1600	143	B

Category and group	Members (individuals)	Staff	Income range
Disability:			
Disablement Income Group	3 000 plus 1 200 (organizations)	N/A	C
Civil liberties/penal reform:			
Liberty	7 000 plus 700 (organizations)	N/A	C
Abortion:			
Society for Protection of Unborn Child	50 000	N/A	C

Notes: Some figures are approximate
Income categories:
A – Over £5 million
B – £1 to £5 million
C – Under £1 million

Sources: Directory of British Associations, 1998; Barings Asset Management, Top 3000 Charities, 1997; *Trade Association Forum Directory*, 1998; personal information.

What is a Pressure Group?

This book is concerned with groups that seek to influence public policy – which can be formulated by central government, local government, the European Union, or, in some cases, by quasi-governmental organizations. The emphasis on public policy is important because any organized entity with the capacity to make authoritative decisions may develop internal pressure groups. For example, a firm may be viewed as a political organization, and groups within it may lobby for a particular investment decision. In the case of a firm, such groups will not normally be formally constituted, but their identity will often be well known to other participants in a decision-making process. Other groups with decision-making authority may see the formation of advocacy groups with a particular purpose: for example, the successful movement for the ordination of women within the Church of England has been replicated by the formation of an as yet smaller movement within the Roman Catholic Church. Groups of this kind have their own fascination, but the focus of this book is on the political processes of society as a whole, rather than on particular organizations within it, however significant they may be either to their own members or to society in general.

This book is concerned with organized entities that have characteristics such as a defined membership, stated objectives in relation to public policy and, often, a paid staff working to attain those objectives. One problem that immediately arises is what we should call such entities. Many of them would object to the term 'pressure group' on the grounds that it implies an improper or at least distasteful exertion of pressure and would prefer the term 'non-governmental organization'. It is certainly a term that is increasingly used by international organizations such as the World Trade Organization which has issued guidelines to cover its relations with such organizations. Other than they are independent of government, it is difficult to give a precise definition of what a non-governmental organization is. The World Bank comments (1990, not paginated): 'The diversity of NGOs strains any simple definition. They include many groups that are entirely or largely independent of government and that have primarily humanitarian or co-operative rather than commercial objectives.' Indeed, even the criterion of independence from government is often difficult to meet, as, for example, many third world aid organizations act as agencies for the distribution of government funds (Burnell, 1997).

It is therefore appropriate to retain the widely recognized term 'pressure group', while emphasizing that its use does not imply any pejorative statement about the methods used by such groups. Nevertheless, there are four important issues of definition that require further attention: the relationship between an 'interest' and the pressure groups that seek to promote that interest; the relationship between a 'social movement' and the pressure groups it generates; the problem of pressure exerted by a single actor such as a firm; and the problem of whether parts of the machinery of government itself can be regarded as pressure groups.

The first of these problems, then, is concerned with the relationship between an interest and the groups that represent that interest. 'Interest' is a word with many meanings. Some of these, such as a legal concern or pecuniary stake in property, or the payment of money to service a debt, need not be discussed here. Other meanings, such as the idea of the selfish pursuit of one's own welfare, have value-laden overtones which are best avoided. The meaning of interest which is particularly relevant here is what the *Concise Oxford Dictionary* terms a 'thing in which one is concerned; principle in which a party is concerned; party having a common interest *(the brewing interest)*'. So defined, interest covers both the pursuit of causes (such as prison reform) and the promotion and defence of particular stakes in the economy (such as those of farmers). However, interest has been especially used to apply to particular economic identities. Not all of these identities have been organized, at least not as a whole. For example, it has been common to speak of the 'City interest'. This has been considered a very influential interest in Britain for a long time. The influence of the City is often blamed for the overvaluation of sterling for long periods of modern British history, an overvaluation which damaged the international price competitiveness of British manufacturing industry. However, the influence of the City did not rest on its possession of well-organized interest groups. The traditional channel for conveying City opinion to the government was through the Governor of the Bank of England. Very often, however, the influence of the City did not require any overt expression of view. Treasury officials and the City shared common, unquestioned assumptions about the need to maintain the value of sterling. Any sign of pressure on sterling as a result of a loss of confidence in the financial markets was often enough to persuade governments to change their economic policies.

Unorganized interests are, however, tending to diminish in significance. In the City, trade associations for various financial interests, formerly of little significance, have assumed a new importance. There are a variety of reasons for this particular change in the City, including a decline in its social cohesion, the removal of traditional barriers between different types of financial institution, a new regulatory regime which has transformed the role of many trade associations, and a greater openness in the relationship between the Treasury and the Bank of England and a change in their respective roles. That is not to say that the Chancellor no longer sounds out City opinion at informal lunches, or that governments do not anxiously watch trends in market sentiment. Even so, the exercise of influence in modern conditions requires organization. The study of pressure groups is the study of organized interests, although one must always be aware that behind well-defined organizations lurk more amorphous but nevertheless significant bodies of opinion.

Social Movements

The discussion so far has focused on 'sectional' economic interests rather than causes, but problems can also arise in exploring the relationship between broad social movements, and the pressure groups that spring from those movements. Just what a social movement is is in many ways less clear than what a pressure group is. Byrne argues (1997, p.2) that 'one of the distinctive features of social movements is their nebulous nature'. Those definitions that are available seem to focus on their methods: 'Social movements ... are populated by individuals sharing collective goals and a collective identity who engage in disruptive collective action' (Klandermans, 1997, p.2).

Jordan (1998a) raises some questions about the value added offered by the social movement perspective. Protest of itself does not establish the existence of a new social movement, for it can occur as a spontaneous act that is not associated with fundamental changes in lifestyle or a rejection of the conventional political system. Jordan cautions that the term has been used in a rather vague and general way:

... it is far from clear whether the primarily sociological term 'social movement' is an analytical concept distinct from the sort of interest group that has been used in political science. There is a tendency to relabel any group using non-conventional strategies and tactics as social movements.

(Jordan, 1998a, p.317)

For analysts of pressure groups, however, the literature on social movements is important because it reminds us that pressure groups are only one, and not even the most important means, by which people secure social change (indeed, the purpose of many pressure groups is to resist change). Consider one of the most important social movements of the late twentieth century: feminism. Women who consider themselves feminists hold a variety of views, and reflect those views in a variety of ways in their lifestyle. They would probably, however, agree that they are concerned with redefining the role, and reasserting the status, of women in a society which has previously been dominated by the assumptions and preferences of men. The required changes can be brought about in a number of ways. For many women, the most important change would be a mental one: thinking about the world in terms of feminist principles and arguments. This change of perception would affect the conduct of a woman's everyday life in terms of her relations with men and with other women; her relations with her family; and her career objectives and behaviour in the workplace. Many important changes can be sparked off by individual women reading feminist literature or watching television programmes with a feminist perspective, or discussing their reading and viewing informally with other women. It is possible for a woman to regard herself as part of the feminist movement without belonging to any organization or even an informal mutual help group. Even so, it is clear that many of the goals of the feminist movement require political action if they are to be achieved. For example, better day-care facilities are necessary if women, particularly less prosperous women, are not to be prevented from pursuing their careers. The feminist movement may have drawn attention to the serious problem of domestic violence, but political action is necessary to ensure that prolonged violence by a man can be a defence for a woman accused in the courts because she made a violent response to continued abuse, and funds are necessary to provide counselling, refuge and general assistance to battered wives. (For a discussion of women's aid, see Stedward, 1987.)

Thus there is here a broad social movement of which pressure group activity forms only one part. Indeed, women's aid groups have stressed such values as complete participation, the authenticity of personal experience, and collective self-organization (Stedward, p.232). When pressure group activity springs from a social movement, it may thus reflect the characteristics of that movement although, clearly, individuals subscribing to a broad goal – such as the abolition of hunting – may differ about how that goal should be achieved: a point returned to later in the book.

Another problem is the question of political pressure exerted by individual political actors, most importantly firms. It is clear that from the 1970s onwards in Britain there was a proliferation of direct political activity by firms, operating either through their own government relations divisions, or through paid lobbyists acting on their behalf (see Grant, 1993a). It would seem wrong to exclude this type of activity because it does not involve an organization with a constitution, membership and paid officials. Jordan and Richardson (1987, pp. 14–18) are surely correct when they argue for a broad definition of pressure group that accepts companies and corporations as groups. After all, such an approach meets the *Concise Oxford Dictionary's* definition of a 'group' as a 'number of persons or things standing close together'.

But then, how wide does one cast the net? For example, should government ministries be treated as pressure groups? After all, the Ministry of Agriculture, Fisheries and Food has often been portrayed as the client of agricultural interests, whilst the Department of Trade and Industry has often been regarded as close to business interests. This could seem to be stretching the term too widely. Ministries do, of course, often fight for the departmental view within Whitehall, and that view often reflects to some extent the perspective and priorities of the pressure groups within the ministry's orbit. However, ministries always have to sift and aggregate the views of their client groups, rather than simply acting as their representatives within the government machine. Aggregation often involves reconciling the divergent views of different groups; it will certainly involve placing their views within the context of both the policy of their own minister and of the government as a whole.

Quasi-governmental organizations pose greater problems. Some of them have been set up in the past with one of their implicit functions being to act as a buffer between the government and particular pressure groups, such as the Countryside Commission or the Equal Opportunities Commission. The 'quangos' set up by the Conservative Governments in the 1980s and 1990s were, however, widely criticized for being filled largely with known government supporters who are then used to implement government policies without adequate democratic accountability. Such bodies may be particularly impervious to pressure group activity.

Quasi-governmental organizations can act as pressure groups; they can belong to pressure groups; they can mediate between pressure groups, or between pressure groups and the government; but they may also be used as a mechanism to insulate policies against pressure group activity. The range of their tasks draws attention to the fact that pressure groups function within a complex system of relationships which link a variety of political institutions and bodies. One sometimes has to look at pressure groups in isolation in order to understand their internal political and organizational dynamics, but one must also relate them to the broader political context in which they operate.

Political Parties

Political parties belong to that broader political context. Pressure groups may exist within political parties, as, for example, the Socialist Educational Association or the Socialist Medical Association within the Labour Party. However, I would argue for a clear distinction between pressure groups and political parties. The cases where there is a lack of definitional clarity are relatively rare (Thomas and Hrebenar, 1995). Political parties seek to win seats in elections with the objective of forming either the government or part of the government. The range of concerns of political parties is typically wider than that of pressure groups. To be regarded as serious, they have to have policies which cover every conceivable issue of public interest leaving aside those moral issues which are seen as a matter for personal judgement by individual MPs. The narrower concerns of pressure groups – with particular issues or interests – do not generally make contesting elections a viable strategy.

Pressure groups may occasionally contest elections as a political tactic, although it is not a very effective one, and is mainly a sign of being outside the political mainstream. It was successfully resorted to by supporters of Charlton Athletic Football Club when they formed the Valley Party to help secure their return to the club's home at The Valley. By securing 14 838 votes (10.9 per cent of those cast) in the Greenwich Council elections, they were able to demonstrate to the local council the extent of popular support for the club returning to its ground (Everitt, 1991). The Referendum Party intervened in the 1997 general election on the single platform of a referendum on Britain's future in Europe, but despite spending over seven million pounds on advertising, 'only a handful of the Conservatives' losses of seats can be blamed on the intervention of the Referendum Party' (Curtice and Steed, 1997, p.308). It may be, however, that there is a long run trend towards the expansion of micro parties (Maloney and Jordan, 1998).

In general, however, the distinction between a political party and a pressure group is a clear one. For example, at a number of points in the history of farmer representation in Britain, the possibility of organising a separate farmers party has been discussed. The National Farmers' Union 'generally regarded a separate agricultural party as impracticable and over-ambitious – as indeed it was' (Self and Storing, 1962, p.44). Agrarian parties have flourished in Scandinavian countries with proportional representation, but have become part of larger groupings as the agrarian share of the electorate has declined, although some of the new democracies in Eastern Europe such as Poland have agrarian parties. Farmers in Britain decided to take the pressure group route to pursue their interests.

A Working Definition of a Pressure Group

We have dealt with the problems surrounding the definition of a pressure group; it is now possible to offer a working definition:

> A pressure group is an organization which seeks as one of its functions to influence the formulation and implementation of public policy, public policy representing a set of authoritative decisions taken by the executive, the legislature, and the judiciary, and by local government and the European Union.

This definition encompasses think tanks such as the Institute of Economic Affairs (IEA) as pressure groups, even though they do not engage in what would conventionally be regarded as lobbying. Stone argues that think tanks are becoming more politicized and that 'The differences between a significant but small proportion of think-tanks and interest groups are blurring' (Stone, 1996, p.225). A think tank may have a close, if informal, relationship with a particular political party, such as that between Demos and the Institute for Public Policy Research and the Labour Party. It is generally agreed that the Institute for Economic Affairs played an important role in paving the way for Thatcherism by making free market ideas better known and more acceptable, while the Adam Smith Institute floated the idea of a poll tax, although in detail only after an informal meeting of ministers had launched the proposal (Butler, Adonis and Travers, 1994).

Think tanks do seek to change the intellectual climate of opinion, which in turn influences the policy agenda and options available to ministers. Stone, however, considers (1996, p.106) that 'the impact of even the best-known think tanks on policy is modest. Policy-making is mainly driven by interests, not by ideas.' Particular instances of influence may be less common than think tank boosters claim, and may not be the result of the efforts of the think tank:

> While there are occurrences of think-tanks being consulted by governments, this is *ad hoc*. Furthermore, political influence may be the result of luck or a host of other factors of work. The window of opportunity for think-tanks may be greatest just before an election and early in the term of a new government when political executives are still establishing their priorities.

(p.109)

Primary Groups and Secondary Groups

The basic definition may be elaborated by making a distinction between primary and secondary pressure groups. Relatively few pressure groups are concerned simply with the representation of the interests or views of their members, although many European level groups offer little in the way of services. Most groups, however, offer services, such as training seminars or insurance, to members as a means of attracting and retaining their membership.

Groups pursuing particular causes usually provide their members with at least a magazine, and perhaps sell various goods on which members are given a discount to raise funds. In practice, of course, many different incentives to join are mixed up in membership appeals. The Aberdeen group give the example of a poster seen there, of which the printed portion said 'Join UNA and help the UN put the world back together again.' A local addition said, 'Drink wine! Meet new people!' (Jordan, Maloney and McLaughlin, 1994a, p.529). Opportunities exist to drink wine while meeting new people without joining a pressure group, but the Aberdeen group make an interesting case for a marketing perspective on pressure group activities:

> Thus, the fact that the RSPB has 852 000 members while Plant Life has 1200 does not necessarily suggest that 'birds' are valued so much more by the population than plants, but that the pro-bird organization has, over time, marketed itself much more successfully.
>
> (Jordan, Maloney and McLaughlin, 1994b, p. 549)

It may be, of course, that the population does have warmer feelings towards birds than plants, and that the RSPB has been very effective in mobilizing those sentiments in an organizational form. A distinction may be made, however, between those organizations where the service function either to members or to others predominates, and those where services are provided as a membership incentive in order to recruit as large a portion as possible of the eligible membership. In the first category are the over seven million members of the Automobile Association (AA) who see its primary function as the provision of a breakdown service, although the AA also lobbies government on transport policy questions. Members are not particularly encouraged to attend the annual general meeting (one can write in for details), and the vast majority of them are concerned with its efficiency as a service club relative to the other alternatives (some of them purely commercial) on the market. Individual members of the AA may not always agree with its statements on transport policy issues, but are generally more concerned with its service function.

Similarly, the Cats Protection League exists primarily to provide a rescue and rehabilitation service for abandoned and unwanted cats, although it does undertake some lobbying on feline welfare issues. Again, there are alternative providers of cat rescue services, although some of these also rescue other animals. Some cat lovers may prefer to identify with an organization that does not also rescue dogs which may be perceived in ideological terms as 'dogist'. In the case of animal rescue services, the rescued animal does not, of course, have a choice about whether it is rescued and by whom.

The distinction between primary and secondary pressure groups is not just one between the predominance of service provision compared with political representation in the organization's work. There is a more general distinction between those organizations whose primary purpose is political, and those whose objectives lead them into political action from time to time. In some cases, this may mean that a particular part of the organization has a special responsibility for political work. Consider the case of the Church of England. Its main purpose is that of a religious organization: to provide facilities, buildings and clergy for worship and the administration of the sacrament in accordance with its doctrinal beliefs, and to propagate its interpretation of the Christian gospel. However, it acts both as a sectional pressure group in relation to its own particular interests and as a cause group on wider social issues. In relation to its own material and institutional interests:

> ministers and/or MPs may be lobbied in order to influence tax or other measures affecting the institution as employer or property owner: examples are continuing attempts to gain exemption from Value Added Tax on repairs to church fabric; efforts to get favourable treatment under the terms of the Land Bill ... and, in 1987, efforts to recoup possible losses flowing from the proposed abolition of rates and their replacement by a community charge.
>
> (Medhurst and Moyser, 1988, p. 313)

The Church also comments on broad social and political issues although some politicians would prefer it to concentrate on redeeming the souls of its members rather than intervening in broader moral questions. Much of the Church's work with a political dimension is undertaken by specialist boards of the General Synod. For example, the Board of Education has the difficult task of linking the Church's network of schools and the government department responsible for education. 'Whereas the Board may be perceived by the [then Department of Education and Science] as a '"peak association", able to negotiate authoritatively on behalf of Anglicans, those in Church House have in reality no real executive power *vis-à-vis* their constituents' (Medhurst and Moyser, 1988, p.329). The prime purpose of the Church of England is, then, a religious one, but it has a secondary function as a pressure group seeking to influence public policy, albeit a rather special pressure group because of its status as an Established Church and the presence of bishops in the House of Lords.

Charities offer another interesting example. Their primary purpose is to collect funds in the pursuit of a defined charitable objective. They are unavoidably drawn into the political process because they are asked by government to offer advice on special policy areas such as the welfare of a particular category of disabled person; or because they act as agents for the dispensation of government funds. Charity law prevents them from engaging in overtly political activity. They do, however, need to engage in such activity from time to time because, for example, changes in tax law can have a significant impact on their ability to raise and retain funds. Thus medical research charities have formed an Association of Medical Research Charities which is able to pursue public policy issues on behalf of its members. This is a clear example of a primary pressure group.

It is apparent from the discussion so far that there are many different types of pressure group. Writers on pressure groups have attempted to categorize the main characteristics of pressure groups through a variety of typologies. The next chapter presents an evaluation of the main alternative typologies.

2

Types of Group

A count of primary and secondary pressure groups in Britain that included locally based groups would almost certainly run into tens of thousands (the Devlin Commission on industrial representation counted 1 800 business associations, which is only one of a number of categories). It is clearly not possible to study all these groups as individual organizations. Hence, a feature of the pressure group literature over the last thirty years has been a variety of attempts to create typologies to classify groups, not only for descriptive purposes, but also in the hope that such typologies might lead to useful generalizations about their behaviour.

One of the most important distinctions has been that between sectional and cause groups. Sectional groups represent a section of the community. Their function is to look after the common interests of that section and their membership is normally restricted to that section. Cause groups 'represent some belief or principle ... They seek to act in the interests of that cause. Theoretically their membership is not restricted at all. Anyone can join and by doing so signify his acceptance of the belief or principle' (Stewart, 1958, p.25). Sectional groups usually seek to organize as large a proportion of their eligible membership as possible. Their standing with government depends to a considerable extent on the validity of their claim to speak for a particular industry, group of employers or profession. Cause groups subdivide into those which seek a mass membership to take part in campaigning and those which seem content with a restricted membership, the implicit emphasis perhaps being on quality rather than quantity.

What useful generalizations does the sectional/cause distinction produce? First, it can be argued that the nature of the demands made by the two groups often tends to differ. Sectional groups are more likely to advance limited, specific goals which, as they are broadly coincident with the values of society as a whole, can be conceded without public controversy (see Jordan and Richardson, 1987, p.21). Sectional groups are often dealing with highly technical issues which do not interest the public at large, or which they would not understand. This does not mean that the resolution of the issue is unimportant to the members of the group concerned: it may have a considerable bearing on the profitability of an industry, or the future of a profession, but usually it will not become the subject of a wider public debate. 'On the contrary, a high-profile area such as nuclear policy or abortion or constitutional reform is unlikely to be resolved without wide participation and parliamentary legitimation' (ibid.).

It could be argued that sectional groups find it easier to recruit members because they appeal to a well-defined constituency with a particular interest at stake. (For a further discussion of this point in terms of Olsonian theory, see Chapter 2.) The research carried out by the Aberdeen group points to a high level of membership turnover among cause groups. Only 35 per cent of those who joined Friends of the Earth in 1991 re-joined in 1992, while Amnesty International lost 24.5 per cent of its existing membership, but still managed to increase overall membership by 16. 5 per cent (Jordan and Maloney, 1997, p.166). Even so, cause groups are not necessarily less well resourced than sectional groups, and even if they have less money, they have more enthusiastic activists willing to devote time and energy to the group's work.

A Classification of Group Strategies

The sectional/cause distinction is of some value as a first step in group classification. However, there is also scope for a classification based on alternative group strategies, and on the receptivity of government to those strategies, which in turn has an impact on group effectiveness. One of the more durable categorizations has been the insider group/outsider group division and its various subdivisions (Grant, 1978). Insider groups are regarded as legitimate by government and are consulted on a regular basis. Outsider groups either do not wish to become enmeshed in a consultative relationship with officials, or are unable to gain recognition. Another way of looking at them is to see them as protest groups which have objectives that are outside the mainstream of political opinion. They then have to adopt campaigning methods designed to demonstrate that they have a solid basis of popular support, although some of the methods used by the more extreme groups may alienate potential supporters.

Outsider groups as a category are by their nature more disparate than insider groups. The very fact of being an insider group imposes certain constraints and patterns of behaviour on a group. (For an example of how an insider group works see Box 2.1 on page 22.) A group which does not abide by the rules may find itself excluded from the consultative process. Groups need to build a reputation of providing information that is accurate, well researched and not exaggerated which decision makers can rely on with confidence. This applies as much at the European Union level as in Britain. One study of Brussels lobbying found that a trade association which 'put forward incorrect arguments ... were finally excluded from the consultation process; and an interviewee who categorically stated, "If I am fed false statistics, I close my door for five years"' (Burson-Marsteller, 1991, p.8).

The basic point about the insider/outsider distinction is that an interest group has to be able to deploy certain political skills before it can be accepted as an insider group. It has to show civil servants that it can, and is prepared, to talk their language; that it knows how to present a case, and how to bargain and accept the outcome of the bargaining process. The language of the British civil service is a language of veiled understatement and it is characteristic of politically unsophisticated outsider groups that their demands are often presented in strident and uncompromising terms.

In the longer run, most groups tend to veer towards an insider strategy because of the potential gains it offers. For example, Greenpeace has 'devoted more resources to research, to report-writing and to conventional lobbying techniques. These changes have in turn annoyed some of the direct action traditionalists, who fear loss of purity and effectiveness' (Edwards, 1988, p.17). Certainly, there are risks in exchanging independence for incorporation. Nettl argues that the 'British consensus' has the effect of emasculating pressure groups 'while preserving their outward shell of autonomy and independence' (Nettl, 1965, p.22). According to Elliott *et al.* (1982, p.91) what was the National Federation of Self-Employed accepted incorporation as the price to be paid for durability.

Above all, an important point about the insider/outsider distinction is that it highlights the way in which the state sets the rules of the game for pressure group activity. Access and consultation flow from the adoption of a pattern of behaviour which is acceptable to government, particularly to civil servants. This creates incentives for groups to act in a particular way; pressure groups are thus tamed and domesticated with only the ideological rejectionists remaining outside the system.

Box 2.1 An example of an insider group

The Royal Society for the Prevention of Cruelty to Animals

Range of concern

- Not a campaigning, single issue organization but has credibility over a wide range of issues

General approach

- Seeks to build on a platform of authority, trust and confidence in relations with government
- Professional campaigning staff use professional methods
- Do not endorse 'the purely emotive campaigning approach of certain single issue pressure groups'
- Has sought consensus and dialogue with field sports lobby resulting in pragmatic legislation
- Exercises campaigning force with caution and responsibility Access to/relationship with decision makers

Access to/relationship with decision-makers

- Scientific, technical and veterinary experts advise government
- Long standing membership of government committees giving advice on use of laboratory animals
- Animal welfare organisation most respected by MPs
- Act as an agent of government in the enforcement of animal cruelty legislation

---

Source: Adapted from Parminter (1996).

A Typology under Attack

Twenty years after it was first proposed, however, the insider/outsider categorization has come under increasing criticism. The following discussion reviews these criticisms and considers whether the distinction is still a viable and helpful one. Before doing this, it is useful to review what the insider/outsider distinction was actually about. First, it is important to note that the distinction was one centred on the idea of interest group strategies, that is, how interest groups go about achieving their goals. One of the associated ideas was that any attempt simultaneously to pursue an insider and an outsider strategy would set up serious tensions within the group and was ultimately unsustainable.

However, deciding which strategy to pursue was not an unconstrained choice by the group itself. The acquisition of insider status by a group involved a decision by government as well as by the group itself: the group had to want insider status, but the government had to grant it. Some groups were more likely to be given insider status than others because their objectives and methods were more acceptable to government. This produced a distinction in the original typology between outsider groups by necessity and ideological outsider groups. Groups of the latter type do not consider that their objectives can be achieved by conventional political means and want to avoid becoming ensnared in the compromises of the political system. Outsider groups by necessity would like to become insider groups but lack the recognition, resources and political sophistication to do so. As Garner observes (1996, p.83):

> It is important to distinguish between those activities that reflect a reluctant outsider status and those that reflect a suspicion of normal decision-making channels. In the latter category we can further distinguish between those that remain outsiders because they are aware of the dangers of being 'captured' by government and those that seek to bypass the public policy route entirely.

It should be emphasized that the original typology did not claim that outsider groups could never be successful, although the odds were stacked against them. It was also emphasized that insider groups had to pay a price for their insider status. They had to abide by established 'rules of the game' and had to moderate their demands so that they were accepted by decision makers as realistic. When Friends of the Earth was 'On the brink of winning its campaign against non-returnable bottles, it was beguiled on to a Government working party and outmanoeuvred' (*Independent on Sunday*, 5 May 1996). Incorporation is classic government tactics, offering access but often little in the way of policy change. As environmental groups have switched to insider strategies, this has often led to problems with their own memberships who sometimes thought that the leadership was not being sufficiently vigorous in their pursuit of the groups' demands. Insider status offers access to incremental change and for many groups that is simply not enough.

Criticisms of the Insider–Outsider Typology

A number of criticisms of the typology have been put forward which may be summarised as follows:

* Achieving insider status is not as difficult as the typology implies.
* Groups are more constrained in their choice of strategy than the typology implies.
* Criticisms (1) and (2) might be dealt with by a modification of the typology, but in doing so its overall validity is undermined.
* It is possible for groups to simultaneously pursue insider and outsider strategies.
* The typology was valid when it was first developed, but has been undermined by the emergence of new forms of politics in Britain in the 1990s. This might be regarded as the most important and challenging criticism.

Each of these criticisms will be considered and assessed in turn.

Achieving Insider Status is Not Difficult

This argument was originally put forward in work carried out by the 'Aberdeen group' of Jordan, McLaughlin and Maloney, but has received further reinforcement in recent work by Page. The basic argument here is that the political entry price is not so high as the original typology implies. Large numbers of groups are placed on departmental consultation lists and are asked to respond to policy proposals. For example, 200 groups are consulted on matters relating to motor cycles. This does not mean that all such groups are equally influential. 'Many groups are granted access to decision makers ... but few have a significant influence over substantive policy outcomes' (Maloney, Jordan and McLaughlin, 1994, p.25.)

The Aberdeen group suggests that the original typology conflates the dimension of strategy and status which could useful be separated for analytical purposes to avoid ambiguity. They suggest that this could be achieved by 'explicitly attaching the insider/outsider term to strategy, and developing a complementary set of terms to distinguish status dimensions from strategy ones' (p.30). They offer a threefold classification of insider groups according to their status:

- Core insider groups – these are characterized by bargaining/ exchange relationships with policy makers over a broad range of issues. Examples would be the CBI, NFU and BMA.
- Specialist insider groups – these are seen as reliable and authoritative, but in much narrower policy niches, for example, the British Poultry Meat Federation.
- Peripheral insiders – participation that has the insider form but carries with it little influence.

'The real issue as we see it concerns the distinction between peripheral, and core and niche insiders' (Jordan, Maloney and McLaughlin, 1992a, p.20). After all, the first distinction between core and specialist groups is one about the range of issues covered. The poultry meat producers are contented if they are consulted about matters that affect them, but they do not wish to be consulted about, for example, dairy products (as the NFU would wish to be).

Page (1998) argues that insider status is much more widespread than has been assumed with insider groups outnumbering pure outsiders by nine to one. In a survey to which 320 groups responded, Page measured three insider characteristics in a survey of delegated legislation which came up with the following results presented in Table 2.1.

Table 2.1 Insider characteristics of interest groups

Criterion	% Insider
Contacts with departments each month or more often	82
Department usually or sometimes makes changes we suggest	73
Consulted most of the time on all relevant statutory instruments	54

Source: E. C. Page manuscript.

There are some methodological problems with this data. Of the answers given in the table above, the response 'Department usually or sometimes makes changes we suggest' is most suspect, not just because of exaggeration by the respondents, but because it may have been a similar submission by another group (or a completely different factor, such as backbench pressure) which may have been influential. In some ways, the most significant finding is in relation to consultation on statutory instruments as this is just the kind of technical, incremental aspect of policy that is of interest to insider groups.

One of Page's central findings is that insider groups predominate over outsider groups – 44 per cent of the responding groups are insider groups if one takes account of all three characteristics, and only 5 per cent have none. This is not a suprising finding in that one would expect insider groups to outnumber outsider groups given the rewards of access and influence that insider status brings. It should also be noted that ideological outsiders are unlikely to be listed in the directories used by Page for his sample.

The general conclusion drawn is that it is relatively easy for some groups to acquire insider status at least in the sense of being placed on a consultation list, although many such groups will have only a marginal influence on policy formation, or their influence will be confined to a very restricted area. Such groups will, however, generally be within the economic and social mainstream. The position will be very different for those groups seeking to represent the 'socially excluded'. For example, Ryan suggests that Inquest, a pressure group concerned with deaths in and around state custody:

> ... would most appropriately be placed among 'ideological outsider' groups; that is, among those groups whose objectives are at odds with many of the basic social and political assumptions of the current political system. The evidence suggests that INQUEST is mostly concerned with those on the border between legality and illegality, the mentally ill, often the poor or the casually employed, those marginal and disadvantaged groups who are subject to state regulation, and whose lot is unlikely to be considerably improved without fundamental political change.
>
> (Ryan, 1996, p.170)

Strategy Choices are Constrained

The insider/outsider typology was in a sense a learning tool for pressure groups because it claimed that groups can make choices which can either improve an initially weak bargaining position or undermine an initially strong bargaining position. The National Federation of Retirement Pensions Associations (NFRPA), formerly the National Federation of Old Age Pensioners Associations (NFOAPA), has seen its insider position deteriorate. From having an 'essential monopoly of organized pension reform advocacy in Britain' (Pratt 1993, p.91) in the 1950s and 1960s when it met regularly with ministers, it has been outflanked by newer retirement organizations. The development of rival organizations reflected in part an assessment of the NFRPA's weaknesses. Age Concern decided to become more politically active after its then director had decided that NFRPA had 'failed to make a very significant impact on the national government' (p. 132).

The decline of the influence of the NFOAPA in part reflected the diminished attraction of the social activities of its local branches as other leisure activities became available, often at discounted prices for older people. However, it also reflected choices made by the organization. Because of the disruption caused by German bombing in the Second World War, the NFOAPA moved its headquarters to Blackburn where one of its leaders lived, and they never moved back. In a centralized political system like that of Britain, effective insider groups need to be in, or close to, the metropolis:

> ... the relative remoteness of its headquarters has not been without its cost in terms of NFRPA's political influence ... the loss of ... preeminence during the 1970s and 1980s was at least partially attributable to its physical remoteness from the center of British government.
>
> (pp. 212–13)

Effective pressure group activity increasingly depends on the ability to develop well researched critiques of existing policy. As policy towards the elderly has become more complex, and developed new dimensions (such as those relating to nursing home care), the NFRPA 'has had difficulty adjusting given its lack of strong policy-analytic capability' (p.136).

The Motor Cycle Action Group (MAG) provides an example of a group which has moved from outsider by necessity to potential insider status. At the end of the 1980s, the organization faced serious difficulties. The newly elected chairman, Neil Liversidge, commented in his 1990 annual report that 'many people were writing MAG off as a shambles' (*Magnews*, August/September 1990, p.6). Improving the political standing of an organization like MAG is not easy. As the then Parliamentary Under Secretary for Transport, Robert Key, who had accepted MAG's offer of 'a serious cross country bike ride' commented 'they are great people ... sometimes the image of motorcyclists is built up by the media, by films ... as 'very macho, very aggressive and one of the things I like about MAG is that they perform a very useful function in the community' (*Magnews*, April/May 1994, p.18). MAG has made a sustained effort in the 1990s to show 'that we are a serious pressure group that we really know what we're talking about' (*Magnews*, April/May 1994, p.28).

This has been done in a way that has made effective use of limited financial resources. MAG still holds demonstrations in the form of mass bike rides, but it has placed an increasing emphasis on discussions with local MPs and the establishment of contacts with civil servants. Recognizing the importance of the European dimension, it was involved in the establishment of a Federation of European Motorcyclists with an office near Brussels staffed by an MAG member. In order to understand the operation of the EU, it sought free advice from political scientists, recommending a list of standard texts to its members. *Magnews* now contains references to, and discussions of, newly issued Commission documents. When it has held discussions with ministers, it has not only raised substantive issues, but also questions about how the consultation process is undertaken and who is included.

Part of the value of the insider/outsider distinction is that it focuses attention on the choices that have to be made by groups and government, and on the exchange relationship that develops between them. The choices that have to be made by groups can be illustrated by the example of the animal protection movement, which exhibits a wide range of strategies. As a very useful contribution to the presure group literature by Garner illustrates, the choice about what kind of strategy to follow is often rooted in fundamental moral choices. Garner draws a distinction (1993, p.48) 'between those groups which emphasise animal rights and those groups which emphasise animal welfare'. Different moral orthodoxies produce 'the key division within the animal protection movement: between those who consider that animal interests should take a subordinate, albeit important, position and those who recognise a higher moral status for animals' (p.49).

Maloney, Jordan and McLaughlin (1994, pp.32–6) argue that most interest groups do not have a real choice of strategies but are constrained by a range of factors. Among those they identify drawing on the work of a number of authors are:

- The group's internal organizational resources, with the larger the staff the greater the propensity to pursue an insider strategy.
- How the group's objectives fit in with those being pursued by decision-makers. If there is a good fit, then an insider strategy is more likely.

- The power and sanctions of the group. If decision makers are aware that a group is powerful, they may be more willing to listen to it and insider status may be readily granted.
- Group finances. Reliance on membership contributions may push a group in the direction of an outsider strategy as a series of 'stunts' may be required to satisfy the membership.
- History of a group. Choices made at an early stage may influence the strategic style of the group.

In particular, Maloney, McLaughlin and Jordan argue (p.34):

> In our view, for groups with incremental demands the appropriate means of influencing policy is by insider negotiations over detail. So it is the nature of their demands on the political system that determines their strategy: they do not have a realistic choice between insider and outsider strategies.

It is evident that the strategic choices made by interest groups are significantly constrained in a number of ways. For outsider groups resource constraints may be particularly serious. As Ryan notes in the case of Inquest:

> Financial constraints in particular have a debilitating effect. Instead of planning ahead in terms of managing and developing their organization, or developing new substantive policies their full-time workers all too often spend most of their time looking to secure next year's grant. This has an obvious impact on morale.
>
> (Ryan, 1996, p.135)

Ryan also admits that an outsider strategy may influence not only the size of the financial resources available to a group, but also the effective management of those resources. In the case of Inquest, it is 'arguable that it has not always made the best of its admittedly slender resources, and that its underlying radical culture has sometimes limited its ability to respond to wider presures for change, pressures that at times threatened its very existence' (ibid.).

It is accepted that the choice of strategies by a pressure group is constrained rather than being an entirely free one. There is a complex interactive relationship between the goals of the group, their acceptability to decision makers and the strategy it pursues. This admission, however, enriches rather than detracts from the insider–outsider distinction. It is also important to remember that this distinction has strong cultural roots. For example, Wilkinson discusses (1998, p.10) how 'insider' and 'outsider' notions have surfaced in 'new' Labour, it being assumed that 'the raison d'etre of outsiders is to wait patiently like Pavlov's dogs to be given access to the inner circle'.

If You Modify the Typology, You Undermine It

The first two types of criticism do not destroy the validity of the insider–outsider distinction. They demand its modification rather than its abolition. The original subdivision of the insider categorization (Grant, 1995a: p.20) might usefully be replaced by that offered by the Aberdeen group. The discussion of the choice of strategies open to pressure groups needs to emphasize that this choice is highly constrained, although that does not mean that there is no element of choice at all. As Page has suggested in a personal communication, there is a danger that once one starts to qualify the original distinction into varying shades of 'insiderness' and 'outsiderness', its utility starts to disappear.

Page takes the robust view 'that to characterise a group as an "insider" or an "outsider" in the process of policy making is at best an oversimplification and at worst possibly misleading' (Page, 1998, p.11). Page argues 'that the apparent dichotomy implicit in the whole notion of an "insider" is a false one; there is rather a gradation of access to executive decision making' (p.8).

As in any modelling process in social science, the insider/outsider distinction involves simplification. Social reality is complex and the only way we can start to understand it, to see the wood for the trees, is by making some simplifications. It is argued that this particular simplification does capture a reality that is faced by pressure groups. In an article that is generally critical of the insider/outsider distinction, Dudley and Richardson note (1998, p.746):

> There is a continual debate amongst the anti-roads groups about the possible limitations of direct action, and the potential advantages in seeking to become 'insiders'. The central issue for them is to decide whether an 'outsider' strategy is effective only in altering the policy image and starting the process of ... change, and an 'insider' strategy is required in order to consolidate these gains.

In some ways a more subtle and challenging critique, although not one specifically directed at this typology, is that we undervalue the contribution of outsiders to our democracy at our peril:

> For the reality is that insiders and outsiders exist in a state of interdependence. Insiders depend on outsiders to act as a check against human fallibility, to keep them connected and informed; insiders teach outsiders the virtues of pragmatism and compromise.
>
> (Wilkinson, 1998, p.10)

The notion that groups might simultaneously pursue both insider and outsider strategies was first developed by May and Nugent when they suggest a third category of 'thresholders' who vacillate between 'pursuing and not pursuing a symbiotic relationship between insider and outsider strategies'. Thresholders can be 'characterised by strategic amibiguity and oscillation between insider and outsider strategies' (May and Nugent, 1982, p.7). Trade unions were offered as an example. Page develops this further by arguing that groups pursue a 'good cop/bad cop' strategy in which insider strategies of reasoned argument are combined with the mobilization of public support. Moreover, he argues that such a combined strategy can be pursued without any penalty in terms of loss of insider status:

> Groups switch strategies themselves without suffering loss of 'insider' status. To initiate a public protest against proposed changes in the law can be pursued at the same time as 'insider' strategies of arguing against them without loss of status. Government departments know and understand the aspirations of and constraints operating on group leaders and expect groups to make a loud noise on some things, and they will still invite them to participate in working groups and other participatory forums.
>
> (Page, 1998, p.11)

Tactics such as peaceful public demonstrations and letter writing campaigns are perfectly compatible with insider status, but more violent forms of direct action are not. It is evident that leaders of insider groups have from time to time tacitly encouraged various forms of protest by their members as a means of generating additional leverage against government in times of difficulty. However, they have always been worried about losing control of their members in such circumstances. This was evident in the mid-1970s when demonstrations by farmers against Irish beef imports led to railway lines being ripped up by 'flying pickets' of farmers and increasing anxiety among the leaders of farmers' unions that they would be accused by ministers of not being able to control their own members. These worries surfaced again in 1998 when farmers' union leaders welcomed demonstrations by members as evidence of the extent of their frustration, but became concerned when these demonstration led to illegal acts.

The tensions of trying simultaneously to pursue an insider and an outsider strategy are well illustrated by the case of the environmental group, Greenpeace. Over the years, Greenpeace has shifted towards more dialogue with government and business while maintaining the direct action activities that attract the donations which sustain the organization. This change of approach was exemplified when Greenpeace held its first business conference in 1996. Those attending were told that the group's latest weapon was '"solutions enforcement". This meant pushing markets to adopt products that solved environmental problems' (*Financial Times*, 26 September 1996).

Although Greenpeace has continued to use direct action tactics, not everyone connected with the organization was happy about the shift of emphasis. As a consequence, divisions over strategy persist: 'The division in the movement between a moderate, rational campaigning approach that appeals alike to governments and to a cautious but persuadable public on the one side and the militant direct action radicalism that still attracts the pure green radicals remains unresolved' (O'Neill, 1995, p.31). As firms try to promote a 'greener' image, the executive director of Greenpeace International has lamented that it is becoming more difficult to pick 'good fights' (*The Economist*, 1 August 1998, p.79).

Nevertheless, Greenpeace is still perceived by decision makers as more radical than other environmental groups. It is the only one of the leading environmental organizations represented in Brussels not to have been commissioned by the European institutions for investigative work (Greenwood, 1997: p.190). It is the only leading environmental organization that 'does not receive funding from the European Commission. This corresponds with Greenpeace's policy of maintaining political and financial independence' (Webster, 1998: p.180). Yet this outsider image is at odds with adverts for senior Greenpeace staff which seek political advisers with a business or intergovernmental background to provide 'strategic direction to campaigns and interface with high-level contacts in government, international secretariats and industry'. Given such a Janus-faced profile, no wonder that stories surface from time to time of tensions within the organization, although its hierarchical character and the fact that it has 'supporters' rather than 'members' help to stifle dissent.

What is really going on is that Greenpeace is shifting towards an insider strategy, but the process is not yet complete: 'Greenpeace is turning away from confrontation and public debate as ways to influence industry and moving to "positive persuasion" of manufacturers by playing their own game' (Eden, 1996: p.49).

Greenpeace's skill at using the media by providing 'a sort of "convenience news" of pictures, imagery and story lines' (Jordan, 1998b, p.16) has helped to maintain their public image as an organization that gets things done by challenging mighty multinationals on the high seas in inflatable boats. Their short term successes such as defeating Shell over its plan to dump the Brent Spar oil platform at sea attract considerable publicity whereas their unsuccessful campaign to stop expansion of oil exploitation in the Atlantic was largely unreported. At some point, however, the declining number of supporters (2.5 million worldwide in 1998 compared with a peak of 4.1 million in 1991) will come to realize that an outsider group has completed the transformation to an insider group, that the 'lounge suits' within the organization have finally defeated the 'rubber suits'. Simultaneously pursuing an insider and outsider strategy is a transitional phase and eventually a group has to opt for predominantly one strategy or the other (usually an insider approach).

The 'New Politics' Argument

The argument that the insider group/outsider group distinction was relevant when it was first developed, but is no longer applicable in a new era of politics is the most fundamental and important challenge to the categorization. It has been particularly developed in the context of discussions of road protests and has been most coherently argued by Dudley and Richardson (1998). They argue that politics is increasingly becoming a 'multi-level, multi-arena game'. They claim that 'the new politics is here to stay' (p.747) and invite a 'reappraisal of the importance of policy "insiders" and outsiders"' (p.743).

A similar line of argument is advanced by Toke (1997, p.114):

> ... insider/outsider analysis of group status and strategy may be less helpful than it used to be in gaining an understanding of the relative effectiveness of different environmental pressure groups. The very fact that environmental groups have shifted towards a more outsider, media oriented strategy and that many groups that continue to pursue outsider strategies have gained more insider status supports this assertion. The rules of the game may be changing.

There is no doubt that the context of pressure group politics has changed throughout the postwar period (for a more detailed discussion see Grant 1997). Three different phases may be distinguished (see Table 2.2).

Pressure group politics in the late 1990s is not the same as it was in the Establishment dominated era of the 1950s. Society has changed and, although the political process has been slower to change in response, it is more open than it used to be. After the end of the Second World War, most pressure groups were organized around one of the great 'Estates' that represented the pillars of society: business, labour, agriculture and the professions. The exceptions were a number of cause groups supported by reformist members of the middle class, often with their own Establishment connections. Today, there is a far greater number and wider range of pressure groups, reflecting a more fragmented society in which personal identity does not derive from membership of a social class or professional grouping, but from a much wider range of possible identities. Supporting a particular pressure group can almost be a lifestyle choice.

Table 2.2 Phases in the development of pressure politics

Time period	Participants in policy-making	Forms of pressure group activity
1950s	Sectional groups, plus limited number of cause groups	Executive focused informal personal links among 'Establishment'
1970s	Tripartism – CBI, TUC very important Environmental groups emerging, overall number of pressure groups on more increase	Still executive focused, but Parliament, media, courts becoming important
1990s	CBI, TUC less important Number of pressure groups greatly expanded across a wide range of fields	Multiple arenas – Executive, European Union, Parliament, courts, media, direct action

Dudley and Richardson and, to a lesser extent, Toke base their case on the example of the roads lobby. Dudley and Richardson argue that:

> ... the environmental lobby failed in the 1980s when the road lobby exploited its insider status to regain its hegemony. The 1990s, however, look rather different for a number of reasons, not least of which is the continuing ability of anti-roads group to exploit the multi-arena politics of the period.
>
> (p.746)

Similarly, Toke argues that:

> The once all-powerful 'insider' influence of the construction companies and the car lobby has been eroded in recent years by a sustained campaign by an alliance of environmental pressure groups, the irreplaceable element of which has been 'outsider' campaigning, much of it militant in nature. This has gradually eroded the political legitimacy of giving planning permission to, and paying for, new roads.
>
> (Toke, 1997, p.113)

The story of what looks to be a permanent cut in the size of the roads programme is a complex one (Robinson, 1998), but in general three alternative explanations are possible (although they are not mutually exclusive):

1. Increasing public opposition to new road building, reflected in sympathetic media coverage of road protesters forced the government to reconsider its policy, particularly as the delays enforced by anti-road activists were pushing up the cost of the programme. This model implies a considerable role for pressure groups both in helping to mould public opinion and in impeding the implementation of policy. If it is correct, it suggests that outsider groups can be highly effective.

2. A second explanation is that opinion within the executive branch on the desirability of road building has changed. Toke dismisses this explanation arguing that 'an "informed debate" about roads policy has been around for a long time among environmentalists, but it just was not taken seriously by mainstream opinion. The point is that the anti-road activists have shifted the policy agenda' (Toke, 1997, p.112). However, this overlooks the influence of the 1994 report from the Standing Advisory Committee on Trunk Roads, an 'insider' committee, which challenged the orthodox 'predict and provide' philosophy of road building, arguing that new roads failed to solve congestion problems because they actually generated more traffic.

Also influential was the 1994 report of the Royal Commission on Environmental Pollution. This second model suggests a more elitist model in which the key actors are civil servants and their expert advisers, together with insider groups (including new insider groups incorporated in the policy process such as Transport 2000 whose director was admitted to the trunk roads advisory committee).

3. A third explanation is that with a political imperative to find budget cuts, the Treasury settled on roads as a popular target, weakly defended inside Whitehall. 'No doubt the Treasury was, as usual, being opportunistic in forcing cuts on one of its spending departments' (Dudley and Richardson, 1998, p.742). The third model implies a centrally directed model of decision making in which external pressures of any kind are subordinated to short run political imperatives.

There are more political arenas for pressure groups to operate in than before, although some of these new arenas, notably the European Union, can readily be analysed in insider/outsider terms. The rules of the game are changing: trust in politicians is at a low ebb, and direct action by protest movements is seen as more legitimate. However, the insider/outsider distinction remains a viable one: there is a new politics, but old political structures and practices persist.

Pressure Groups and Democracy

There is a fundamental link between the existence of pressure groups and the very survival of a system of democratic government. Freedom of association is a fundamental principle of democracy. Democracy permits the existence of groups, but it could also be argued that groups contribute to the quality of the decision-making process. Those that have axes to grind may have something to say that is relevant to the issue under consideration.

A system of representative democracy offers electors a relatively infrequent choice between alternative party programmes. Systems which permit referenda to be held on specific issues extend the range of choice, but one consequence is often that the protaganists spend large sums of money on advertising to influence the outcome, with an unfair advantage being given to the side with more money (Grant, 1996). Pressure groups permit citizens to express their views on complex issues which affect their lives. In most systems of voting, each vote (at least in principle)

counts equally, but numerical democracy finds it difficult, without elaborate systems of weighting votes, to take account of the intensity of opinion
on a particular issue. Democracy cannot be simply reduced to a head-count-
ing exercise: it must also take account of the strength of feelings expressed,
and of the quality of arguments advanced. Moreover, group membership
and activity offers an additional mechanism for citizens to participate in
'the experience of ruling and being ruled' (Lively, 1975, p.117).
This rather benign view of pressure group activity can be challenged
in two ways. It can be argued that pressure group activity simply rein-
forces existing patterns of political inequality in society. For example,
consider the position of business in society. Business already has considerable influence over people's everyday lives because of the economic
assets at its disposal, assets which allow it to make decisions about the
location of plants, the range of products to be produced, the number and
type of people to be employed and so on. Business is able to reinforce
this economic power through pressure group activity, either at the level
of the individual organization, the firm, or through organizations representing particular industries or business as a whole.
    Why is business allowed these dual advantages? At a fundamental
level, it could be argued to reflect a value choice by society, expressed
through the outcome of elections, in favour of a capitalist, free-enter-
prise society. In that society, businesses are corporate citizens, paying
taxes and being required to obey a wide variety of laws and regulations. It therefore does not seem unreasonable that business should be
allowed an opportunity to express its views on public policies that
affect it. On a practical level, it should be noted that there are two
additional reasons why governments consult business interests. First,
business can advise government on the practical consequences of a
particular policy, thus helping government to avoid policies which are
ineffective, or which have undesirable and unintended side effects.
Second, business is often called on to assist in the implementation of a
particular policy, such as a training policy, making it desirable to maintain its goodwill.
    Even so, it can be argued that pressure groups that represent organiza-
tions rather than individuals have certain advantages in terms of their ability
to exert effective influence on public policy. An institution has interests
that are independent of its particular members, and its leadership has greater
latitude in making decisions about how those interests can best be served.
'Institutions have less need to justify their political efforts by reference to
membership approval or demand' (Salisbury, 1984: p. 68).

One should not dismiss too readily the concerns which have been expressed about the tendency for at least some pressure group activity to reinforce existing concentrations of power. However, it is difficult to take a position on these issues without having some general theoretical perspective on the role of pressure groups in the policy-making process, and a number of alternative theories are set out in Chapter 3.

The other challenge that has been mounted to pressure groups questions their impact on the overall decision-making process in a society. In summary, it is argued by some liberal writers that the presence of what are referred to as vested interests makes it difficult to bring about necessary changes in a society. By mounting an effective defence of the status quo, group activity leads to ossification in a society. At the opposite end of the spectrum are the prescriptive corporatists who argue that a close relationship between groups and government is not only the most effective way of governing a polity, but also one that contributes to social progress. These alternative perspectives will also be considered more fully in Chapter 3.

3

Theoretical Perspectives

This chapter reviews a number of alternative theoretical perspectives on the place of pressure groups in the political system. The focus is on theories which help us to understand the role of pressure groups in the democratic political process as a whole. Theories which consider, for example, the problems of recruiting or retaining group members, or the internal dynamics of interest groups, will be discussed only in so far as they are relevant to these broader issues.

One important point to bear in mind when reading about the various theories is the distinction between analytical and normative theories. There is, of course, a sense in which all theories are normative because the process of theory formation is not value free. Even so, a distinction can be maintained between those theories which set out to describe and explain a particular set of political phenomena, and those which seek to prescribe a preferred set of political arrangements: the distinction between is and ought.

One of the problems with pressure group theory is that this distinction between analytical and normative theories has often not been maintained, or at least has become confused in the minds of those writing about the subject. Consider corporatist theory, which is discussed later in the chapter. Many of the writers on corporatism are prescriptive corporatists, that is, they believe that neo-corporatist arrangements enhance the quality of decision-making in a democratic society, and that countries with such arrangements are, in general, better off than those without them. Other writers have been interested in corporatism simply as a means of trying to understand changes which took place in the relationship between the state and pressure groups in a number of western societies in the postwar period. They are not arguing that corporatist arrangements are particularly beneficial: simply that they have occurred, and need to be studied if we are to have a better understanding of the democratic process. However, the distinction between these two approaches often becomes blurred, so that analytical writers on the subject are often labelled corporatists along with the prescriptive corporatists.

Ideas and Interests

Before considering the various theories which have been used to examine pressure group activity, there is a broader issue that needs to be tackled: the relative importance of ideas and interests in explaining political outputs and outcomes. A crude interest-based model of the political process would argue that what is important in determining political outcomes is the clash of divergent interests in society, for example business and labour, and the relative power that they are able to deploy. Ideas are then used as a camouflage for these interests to give them respectability and legitimacy and to make their rent seeking behaviour seem less blatant and selfish. Thus, for example, farmers seeking to maintain their state subsidies would deploy whatever argument seemed convenient to justify their position. For instance, in the immediate postwar period they would emphasize food security whereas at the turn of the century they would portray themselves as guardians of the countryside and of a particular kind of landscape and way of life. In this perspective, then, ideas are seen as the servants of interests, rather than having any independent life of their own.

Such a perspective was always a caricature. As Keynes once observed, 'the ideas of economists and political philosophers, both when they are right and when they are wrong, are more powerful than is commonly understood' (1936, p.383). Despite that influential insight:

> Ideas are commonly seen as part of the superstructure rather than the base of political economy or portrayed as so much froth on the long waves of economic development. Even the study of politics has recently moved away from an emphasis on ideas, as structuralist accounts of public policy and political change have superseded more traditional lines of analysis.
>
> (Hall, 1989, p.361)

However, Marxist notions of superstructure are less influential than they once were. Grand theories and meta discourses have seemed less useful as society has become more fragmented. The displacement exerted by the great producer interests has become less securely based, leaving more space for a variety of ideas to fill the resultant vacuum – and more ways to disseminate such ideas, for example through the Internet. The resultant moral relativism in which every idea is seen to have equal value has its dangers, but there is an evident need for a systematic means of bringing 'ideas back in' to the debate about how policy change occurs or does not occur. Such a framework is provided by Sabatier's 'advocacy coalition' approach.

Sabatier's writing needs to be distinguished from the traditional interest group literature because it is focused on ideas rather than interests: This framework uses belief systems, rather than 'interests', as its focus because beliefs are more inclusive and verifiable than interests (1993, p.28). Hence, one of the most important aspects of Sabatier's approach is the contention that 'policy change is not simply the result of competition among various interests ... but rather that "policy-oriented learning" ... is an important aspect of policy change' (Sabatier, 1998, p.117).

Sabatier's basic unit of analysis is the 'advocacy coalition' which is made up of people 'who share a particular belief system – that is a set of basic values, causal assumptions and problem perceptions – and who show a nontrivial degree of coordinated activity over time' (Sabatier, 1993, p.25). He emphasizes that advocacy coalitions are 'not simply constellations of interest groups; their 'members' also include legislators, agency officials, researchers and journalists' (p.37).

Sabatier organizes the belief systems of each coalition into three levels. The highest or deep core level is concerned with basic normative beliefs 'such as the relative valuation of individual freedom versus social equality' (Sabatier, 1998, p.103). The lowest level is made up of secondary beliefs concerning such matters as desirable regulations or spending decisions. The intermediate level of policy core beliefs are in many ways the most important in Sabatier's model. These cover such matters as perceptions of the importance of the problem, the role of governments versus markets, and the policy instruments to be used to tackle a problem. Deep core beliefs are very resistant to change, while secondary beliefs can be more easily adjusted. If one wants to understand policy change, then it is the core beliefs that are most interesting and Sabatier hypotheses that some shock originating outside a policy sub-system is the most likely source of such change.

Sabatier's work is an important contribution to the study of policy change and learning, but how far does it help us in the study of British pressure groups, other than acting as an antidote to a misplaced belief that politics is all about the clash of interests? As Sabatier admits, 'The

ACF (Advocacy Coalition Framework) was originally developed primarily with the American experience in mind' (ibid., p.120). The American system of government is more fluid than that of Britain with multiple access points and without strong and disciplined political parties. The policy process is much more unpredictable than in a polity dominated by a strong executive. There is therefore more scope for the building of broadly based coalitions advocating policy change and bringing together legislators, interest groups and technical experts. Participants in the policy process adjust to fragmentation and unpredictability 'by having fewer inhibitions about coalition-building across political divides' (Grant, 1995b, p.73). Indeed, building such a coalition may be a precondition of policy success.

There is a sense in which the Sabatier framework may be becoming more applicable to British circumstances as a consequence of the increasing involvement of the EU in policy making. This introduces a federal element into policy making, proliferating the number of access points and increasing unpredictability. The EU also has a decision-making process in which technical information is important, a dimension of policy making very much emphasized by Sabatier. These factors lead to a greater use of coalition building, even if this practice and its study is still at an early stage of development (Pijnenburg, 1998).

Just how useful one finds Sabatier's framework in the study of pressure groups depends in part on how the dependent variable is specified. Sabatier is focused on the study of policy change (although his framework does have some limitations in the explanation of such change as he is the first to admit). Pressure groups in Britain have often had as their principal mission the resistance to change and there are a number of features of the British political process which assist them in that task. Moreover, one of the principal concerns of this book is the extent to which pressure groups enhance, or detract from, the democratic process. The concern here is not just with outputs or outcomes, but with the quality of the process that produces those outcomes.

Pluralism

Pluralism offers the most influential and resilient account of the role of pressure groups in a democratic society. In part, its resilience is due to its elasticity: pluralists hold a variety of positions, particularly on the role of the state in a democracy. Jordan complains, 'Since pluralism is so vague a set of ideas it is difficult to understand how opponents can have rejected it with such confidence' (1990, p.286). This vagueness does, however, undermine the theoretical claims of pluralism, even if it makes it easier to deflect criticisms from any quarter.

One of the key charcteristics of pluralism is the emphasis placed on the role of pressure groups in society as a means of providing access to the political system, and as a counterweight to undue concentrations of power. Thus, 'The pluralist case ... rests on the argument that the essential thing is competition and participation among organized *groups*, not among individuals' (Presthus, 1964: p.19).

Pluralist theory is often caricatured by its less well informed critics, and it must be emphasized:

> Despite the accusations of many critics, pluralists do not see all pressure groups as having equal access to the policy process ... pluralists accept that relationships between interest groups and government agencies can become very exclusive ... Pluralists do not expect a free flow of groups and ideas into the policy arena, nor do they regard all groups as having equal access and power.
>
> (Smith, 1990a, p. 303)

Pluralist theory combines within it a mixture of normative and analytical elements: pluralist theorists often seem to be simultaneously offering both an account of how society ought to be organized, and a working model of how society is actually organized. In this description, pluralism will be treated as an analytical theory, but it should be emphasized that it has considerable normative undertones.

Pluralists believe that power in society is fragmented and dispersed, a 'system of dispersed inequalities' (Jordan, 1990, p.288). In particular, they believe that power is non-cumulative in the sense that those who are powerful in one arena are not necessarily powerful in another. This idea of distinct issue areas has given rise to the neo-pluralist notion of policy communities which is discussed more fully below. The dispersal of power is assisted by the presence of a large number of groups, and by the existence of a rough balancing equilibrium in the society which operates through the presence of countervailing groups, for example labour countervails capital. If a particular interest is neglected, then a 'potential' group will be mobilized to represent it (see Truman, 1951). This theory does have some practical relevance: in research on the CBI, Marsh and I discovered that its members thought that a principal reason for its existence was the need to provide a counterweight to the TUC, a consideration mentioned by almost every director we interviewed (Grant and Marsh, 1977, p.49). However, Smith (1993, p.27) makes some telling criticisms of the notion of potential groups:

> It seems likely that potential groups are those that have great difficulty organizing, such as consumers or the elderly, who do not meet collectively, lack resources, often have conflicting interests and lack economic power. However much their interests are threatened, they are unlikely to become actual groups. Indeed the concept of a potential group is questionable. How can a potential group exist when the concept group involves some form of collective identity? A group can only exist once it is formed.

It is important to bear in mind is that 'The major literature on pressure groups is American. There is no major British contributor to theory' (Jordan and Richardson, 1987, p.53). (A subsequent exception is Dunleavy, 1988, 1991.) One consequence is that pluralist theory often seems to reflect a more open, fragmented political system than applies in the case of Britain. In particular, government is often presented as highly fragmented. such a picture has considerable validity in the US with its autonomous executive agencies, but less so in Britain.

Pluralism: an Assessment

Much of the pluralist case rests on the assumption that access to the political system is relatively easy, that forming a group which will be listened to is not particularly difficult. In 1965 Mancur Olson published a book called *The Logic of Collective Action* which cast doubt on some of the central assumptions made by pluralists in 'an apparently devastating critique' (Dunleavy, 1988, p.23). Olson argued that there was a logical flaw in the pluralists' treatment of economic interest groups. They assumed that individuals in a large group would make sacrifices to attain the political objectives of the group. Olson pointed out that the individual member of a large organization was in a position where 'his own efforts will not have a noticeable effect on the situation of the organization, and he can enjoy any improvements brought about by others whether or not he has worked in support of his organization' (Olson, 1965, p.16). Olson argued that the relatively small groups, which he termed privileged or intermediate groups, would be much easier to organize:

The small oligopolistic industry seeking a tariff or tax loophole will some-times attain its objective even if the vast majority of the population loses as a result. The smaller groups – the privileged and intermediate groups – can often defeat the large groups – the latent groups – which are normally sup-posed to prevail in a democracy.

(Olson, 1965, pp. 127–8)

Olson explained the existence of large numbers of groups in terms of a by-product theory of pressure groups. Members did not join because of the collective goals the groups pursued, but because of the selective incentives (services, discounts and so on) which were available only to members. Olson drew a picture of the pressure group system in which the business community was by far the best organized sector. It should be noted that Olson admitted that his theory did not apply to 'philan-thropic' groups, where those organized were concerned about persons other than those organized in the group itself. It is in this area, of course, that there has been a considerable expansion of group activity since Olson wrote his book.

It would be no exaggeration to say that in the years after the publica-tion of Olson's book, the study of pressure groups lived through 'The Olsonian years'. At the 1988 annual meeting of the American Political Science Association it was observed that there was now a need in the study of pressure groups to move 'beyond Olson-type questions'. A sub-stantial and growing literature has attempted to do so:

The history of the literature is of a battle to re-insert non-material incentives into the calculation. The most obvious explanation for action which does not conform to Olson's model is that there are non-economic inducements oper-ating – i.e. action is rational, but rationality is not the self-interested eco-nomic calculation set out by Olson.

(Jordan and Maloney, 1997, p.85)

In the decades since Olson's book was published, pressure groups have continued to multiply. This is, of course, what was argued by Truman in terms of a proliferation thesis. As processes of economic and social dif-ferentiation took place, more grounds for group emergence appeared (Jordan, 1994, p.3). Walker observes that 'the recent increases in the number of groups suggests that Truman has the data on his side' while admitting that 'An increase in the number of groups, by itself, would not disconfirm Olson's theory' (Walker, 1991, p.75). How can this increase be explained in Olsonian terms? Dowding is sceptical of the by-product theory, arguing that 'selective incentives cannot be the primary incentive for members of an organization primarily devoted to lobbying' (Dowding, 1994, p.542). This observation is supported by the survey work undertaken by the Aberdeen group. In the case of Friends of the Earth, '86.2% of existing members claimed that they would rejoin if direct member services were reduced, but only 31.5% would remain in membership if core campaigning was reduced' (Jordan, 1994, p.12).

In many cases, of course, the cost of joining a group is so small relative to an individual's income or a firm's turnover that the decision to join falls below the rationality threshold. Deciding whether to join could consume more resources in terms of opportunity cost than the actual cost of joining. There is, moreover, an important distinction between membership and participation. As Moe points out, 'An individual may, for instance, derive a sense of satisfaction from the very act of contributing, when he sees this as an act of support for goals in which he believes' (1980, p.188). Participation involves much higher costs in terms of the time expended by an individual or an employee attending meetings in the firm's time, but it also brings greater benefits with it: the solidaristic benefits of participation, and privileged access to a shared exchange of information. The former is generally of greater importance in cause groups, the latter in sectional groups.

Work in the United States by the late Jack Walker suggests that the Olsonian dilemma may be resolved by groups locating sources of funding outside their organization. Walker focuses in his work on the role of external patrons of political action such as the federal government, major institutions, and, most significant in the case of American citizen groups, wealthy individuals who 'are still a crucial source of the venture capital needed by aspiring political entrepreneurs' (1991, p.81). Walker himself poses the question of whether this is a distinctively American phenomenon, and uses French data to suggest that it is not. It would seem evident, however, that Britain has fewer independent foundations and wealthy individuals than the United States, but this does not mean that Walker's perspective is irrelevant. The Rowntree Trust did help Friends of the Earth by providing free office space in its early years, while Amnesty International benefited from a legacy (Jordan, 1994, p.16). The most striking example, however, is the Royal Society for the Prevention of Cruelty to Animals (RSPCA). Of a total income of £21.7 million in 1990, £17 million came from legacies and only £128,000 from subscriptions (Garner, 1993, p.46). Radical activists believe 'that the growing reliance on alternative means of income is a convenient means of preventing the influx of those who want to change the direction of the Society' (p.45).

Jordan and Maloney have developed a 'supply side' perspective which emphasizes the role of marketing in recruiting and retaining members through the manipulation of the decision to join. In a sense, group membership becomes a mail order purchase rather like the purchase of other consumer goods, only in this case people feel good about themselves because they are supporting an organization like the RSPB. Making use of professional marketing techniques, 'Groups offer a mixture of organizational and psychological strategies which help place the joining decision on individuals' agendas, and helps shape the decision-making process' (Jordan and Maloney, 1997, p.144). For an example of how a group markets itself, see Box 3.1.

Box 3.1 How a pressure group markets itself

The Association of Retired Persons Over 50

[Benefits of membership referred to in recruitment literature are categorized below according to a standard political science typology.]

Selective benefits

At an individual level, membership of ARP/O50 gives you a whole host of tangible benefits – such as free insurance cover, free telephone helplines, and substantial discounts on all sorts of goods and services.

Collective benefits

Since our inception, ARP/O50 has been a vigorous and effective campaigner ... We've recently seen significant successes in three areas: free eye tests, increased pensions for the most needy, and half-price travel for seniors ... we form a powerful lobby for the rights and interests of the Over 50s, through regular meetings with Government, MPs and other influential figures.

Solidaristic benefits

At a local level, our thriving network of Friendship Centres provide both a highly congenial forum for social activities ... first and foremost, they are a great way to meet new people, make new friends and share in an amazing variety of activities and events.

Source: ARP Over 50 recruitment literature, 1998.

It could be claimed that Olson's theory should really only be applied to economic interest groups which were the organizations he was concerned with in Olson (1965) and in his subsequent work. If, however, his theory is restricted to economic groups, Olson is 'no longer the missile aimed at the heart of pluralism' (Jordan, 1994, p.25). Olson's work does, however, provide an explanation of the special advantages that business enjoys in pressure politics. 'Where businesses do have to join together, the benefits of their actions are often enjoyed by a small number of firms and so the incentives to organize are high' (Smith, 1993, p.27). There are, of course, other ways of arguing that business enjoys a special position of power (Lindblom, 1977), but Olson provides a formal model which exerts a particular influence given the growing popularity of public choice approaches.

Offe and Wiesenthal (1985) have argued that there are 'two logics of collective action'. Labour is powerless unless it organizes: organized action is only one of a number of alternatives open to employers. Labour has been able to organize, but when groups such as the unemployed, the homeless, and those in prison attempt to organize, they face special difficulties. Outside patronage may be difficult to obtain (Walker, 1991), but the individuals in these categories may consider that their needs will be misinterpreted by well meaning professional outsiders who have not shared their particular experience.

Another set of problems arises from the absence of democracy within many pressure groups themselves. Either arrangements for democratic control are limited, or they tend to fall into disuse. Control of an organization can pass into a self-perpetuating oligarchy. Activists tend to be those who have the time and money to devote to organizational work, so that doctors' organizations may have a disproportionate number of doctors with private practices in leadership positions, whilst farmers organizations may be led by the more affluent arable farmers who can afford to be away from their farms. However, such leaderships must be careful not to move too far away from the opinions of their members, or they may lose large segments of the membership, as, for example, in the case of the separate organization of a Welsh Farmers' Union.

A more fundamental criticism of pluralism is that there are two levels of power in society, and that pluralism really only tells us about the lower level. The upper level is that of the core assumptions of society, such as private property, which largely go unquestioned. These core assumptions set the terms of reference for conflicts and outcomes at the lower level where 'the picture will look something like the polygon of

forces found by pluralist analysis' (Westergaard and Resler, 1976, p.248).
It could be argued, however, that if the core assumptions of society are
to be challenged, it should be done through the party system where electors can be offered a radical alternative to the status quo such as that
offered by the Green Party. Within government itself, the battle for resources between different departments does, in some senses, resemble a
competition between particular institutionalized interests (health, education, industry, agriculture, and so on).

Policy Networks and Policy Communities

'Policy network analysis has become the dominant paradigm for the study
of the policy-making process in British political science' (Dowding,
1995, p.136). In relation to the study of pressure groups, it has been
argued that it offers 'a model of interest group intermediation ... which
is superior to the pluralist or corporatist model' (Daugbjerg and Marsh,
1998, p.53).

In its original form, the notion of a policy community represented a
useful adaptation of the pluralist notion of distinct issue areas to the
particular circumstances of modern British government. As first developed by Richardson and Jordan (1979), it could be characterized as 'the
plurality model, in which disaggregation and plurality are seen as synonymous with pluralism' (Daugbjerg and Marsh, 1998, p.58). More
recent literature has led to the conclusion that 'there is not much here
which would naturally relate policy networks and pluralism, unless we
accept a very weak notion of pluralism'. Indeed, empirical studies perhaps provide more support 'for a statist interpretation of the distribution
of power' (Marsh, 1998b, p.189).

In their original work, Richardson and Jordan were seeking to emphasize the way in which policy-making in Britain was disaggregated
into a number of sub-systems which gave pressure groups ample opportunities to influence policies of concern to them. Thus, the president of
the NFU has a substantial influence on agricultural policy, but has no
interest in health policy; the president of the BMA can influence health
policy, but agricultural policy is not a matter for concern. It was argued
that the policy-making map was made up of a series of distinct vertical
compartments, generally organized around a government department and
its client groups, and largely closed off to the general public:

The term 'community' was chosen deliberately to reflect the intimate relationship between groups and departments, the development of common perceptions and the development of a common language for describing policy
problems.

(Richardson, 1993, p. 93)

In recent literature the term 'policy network' has largely displaced
that of 'policy community'. This may be because there are in fact relatively few networks which have the internal stability and insulation from
other networks typical of policy communities. Richardson's work suggests a gradual shift in emphasis from a policy-making world of tightly
knit policy communities to a policy process which is more loosely organized and hence less predictable. Many of the examples of stable and
predictable policy networks are to be found in agriculture. However,
'While agriculture may represent the archetypal case, continuity, resulting to a significant extent from the existence and activities of a policy
network' has been observed in a diverse range of policy areas including
smoking, nuclear power, diet and health, health services and sea defence (Marsh, 1998a, p.11).

The fire service offers a good example of a closed policy community,
albeit one characterized by considerable internal conflict, both between
local providers of fire services and the Home Office and between the
employers and the Fire Brigades Union (Rhodes, 1986, pp.304–25). What
does make the fire policy community a typical example of a policy community is its stability and its insulation from public discussion. Fire
service is provided in accordance with Home Office risk categories which
have 'been in place since 1958 and had their roots in work conducted in
1936'. Standards of cover are deteriorating in the absence of any public
awareness of how they are arrived at, or any discussion of the problems:

These standards effectively constrain and preclude radical changes in how
we provide the service. They also dictate how resources are deployed. The
public has never debated any significant changes. Budgetary pressures now
challenge our ability to meet these standards.

(http://www.cheshire.gov.uk/fire, 16 January 1999)

One can distinguish between five types of network 'ranging along a
continuum from highly integrated policy communities to loosely integrated issue networks' (Rhodes and Marsh, 1992, p.13). At one end of
the spectrum is the policy community 'characterized by stability of relationships, continuity of a highly restricted membership, vertical

interdependence based on shared service delivery responsibility and insulation from both other networks and, invariably, the general public (including Parliament)' (ibid.). At the other end of the spectrum, 'Issues networks are characterized by a large number of participants with a limited degree of interdependence. Stability and continuity are at a premium, and the structure tends to be atomistic' (ibid. p.14). The Rhodes and Marsh distinction has been adapted by Daugbjerg (1998a) to present policy communities and issue networks as two extreme network types on a continuum (see Table 3.1).

Table 3.1 Extremes on the policy network continuum

Dimensions	Policy community	Issue network
Membership	Very limited number of members; narrow range of interests represented	Large number of members; wide range of interests represented
Integration	Bargaining and negotiation; frequent interaction	Consultation; unstable pattern of interaction
Institutinalization	Consensus on policy principles and procedures to approach policy problems	Conflict over policy principles and procedures to approach policy problems

Source: Daugbjerg, 1998a, p. 44.

As an analytical proposition, the idea of policy communities clearly provides a good fit with the available empirical evidence on how decisions are made in British government. Dowding has, however, expressed doubts about whether the model can take us beyond description to any explanation of transformation or change. He comments, 'whilst we have learned much about the policy process by cataloguing the policy world into different types of networks, the approach will not, alone, take us much further' (Dowding, 1995, p.136). Marsh suggests (1998a, p.13) that the way forward is to stress the dialectical relationship between the structural aspects of networks and the interpersonal exchange of resources. As developed by Daugbjerg and Marsh, the policy network approach is seen as 'a model of interest group intermediation which needs to be integrated with macro-level theory and analysis if it is to contribute to an explanation of policy outcomes' (Marsh, 1998b, p.186). Work in progress by Kiernan that seeks to explore the compatibility of macro level Marxist theories and network analysis of particular issue arenas represents one interesting contribution to this debate.

Perhaps the most important but often neglected aspect of the policy networks approach is its implications for normative democratic theory. It is clear that these policy communities have rather high entry barriers around them (although the entry barriers are probably higher in longer-established communities such as agriculture than in younger ones such as conservation). Policy communities can become rather exclusive networks made up of well-established insider groups. Daugbjerg notes (1998b, p.79) 'Policy networks structure the decision-making process and provide outsiders and insiders with different opportunities for respectively changing or maintaining the existing order within a sector.' Thus, for defenders of the status quo, not least pressure groups, 'a sectoral policy network which has a high degree of cohesion among its members is a very powerful political resource' (Daubjerg, 1998b, p.79). Marsh and Rhodes noted (1992, p.264) that the case studies in their volume 'consistently show that producer groups and professional groups are the groups which, together with the government, dominate the policy networks'.

What emerges is rather like an elite cartel in which participants collude to preserve the existing parameters of the policy-making process. Not only is the range of participants limited, but there are good grounds for concern about the quality of the decision-making process. Stringer and Richardson (1982, p.22) argue that 'The objective of the policy-making process within these communities is often not the solving of real problems, but the management of avoidance of conflict, the creation or maintenance of stable relationships, and the avoidance of abrupt policy changes.' If the policy network is the best encapsulation we have of the policy-making process in Britain, there are normative grounds for concern.

Corporatism: Yesterday's Theory?

Tony Blair has repeatedly stated that 'old style' corporatism has no place in his 'new Britain'. He has stated in relation to what he terms '1960s corporatism' that 'I don't think that is where the world is any more' (*The Independent*, 26 September 1998). Although corporatist explanation has not been entirely abandoned by academics, and is still being deployed in current research in countries such as Venezuela and South Africa, its utility as an explanation of British pressure groups came to an end with the abandonment of neo-Keynesian politics. What happened was that 'neo-corporatist arrangements could no longer perform the imperative tasks that had been assigned to [them] by neo-Keynesian policy makers operating within the confines of their respective nation-states' (Schmitter and Grote, 1997, p.6). Nevertheless, corporatism was very influential for a while and at least an autopsy is necessary.

One of the problems about the corporatist debate was that there was little agreement about what the term meant. In its most basic form, tripartism, corporatism can be taken to refer to bargaining between the state, organized employers and the trade unions about the conduct of economic policy. The employers and unions were supposed to secure the adherence of their members to the agreements arrived at, thus reducing enforcement problems for the state.

Corporatist theory was attacked from all directions: by pluralists, who resented this attempt to invade their intellectual territory; by neo-marxists who regarded it as an inadequate theory, because of its pluralist roots and its failure to develop a theory of the state; and by Conservative politicians who saw corporatism as one of the major sources of British economic decline, even though Britain had experimented only with very weak forms of corporatism. In the context of incomes policy, which was one of the main drivers of corporatism, it quickly became apparent that the employers and the unions in Britain had difficulty in delivering their side of the bargain, even if they really wanted to.

Thatcherism and corporatism proved to be incompatible, and the remaining tripartite institutions such as the National Economic Development Council (NEDC) were gradually abandoned, although it was John Major who finally go rid of an already weakened NEDC. This move away from liberal corporatism was not just a British phenomenon as throughout the world, globalization made it increasingly difficult for governments to adhere to a full employment commitment 'which many have seen as the underpinning of corporatist exchanges between states, capital and labour' (Ainley and Vickerstaff, 1994, p.543).

As someone who would have to reply in the affirmative to the question 'Are you now, or have you ever been, a corporatist?', at least in the analytical sense, can any defence of corporatist theories be mounted? Schmitter, the doyen of corporatist theory, has attempted to do so, arguing that there is a twenty to 20–25-year cycle in corporatism and that it will enjoy a revival towards the end of the 1990s. This is in spite of the fact that he and his co-author admit that 'the very core interest categories upon which macro-economic compromises had been built were increasingly becoming disaggregated and dispersed' (Schmitter and Grote, 1997, p.29). The core of the argument advanced is that the future of macro-corporatism depends on the future evolution of the EU. There is, of course, a philosophy and practice of social partnership at the EU level which has Christian Democratic roots. Schmitter's argument is not, however, that some new edifice of Euro corporatism will be constructed around the social dimension or sectoral policies at the EU level. Rather, the argument is a more subtle one: the effective achievement of economic and monetary union will require national governments to obtain the active assent of their social partners through negotiation to secure competitive success.

There may be member states in which such arrangements develop, but Britain is unlikely to be among them. 'New Labour' involves an acceptance of much of the Thatcherite restructuring of British politics, not least the permanent weakening of organized labour. The much vaunted 'Third Way' may thus be seen as a compromise between neo-liberalism and social democracy which leaves room for a closer relationship with business but not a revival of tripartism.

The Liberal Critique of Pressure Groups

The study of pressure groups in Britain was pioneered by two American political scientists, Samuel Beer (1956; 1965) and Harry Eckstein (1960). Their starting point was the American pluralist perspective on pressure groups, but they also found in Britain an older corporatist tradition which reinforced the legitimacy of group activity. Their view, then, of the pressure group system in Britain was essentially a benign one, although Beer took a more pessimistic view in a later (1982) work. Their view was echoed by a leading British writer on pressure groups of the period, Finer (1958), who concluded his book with a plea for 'Light, more light!', that is, more transparency about the operation of the pressure group system.

This benign view happened to be reinforced by wider developments in political life. The year 1960 saw the so-called Brighton Revolution, named after a major conference on the economy held in the town by the then Federation of British Industries. This marked a shift towards a more interventionist approach to the management of the economy which went beyond the aggregate demand management of the 1950s. (For an excellent analysis of this shift, see Hall 1986, chapter 4.) Held against the background of increasing concern about Britain's economic performance, the Brighton conference led to a new enthusiasm for a limited form of economic planning among business leaders.

The significance of what developed into a shift to incomes policies and industrial policies was that it necessarily involved government in a closer relationship with key producer groups. The role of incomes policy in encouraging a tripartite style of government–industry relations has already been mentioned earlier in the chapter. Sectoral industrial policies usually draw government closer to pressure groups because their success 'is dependent on how readily producer groups will agree to accept the inevitable dislocations associated with economic adjustment' (Atkinson and Coleman, 1985, p.27).

The 1970s saw the collapse of the postwar Keynesian consensus, and its eventual replacement by a new monetarist orthodoxy. The exact reasons for this collapse do not concern us here, nor does the timing of the collapse or the extent to which the 1974–9 Labour Government repudiated Keynesianism. (For a fuller account, see Grant, 1993b.) The first oil shock of 1973, alongside serious industrial disputes in Britain, precipitated the crisis of Keynesianism, but it can be argued that these particular events simply revealed more fundamental flaws in Keynesian political economy. Against a background of considerable economic and political disruption, constituting the most serious crisis in Britain's postwar history, a new critique of pressure groups developed.

This background has been sketched in to suggest that the time was ripe for some new thinking about the durability and viability of the postwar political settlement in Britain, which had involved a new emphasis being given to the role of pressure groups, particularly trade unions, in the political process. Indeed, a general debate about British 'ungovernability' was sparked off, although this has not stood the test of time very well given that Mrs Thatcher showed that the British state has considerable powers at its disposal if it is directed by someone with strong and clear political convictions.

The most important piece of writing to appear at the time on the subject of pressure groups was an article by Samuel Brittan (1975). Brittan argued that liberal representative democracy was threatened by the generation of excessive expectations, and the disruptive effects of the pursuit of group self-interest. Producer groups had not in the past made full use of their potential power, 'but have tended to make increasing use of it as time has passed'. Brittan was particularly concerned about the activities of trade unions, which differed from other organized groups in terms of their willingness to withdraw output from the market until paid more. The kinds of demand being made strained to breaking point the sharing-out function of democratic society.

The power of trade unions has diminished significantly since the 1970s, but Samuel Brittan has provided through his later work a more general critique of the role of pressure groups in democracy from the perspective of an economic liberal. His arguments are a healthy corrective to a period when extensive pressure group activity was seen as an inevitable part of a modern democracy. Although he occasionally does have some good things to say about pressure groups, his perspective is based on a wish to defend the values of freedom and an open society. Reviewing an influential critique of pressure group activity which he wrote in the mid-1970s (Brittan, 1975), Brittan reflected (1987a, pp. 197–8):

> My theme ... became the incompatible claims of rival interest groups which increase in influence when government takes on overambitious economic functions. Interest groups do not merely reduce the national income when they become embedded in the political process. They embody rival claims which more than exhaust the national product and threaten the survival of liberal democracy itself.

Brittan argues (1987b, p.79) that interest group pressure constitutes one of a number of threats to individual freedom and popular government. Analysing the interest group threat, he notes (p.74) that: 'The main theme of Hayek's latest work is that democracy has degenerated into an unprincipled auction to satisfy rival organized groups who can never in the long run be appeased because their demands are mutually incompatible.' Brittan's clear message (1987b, pp.262–3) is that 'the entrenched position of industrial, economic and political interest groups will limit what can be achieved by any form of economic management, new or old'. Constitutional and political reform is necessary to reduce the role of interest groups and increase that of the individual citizen.

It might appear that with Mrs Thatcher's declared opposition to 'vested' interests, and her distaste for any kind of corporatism, the power of interest groups was fundamentally diminished. Certainly, the TUC, and even to some extent the CBI, became infrequent visitors to Downing Street. The implementation of policy continued, however, to be negotiated with affected interests, while the changes in policy-making that were introduced were not necessarily lasting. Under John Major 'there was a return to the more traditionalist style of policy-making in Britain ... civil servants remarked that they now felt more able to return to a previous form of intimate dialogue with groups, less fearful of a prime-ministerial dictat' (Richardson, 1993, p.98). Even when Mrs Thatcher was in office, Brittan considered that Mrs Thatcher's Goverment had done very little to reduce certain areas of middle-class privilege. He notes, 'Many interest group privileges, for instance for pension funds, mortgage holders or concessions to farmers, appear as tax reliefs' (Brittan, 1989, p.17). Even in the privatization programme, Mrs Thatcher's governments were very willing to make concessions to the existing managements of nationalized industries.

Another important contribution to the liberal critique of interest groups has been made by Mancur Olson (1982). Indeed, Brittan notes that 'There was a natural link between my thesis on collective pressures on democracy and the Mancur Olson thesis that the longer a country has enjoyed stable democratic political institutions, the more time there will be for interest group coalitions to form, which undermine performance' (Brittan, 1987a: p.198). Olson argues that stable societies with unchanged boundaries tend to accumulate more special interest organizations over time. The general effect is to reduce efficiency and aggregate income, and a society's capacity to reallocate resources and adopt new technology in response to changing conditions. Olson admits that a broadly based, 'encompassing' organization has an important incentive to take account of the consequences of its actions on the society as a whole. He points out, however, that many of the 'peak associations' (such as the CBI and TUC) studied by political scientists lack sufficient unity to produce coherent policy.

Britain has a particularly powerful network of special interest organizations, a phenomenon which Olson links to the country's poor growth record. 'British society has acquired so many strong organizations and collusions that it suffers from an institutional sclerosis that slows its adaptation to changing circumstances and technologies' (Olson, 1982, p.78). He concludes that special interests are 'harmful to economic growth, full employment, coherent government, equal opportunity and social mobility' (p.237). One possible remedy might be the repeal of 'all special-interest legislation or regulation and at the same time [the application of] rigorous anti-trust laws to every type of cartel or collusion that uses its power to obtain prices or wages above competitive levels' (p.236).

Much of what we know about the history of pressure group activity would seem to support Olson's argument. The number of pressure groups has increased over time, and the exit barriers preserving groups tend to be higher than the entry barriers in the way of new group formations. It would also seem to fit in with much of what we know of interwar economic history, particularly when viewed from the perspective of the institutional school of economic historians (Elbaum and Lazonick, 1986). This was an important period in Britain's economic development because a recognition of the problem of poor British economic performance was accompanied by only partially successful attempts to do anything about it.

Olson's analysis is thus of value in pointing to a problem of political adjustment in countries like Britain. Older industries were able to develop a dense network of institutional protections (a well-developed, closed policy community to use one language of analysis) which enabled them to slow down the transfer of resources to newer industries through protectionist measures, government subsidies and so on.

Where his analysis is more open to question is in relation to the argument that Britain was particularly afflicted by such problems. Just as some analysts tend to exaggerate the extent to which German industry was devastated by the Second World War, so Olson tends to overstate the institutional clean break that occurred in Germany and Japan (see Olson 1982, p.76). Lynn and McKeown (1988, p.173) argue that Olson very much exaggerates the extent to which special interest groups were abolished in Japan under the rule of the militarists during the war and under the Occupation after it. Similar continuities may be observed in Germany (Grant, Paterson and Whitston, 1988; Streeck, 1983, p.143.) A broader, cross-national study also suggests considerable elements of continuity in countries disrupted during the war by defeat or occupation (Grant, Nekkers and van Waarden, 1991). In the case of Germany, van Waarden notes (1991, p.297) that 'the war did not really entail a break in the development of structures of interest intermediation'.

The liberal critique of pressure group activity has obliged those of us who take a relatively benign view of organized interests to re-examine some of our fundamental assumptions. The liberal analysis has helped to revitalize the analysis of pressure groups in so far as it was becoming increasingly focused on relatively narrow questions such as the merits of different typologies of pressure groups. Even if one does not agree with their particular analysis, writers like Brittan and Olson have made an important contribution towards lifting the debate on to a higher plane. They have redirected our attention towards broader issues such as the relationship between pressure group activity and basic societal goals such as the preservation of freedom and economic success. As Brittan (1987a, p.198) notes:

> The dilemma is that many of the same groups – e.g. trade associations, unions, farmers, clubs or users' councils – which appear in political theory as beneficent intermediate associations between the citizen and the state, and the very cement of democracy, appear in political economy as threats to economic performance and stability.

The Tory Defence of Interest

The liberal critique of interest group activity, imperfectly reflected in Thatcherite thinking and action, stands in strong contrast to the traditional Tory analysis of the role of interest organizations in society. This traditional Tory or moderate Conservative strand was once the dominant tendency in the Conservative Party, but was supplanted after 1979 by Thatcherite neo-liberalism.

Tories reject the atomistic individualism inherent in neo-liberalism, and see interests as necessary and desirable intermediaries between the individual and society as a whole. Whilst not accepting Mrs Thatcher's view that there is no such thing as society, that is, that society is a totally artificial construct, they would argue that the individual cannot experience society as a whole. Organizations which link the individual to a wider community are valuable both for engendering a corporate spirit and for the communal good that they achieve. Indeed, the traditional Tory view comes close to being a prescriptive corporatist one, with its emphasis on the role of interests in governance, and proposals for an 'industrial Parliament'. (This is a recurrent Conservative theme: see Churchill, 1930; Amery, 1947; Gilmour, 1983.)

The most articulate exponent of the Tory interpretation of interests in the 1970s and 1980s has been Lord Gilmour (formerly Sir Ian Gilmour). He argues that 'Tories were never enthusiasts for *laissez-faire* with its glorification of individual self-interest and its distrust of groups' (1983, p.203). 'A Tory, then, rejects the simple idea that individuals are selfish and good and groups selfish and bad' (p.204). That is not to say that Gilmour views all groups benignly. He was very critical of the British trade union movement, arguing for the need 'to make trade-union activity less self-destructive and to bring home to the average trade-unionist that union power is only legitimate within limits' (1978, p.239). However, he has also been very critical of the CBI, which he portrays as weak, divided, lacking in political intelligence and sophistication, and subservient to the Conservative Party (1983, pp.194–5, 207). More generally, Gilmour echoes earlier arguments about the role of interest groups by arguing that their activities should be made more visible, with greater democratic influence being exerted over them (p.208).

Socialist Views of Pressure Groups

There is not really a distinctive socialist view of pressure group activity, although there is obviously a strong suspicion of business interests, particularly multinational big business. Centre-left postwar Labour governments in Britain, because of their wish to manage the economy, tended to veer towards a weak form of prescriptive corporatism. This was marked by intensive consultations with the unions and the employers although all the major tripartite institutions were set up by Conservative governments. There have also been some half-hearted attempts by Labour governments to improve the position of under-organized interests, for example with the formation of the National Consumer Council.

In general, however, the impression that emerges from reading the many books by former Labour ministers is the extent to which they took an orthodox approach to pressure groups. That is to say, they viewed them as a legitimate part of the political system which had to be consulted, although this might often become a chore. They were certainly irritated by organizations which went outside the conventional channels and resorted to demonstrations. In general, however, they worked the system as they had inherited it, although developing it through closer partnership relationships with selected pressure groups.

The Blair Government falls more clearly within the Thatcherite tradition than the 'old Labour' weak corporatist tradition, particularly in terms of a determination to challenge vested interests. This has been particularly true in relation to some of the well established professional interests such as those of teachers and doctors. Although the trade unions have been consulted more frequently than under the Conservatives, they have not been treated as a group with special status and their influence has been limited. From the Blair perspective, pressure groups are part of the problem rather than part of the solution.

4
Pressure Groups and the Executive

Pressure groups do not have the power to make authoritative decisions themselves. They do not constitute governments, or control legislatures, or staff courts. Hence, their success in achieving their objectives depends on influencing political institutions to adopt the policies and measures they advocate. This may involve securing the attention of political influentials, which could entail using the media to win public sympathy for the case advocated. Even so, it must be stressed that the bulk of pressure group activity is very undramatic and routine, and is invisible to the public eye. It involves a series of detailed discussions with civil servants, MPs or peers about the content and implementation of legislation.

It should also be remembered that pressure groups spend a lot of time talking to other pressure groups. Sometimes this may be to try and build a coalition on a particular issue and thus strengthen a particular case being put to government. Alternatively, producer pressure groups engage in discussions with other groups with whom they are potentially in conflict. A trade association will usually have more or less formal arrangements for maintaining contacts with its suppliers and its customers. For example, food industry associations talk to retail associations about questions ranging from discounting to the conflict between 'own label' and manufacturers' brands.

There is no one route by which pressure groups exert influence. The general features of the process can, however, be presented in the form of a simplified flow diagram (see Figure 4.1 below). Not all the stages presented in the diagram will be relevant to every instance of a pressure group exerting influence. For example, some cause groups have been able to achieve their objectives through the passage of a private member's bill, as happened with abortion law reform and the abolition of capital punishment. There will be further consideration of the role of

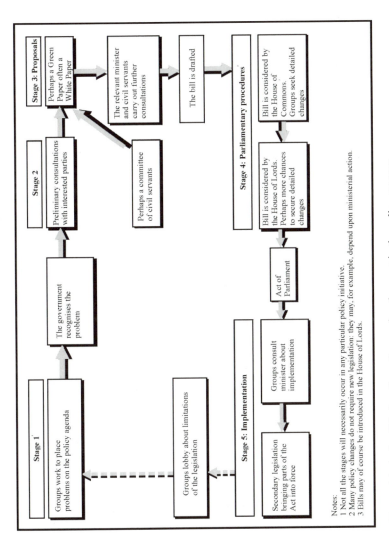

Notes:
1 Not all the stages will necessarily occur in any particular policy initiative.
2 Many policy changes do not require new legislation: they may, for example, depend upon ministerial action.
3 Bills may of course be introduced in the House of Lords.

Figure 4.1 A simplified outline of group involvement in the policy process

legislation in Chapter 8. However, many cause groups are more concerned to influence government than they are Parliament, for all insider groups issues will usually be pursued first through discussions with ministers and civil servants. 'A general characteristic of parliamentary constitutional structures is that interests direct their attention and activity first towards the executive rather than elsewhere' (Mitchell, 1997, p.156).

Influencing the Executive Branch of Government

In reviewing the literature published on pressure groups in the mid to late 1990s, it is remarkable how little touches on the question of relations between groups and the executive. In part, this is because the focus of attention has been elsewhere, either at the EU level or domestically, on such subjects as the role of commercial lobbyists and the rise of direct action groups. However, it also reflects the fact that relatively little has changed in relations between the executive, or more specifically civil servants and pressure groups (and it is with civil servants that the greatest volume of interchanges takes place).

Recent literature has distinguished between the core executive and the rest of the executive branch. The term refers to the bodies which coordinate government policies and resolve interdepartmental conflicts:

> In brief, the 'core executive' is the heart of the machine, covering the complex web of institutions, networks and practices surrounding the prime minister, cabinet, cabinet committees and their official counterparts, less formalised ministerial 'clubs' or meetings, bilateral negotiations and interdepartmental committees. It also includes coordinating departments, chiefly the Cabinet Office, the Treasury, the Foreign Office, the law officers, and the security and intelligence services.
>
> (Rhodes, 1995, p.12)

It is only a very limited number of core insider groups who have access at this level. Even during the Thatcher years, organizations such as the CBI continued to meet the prime minister and chancellor, both formally and informally. The case study presented later in the chapter of the formation of a Food Standards Agency under the Blair Government refers to an instance where a senior industrialist went straight to Downing Street to resolve a problem. The day after its formation in 1997, the chair of the Local Government Association met the deputy prime minister. There is a quarterly meeting between the association and senior cabinet ministers. In general, however, pressure groups are not involved in the resolution of interdepartmental conflicts, in which one department may be putting their point of view, or the final allocation of resources between competing demands on the budget.

Mrs Thatcher's distaste for 'vested interests' did affect the seriousness with which representations from bodies such as the CBI and TUC were regarded. 'Other lobbies such as doctors, teachers, the broadcasting industry, lawyers and the local authorities experienced a deterioration in their relationship with the executive and could not prevent the adoption of radical policies hostile in many ways to their interests' (Baggott, 1995a, p.489.) However, the deeply ingrained civil service tradition of consultation with affected interests meant that routine contacts continued. 'Even where ministers were hostile, some pressure groups continued to maintain fairly cordial links with civil servants, especially on low-profile issues' (p.491). A senior civil servant denied claims that consultation declined under the Thatcher administration, stating 'Of course we consult. I do not think the Government would survive long if we did not' (Maloney, Jordan and McLaughlin, 1994, p.23). The Aberdeen group take the view that 'the practice of consultation has been growing in importance over the past decade' (p.23). Reviewing the development of the system of business representation since 1979, May, McHugh and Taylor (1998, p.275) emphasize that what is striking is not the extent of change but its limits: 'The consultative relationship with central government departments was not seriously disturbed after 1979. Where change occurred it was attributable to the widening impact of legislation from the European Union than to changes in Whitehall practice.'

The Devlin Commission on Industrial Representation argued that 'All executive policy and most legislation is conceived, framed, drafted and all but enacted in Whitehall' (1972, p.5). This statement was an exaggeration when it was made; moreover, Parliament has almost certainly acquired greater influence since it was made. Even so, it contains a substantial element of truth. As a senior official of the National Farmers' Union has commented:

> Getting in early is a very important golden rule. We have a sort of intelligence role on behalf of the farmers to keep our ears to the ground to find out what new initiatives are being proposed and what legislation may be coming on with the object of influencing it from the outset ... Whatever it is we shall be

wanting to take an interest from the earliest stage. There is no question that once a piece of legislation reaches Parliament you may be able to tinker around the edges, but the prospect of getting any significant changes at that stage are very remote indeed ... Therefore it makes it much more important to try to get it right before it ever enters Parliament.

(Holbeche, 1986, p.46)

In a survey of business associations and unions, Mitchell (1997) found that 55 per cent of respondents reported meeting civil servants 'often'. Ministers were met 'often' by 27 per cent of respondents with 46 per cent meeting them 'sometimes'. The respondents found meeting civil servants the most effective of seven types of pressure group activity rated on a five point scale (34 per cent); meeting ministers was ranked second (22 per cent). When asked to select the most effective means of using influence, 58 per cent of business association respondents chose meeting civil servants, followed by 27 per cent who selected meeting ministers. If one adds in the 6 per cent of respondents who chose written submissions, then over 90 per cent of respondents selected a channel of influence involving the executive branch as the most effective (p.156 and p.158). Admittedly, the pattern of answers was somewhat different for trade unions who were forced into more of an outsider role during the period of Conservative government. As Mitchell notes (p.157), 'Business interests are the consummate insiders.'

Insider groups will try to influence policy when it is at the formative stage by talking informally to civil servants and ministers. In this respect, membership of some of the large number of advisory committees maintained by government may be important. As Jordan and Richardson observe (1987, p.185), 'Through regularized participation in these structures, groups are able to shape the definition and perception of problems, influence the political agenda in those policy areas of direct concern to them, and influence the perception and emergence of "practicable" solutions.' The more solidified the proposal becomes, the more difficult it is to change. Even once a consultative Green Paper has been published, there are limits to the extent to which government will be prepared to modify its policies; this is even more true in the case of a white paper, which can be seen as a statement of the government's intentions. Of course, consultations will go on in between the publication of the white paper and the presentation of a bill to Parliament. However, by this stage they will be increasingly formal and even ritualistic, and the government's room for manoeuvre without losing face will be seriously limited.

As Bruce-Gardyne (1986, p.152) explains in the light of his experience as a minister:

> the safest solution for the corporate lobbyist is to fix his trade association, and then to watch his trade association fix the civil service. For once the deal is done, the honour of the civil service is engaged. If it then fails to deliver its Ministers bound hand and foot, it hangs its head in shame. Whereas the lobby which converts the politicians is inevitably confronted by the resistance of the civil service.

The Structure of Government

In understanding how insider groups influence policy at the formative stage, it is really necessary to start with the structure of government itself. Policy communities and networks tend to form around government departments, and pressure groups are often concerned when departments are reorganized. For example, the roads lobby was unhappy when the Ministry of Transport was incorporated into the Department of the Environment in 1970. In 1976 a new Department of Transport was created. 'The experience of the DoE suggested that the transport community was not happy to form part of an integrated land-use planning department, and possessed the political power to withstand this assault from those campaigning for greater integration' (Dudley 1983: p.113). The disappearance of a separate Department of Transport after the return of a Labour government in 1997 was an indication that the influence of the road lobby was not as great as it once was.

Although most insider pressure groups will have contacts with a range of departments, they tend to have particularly close contacts with one department. Indeed, they may encounter difficulties in establishing relations with departments with which they are not familiar. This is partly because each department is anxious to defend its clients. For example the Energy Department, before it was absorbed by the Department of Trade and Industry, tended to defend interests of energy-producing industries against energy users. It is also a reflection of the importance of departmentalism within the culture of the British civil service. 'The distinctive culture of the department is at least as important as the culture of Whitehall as a whole' (Plowden, 1985, p.26). Whiteley and Winyard (1987, p.94) noted the existence of different 'house-styles' and bureaucratic cultures from department to department, while a study of the

chemical industry found considerable differences in departmental attitudes towards the industry (Grant, Paterson and Whitston, 1988).
It is also important to take account of the relative importance attached
to different functions within a department. Discussing the organization
of MAFF in the immediate postwar period, when there was a distinct
Ministry of Food, a then senior official of a food-processing industry
association has commented:

> All Ministers at Whitehall Place do from time to time assure the food industry
> of their awareness that they are ministers of Food *too* but in recent times they
> have in reality been, according to party, an extension of Ministers of Con-
> sumer Affairs or simply Ministers of Agriculture and, perhaps, fisheries. Their
> policies have, it is true, sometimes been of benefit to this or that part of the
> food industry but that has been almost entirely coincidental.
>
> (Stocker, 1983, pp.250–1)

This version of events received confirmation from the former permanent secretary at MAFF, arguing the general thesis that from the merger
of the two departments in 1955 to the late 1980s:

> food policy, if it existed at all was very much the junior partner in the MAFF.
> This was so from the outset. Much as we pretended to our colleagues that it
> was a true merger of the Ministries of Food and Agriculture, in fact it was a
> takeover. For the rest of my official career (and I retired in 1987), agricultural
> policy was in the driving seat.
>
> (Franklin, 1994, p.4)

Some interest groups may have a close relationship with a particular
junior minister who is perceived as an advocate for their particular needs;
indeed, they may have lobbied for the particular post to be established.
Examples include the creation of a post of Minister for the Arts in 1964,
probably most successful as a means of promoting the arts under its first
incumbent, Jenny Lee, and a Minister for the Disabled in 1974. Although
the effectiveness of such ministers has been questioned, Theakston (1987,
p.161) points to 'the increased expenditure secured through their cham-
pioning of their clients; their liaison work with organizations at arm's
length from Whitehall, local authorities and interest groups, helping keep
the government in touch with problems and views outside; and the con-
solidation of responsibilities within Whitehall achieved under them'.

The Dullness of Lobbying

A few years ago the author was sitting in the reception area of a trade association. Two other people were there, and one, clearly unfamiliar with trade associations, asked the other, 'What do they do here?' The reply was, 'It's very dull really, collecting statistics, and talking to civil servants.' It has to be emphasized that most lobbying is a rather dull business carried on between two sets of bureaucrats. Pressure groups employ professional staff, usually structured on relatively hierarchical lines. They then go and engage in detailed discussions with other bureaucrats working for the civil service about the details of, for example, a statutory instrument implementing an EC directive. A lot of the negotiation takes place with relatively junior or middle-ranking officials. Miller notes (1990, p.94) that 'the great proportion of administrative judgements made and communicated to the public are by officials who have been well trained in the largely fictional convention of Ministerial Responsibility'.

Most representations should thus be directed at a relatively low level of the administrative heirarchy. As one under-secretary is reported as commenting, 'Action is taken at the lowest level in the Civil Service at which it can be competently handled' (Public Policy Consultants, 1987, p.16). Busy permanent or deputy secretaries are not usually going to contradict the advice given to them by junior officials who know much more about the issue under consideration. A booklet on working with Whitehall prepared for the CBI notes, 'it is the senior executive officer or higher executive officer in charge of a section of a policy division whose work is most likely to be relevant to the businessman' (Coffin, 1987, p.32). Whether such advice is taken is another matter; Public Policy Consultants (1987, p.15) found that 77 per cent of the ministers and officials in their sample thought that pressure groups suffered from a mistaken desire to take things to the top.

The frequency of contact will vary from one group to another. Whiteley and Winyard (1987, pp.92–3) make a distinction between regular, periodical and infrequent contacts, ranging from day-to-day relations to a major meeting once a year. Similar distinctions would apply to sectional groups. However, it should be noted that a particular issue may lead to more intensive contacts than usual. For example, the Ice Cream Federation had more than its usual level of contact with MAFF while an EC directive on ice cream was under consideration.

The process of consultation usually starts with the department sending out a proposal for comment to a range of groups. The number of consultative documents increased considerably in the 1970s and 1980s: from 11 in 1976 to 112 in 1983 and 267 in 1990. (Hansard Society, 1993, quoted in Maloney, Jordan and McLaughlin, 1994, p.24). Lists are maintained for the purposes of circulating such documents; they are usually rather long:

> Consultation processes related to food labelling issues (according to the relevant civil servant) involve approximately 500 groups within which some 20 to 30 organisations are seen as particularly influential. But it would not be unusual for them to receive somewhere between 30 and 60 responses to a particular aspect.
>
> (Jordan, Maloney and McLaughlin, 1992b, p.19)

The civil service considers that it is better to over-consult than to under-consult. As one senior civil servant has commented:

> We consult on any proposal those organisations which seem to be representative of the subject or interests under discussion. It is a subjective judgement on every occasion but we work on the basis that we would sooner over-consult rather than under-consult because you cannot from our position judge the importance on occasions of a particular proposal to a particular group of people.
>
> (Quoted in Coates, 1984, pp.146–7)

The initial consultation process could be viewed as a trawling exercise in which not everything that is obtained will be of value. A further process of sifting and grading has to follow. Most of the meetings that take place will be between pressure group representatives and civil servants, although occasionally ministers will become directly involved. When that happens the meeting will often be a rather formal, set piece affair in which both sides state their positions. Indeed, one of the chores given to junior ministers is to 'receive a large number of deputations and delegations to save them going to the top minister' (Theakston, 1987, p.139). Sometimes such meetings often seem to be held for the benefit of the vanity of the pressure group's members. One experienced director of a regionally based association told me after his retirement that his members were great believers in delegations to London. He recalled, 'They would put their case bluntly to the minister – with little effect – and the man from the *Yorkshire Post* would be waiting outside the building and they would say, "We told him!"'

The annual 'Budget representations', made by a variety of associations to the Chancellor, often seem to have a rather ritualistic character, amusingly recalled by Bruce-Gardyne (1986, pp.157–9). He suspects that often the whole exercise is for the benefit of the trade press photographer waiting on the Treasury doorstep. The delegation is duly displayed 'to advantage over a story reporting that they have "made the strongest representations" and "received a sympathetic hearing"' (p.159). Nevertheless, lobbying the Chancellor does sometimes lead to a favourable outcome from the point of view of the pressure group in the Budget.

Even so, there are times when it is useful to involve the minister; often it may be more appropriate to approach a junior minister who is handling a particular area of policy. For all the constraints and limitations that they face, 'It is indisputable that in the 1970s and 1980s junior ministers in general have played more significant roles and carried more weight in Westminster and Whitehall than in the 1940s, 1950s and early 1960s' (Theakston, 1987, p.79). More generally, as Whiteley and Winyard note (1987, p.93), 'the view that civil servants run things and that the minister has to go along with this is an over-simplification. Individual ministers were perceived to make a real difference to outcomes'. Some key decisions, such as whether to refer a proposed takeover bid to the Monopolies and Mergers Commission, ultimately have to be made by the minister personally, albeit on the basis of advice offered by his civil servants. Such decisions are generally taken in the political limelight, with the political and media spotlight on the minister.

It must also be emphasized that some contacts take place at a very high level within government, particularly when major companies are involved. For example, when ICI was worred about a change in tax law which it thought would adversely affect its operations, meetings took place between the chairman of ICI and the then chancellor of the exchequer, the chief secretary of the treasury, and other ministers and senior officials of the Inland Revenue. It is not unknown for chairmen and managing directors of major companies to have meetings at prime ministerial level.

One of Mitchell's respondents noted that 'the most effective way of influencing Government on a detailed issue without wide political implications would usually be by meeting the relevant civil servants' (1997, p.157). However, even when one is dealing with a high profile issue where a new government is committed to action, there are many opportunities for the exercise of influence. This is apparent from the following case study of the decision to set up a Food Standards Agency. Public concern following the policy disaster of BSE forced the issue on to the policy agenda and led to a shift in the prevalent elite consensus. However, the actual design of the agency then became the subject of intense and classical forms of lobbying.

Case study: the Formation of a Food Standards Agency

The 1980s saw a growth in public concern about the maintenance of food safety standards. In part this reflected the growth of new campaigning organizations such as the Food Commission and the National Food Alliance, concerned with issues such as food additives and the effect of diet on coronary heart disease. These concerns were reinforced by a number of 'food scares' which were not seen as being accidents, or simply the result of inadequate enforcement, but were seen as having a systemic relationship with more intensive and industrialised forms of agriculture. Animals kept in high densities, often among their own faeces, mean that bacteria could spread more widely. The extensive use of antibiotics to keep animals healthy can lead to resistant strains of bacteria entering the human food chain. For example, there has been a growth in food poisoning from a particular type of salmonella which is resistant to five antibiotics. Cases of food poisoning in Britain quadrupled over a 10-year period with more than 81 000 cases reported in 1994 (*Farmers Weekly*, 6 December 1996). 'In summary, intensification of agriculture and its exposure to world markets increased the risk of consumers being exposed to potential hazards' (Meat and Livestock Commission, 1997, p.2).

A new food safety law was introduced in the 1990 Food Safety Act and MAFF was reorganized internally in 1993 to create a Food Safety Directorate, while quarterly meetings were organized with a consumer panel. 'The Food Safety Act ... enhanced hygiene control in the downstream industry (retail and processing) but it had little effect on the primary industries because farming was regarded as a food source, and was largely exempt' (Meat and Livestock Commission, 1997, p.2). However, the Conservative Government also created strong pressures for deregulation, commissioning the 1993 report of the Food and Drink Agriculture Task Force and the 1995 report of the Deregulation Task Force 'Both saw overregulation as an issue for the food industry' (Marsh, 1997, p.18). For the Conservatives, deregulation was a key policy of MAFF, although they claimed that it was not about 'removing essential protection' (Browning, 1997, p.13).

For critics of the existing arrangements, MAFF was being asked to fulfil a contradictory mandate which demanded reform:

> These contradictions are rooted in the fact that MAFF is charged with both sponsoring and regulating an industry and that it is supposed simultaneously to promote commerce, yet respond to consumer demands, notably for sound public health.

(Lang, Millstone, Raven and Rayner, 1996, pp.1–2)

Such arguments had been made for some time, but what transformed the situation was the government's admission in 1996 of a possible link between Bovine Spongiform Encephalopathy (BSE) and a new variant of the invariably fatal Creutzfeld Jakob Disease (CJD). The full story of the handling of the BSE episode was still under investigation at the time of writing, but it bore all the characteristics of a policy disaster (Grant, 1997). In any event, the immediate consequence was that 'British food policy and the role of the state in relation to food has been scrutinised to a level not seen since World War II' (Lang, Millstone, Raven and Rayner, 1996, p.1).

A new consensus quickly emerged among the key actors in the policy arena who were brought together at a conference organized by the European Food Law Association in December 1996. Retailers, food companies, farmers, environmental health officers, and consumers' representatives all called for the establishment of an independent food agency. However, it was evident that what the farmers had in mind was more modest than the other key actors: either an independent food safety professional attached to the existing Food Safety Directorate or an audit body which would supervise MAFF and some activities of the Department of Health. In fact, this was rather close to what the outgoing Conservative government proposed in January 1997, an independent food safety adviser chairing a new Food Safety Council which would 'take a strategic view of the longer term agenda and identify issues cutting across the work of the existing network of independent expert advisory committees' (MAFF News Release, 30 January 1997).

It was in fact quite difficult for the NFU to decide how it should handle the issue. It was initially against the whole idea of a food safety agency but 'weakened in the face of public demand ... it has concluded that, on food safety issues, MAFF is no longer being taken seriously and that this is counterproductive' (*Farmers Weekly*, 3 January 1997). The NFU sought the views of its members who turned out to be 'split evenly on whether an independent food agency should have executive status or should be an audit body' (*Farmers Weekly*, 17 January 1997). This illustrates that pressure groups sometimes have to respond to public opinion, and that it is not always immediately apparent what their optimal strategy is in a situation in which the underlying policy paradigm has shifted. The public debate, and, more importantly, the debate in the policy community had moved beyond what was readily acceptable to the NFU's membership.

Tony Blair as leader of the opposition commissioned a report from Professor Philip James, an acknowledged food safety expert. In order to carry out his work he was provided with office facilities by the Consumers' Association. It was evident that he had in his mind a distinction between 'vested interests' (essentially bad) and 'public interests' (essentially good). He argued that 'inappropriate political and industrial interests are perceived to determine decisions on food safety to the detriment of public health and consumer interests' (James, 1997, p.5). 'Many public interest groups ... consider that there are real failings in the present system' (p.14).

James's solution was to propose an agency modelled on the Health and Safety Commission/Executive, but with more 'consumer and other public interest involvement within its structure' (p. 5). The agency should be free of 'interference from vested interests' (p.16) and the majority of the members would be nominated by public interest groups. James's rather naive belief in the purity of public interest groups was, however, offset by his own statement that 'It is also important to note that any reforms must gain the confidence of the food and agricultural industries whose interests are crucially affected by the reputation and performance of government department and agencies' (p.15). Presenting the report to Mr Blair at a photo opportunity just after the election, Professor James forecast that an 'enormous battle' had begun over his proposals (*Financial Times*, 10 May 1997).

In preparing his report, Professor James consulted a range of experts and interests. The main categories of associations consulted were public and environmental health organizations (10), for instance the Chartered Institute of Health; consumer and environmental associations (9), for instance the Food Commission; and associations connected with the food chain (5), for instance the Food and Drink Federation. No trade unions were consulted. In drawing up a white paper, the government invited anyone with views to write in which, if nothing else, showed the wide range of associations in existence that are prepared to express a view on public policy. There were over 600 replies. Many of these were from local authorities or private individuals. Nevertheless, no less than 66 associations concerned with the food chain appeared, along with 27 environmental and consumer organizations, 22 public health organizations, and 13 miscellaneous trade associations. Three trade unions also gave their views. Some of the bodies which produced responses were relatively obscure or had highly technical concerns, such as the Automatic Vending Association of Britain, the British Goat Society, the Cornish Guild of Smallholders and the Gin and Vodka Association of Great Britain.

What was made clear in the white paper was that interest groups were seen as active participants in the policy-making process:

> The consultation process has already highlighted a variety of issues where interest groups would like to see changes in the way policy is formulated and the existing legal controls are interpreted and applied, as well as some areas where those existing legal controls are considered to be inadequate.
>
> (Cm. 3830, p.10)

Although one of the guiding principles set out in the white paper was that 'the Agency should act independently of specific sectoral interests' (p.5), the tone of the report gave a greater emphasis to the role of producer interests than the James Report. 'In assessing costs and benefits the Agency will need to take account of the effects of its actions on those affected ... it will be essential for the Agency to secure the confidence, support and co-operation of all sectors of industry' (p.6).

The production of the white paper was delayed by disagreements within the government about the scope of the new agency. The cabinet sub-committee considering the white paper received a letter from Peter Mandelson in his role as minister without portfolio about the agency's role on nutritional issues. He argued that it could be distracted from its main purpose if it became a campaigning body on food health. Unsafe food was not the same as undesirable food. His stated intention was to 'clear up "muddled thinking". However, his ministerial colleagues saw an uncanny resemblance between Mandelson's musings and lobbying by the food industry, which was worried that the new agency would turn nannyish ... Ministers felt that they could not be seen as responding to industry pressure' (*Financial Times*, 4 December 1997).

The divergence of views between consumer and public health organizations and food and farming organizations about including nutrition in the agency's remit was referred to in the white paper. It noted that 'The area of nutrition has been the subject of vigorous debate ... the Government expects there will continue to be debate' (Cm. 3830, p.33). Translated out of the restrained language of Whitehall, this means 'there has been a row about this and it isn't going to go away'. The government hedged its bets about whether the definition of a healthy diet should rest with the agency or the agency and health departments jointly. It was this kind of unresolved issue that was referred to by an official who stated that 'Bits of the white paper will have green edges, and will be subject to further discussion' (*Financial Times*, 8 January 1998). As far as the government was concerned the white paper was just one further stage in a continuing process of consultation:

> The Government intends to make full use of the time which is required for the preparation and passage of legislation to continue detailed discussions with representatives of the public, consumer organisations, the enforcement authorities, the scientific community and the food and farming industries. Close cooperation between all those with an interest is essential to achieve a smooth transition and to construct a secure foundation for the new Agency.
>
> (Cm. 3830, p.46)

The white paper did not take up the James Report's recommendation that the agency should be made up of representatives of public interest groups, but nor was it intended to follow the Health and Safety Commission model of appointment after consultation with representatives of employees and employers and so on. It was claimed that the range of affected interests was too wide and it would not 'be feasible for the Commission to cover all the relevant fields' (p.35). Decoded, this means that appointing people on the basis of interest affiliation would cause too many disputes about which interests should be represented and in what proportions. Hence, the preference for appointing individuals with relevant expertise 'from a wider public interest background without any specific affiliation' (p.36).

The government minister who drew up plans for the agency, David Clark, confirmed after his subsequent dismissal that he and fellow ministers were 'lobbied hard by the food industry' (*Financial Times*, 20 October 1998). The food industry did make some progress on the nutrition issue, as the agency's role in that area was less powerful than many food lobbyists had hoped for. They had hoped that it would offer specific advice on what people should eat. Where the industry did not make headway was in relation to the government's insistence that the greater part of the cost of running the agency should be met by a system of licensing charges across the industry. Indeed, some food lobbyists and trade unions were worried that an industry financed body would be opened to pressure from producers.

The then agriculture minister, Jack Cunningham, was angered by comments by the Food and Drink Federation that the proposed licence fees represented a tax on food, particularly as he was reported as favouring the agency being taxpayer-funded. Sir Dominic Cadbury, president of the Federation, bypassed the agriculture ministry and took his concerns direct to Downing Street. The government's own better-regulation taskforce, chaired by a Labour peer, Lord Haskins (also chair of Northern Foods) was another ally, arguing that licensing 600 000 outlets would incur high transaction costs. At a high political level, the government became concerned about being seen as 'nannying' the nation after the adverse reaction to the ban on beef on the bone, while the Countryside March had caused a determination within the government to be seen as concerned about the special problems of rural areas. However, the Treasury and Downing Street were reported to be opposed to using taxpayer funds, no doubt concerned about any new source of upward pressure on taxes (*Financial Times*, 14 July 1998). The extensive consultation process, and the complicated issues arising from it, led to fears that the legislation would not be ready for the 1998–9 Parliamentary session.

By the autumn of 1998 it became apparent that the legislation would not be included in the legislative programme for the new Parliamentary session. The government had a number of other major pieces of legislation to which it gave higher priority, not least House of Lords reform. One food industry source claimed, however, 'We hijacked this from the start'. Even a 'government insider' conceded, 'There is now real confusion over when, whether and how this agency will ever take shape' (*Sunday Times*, 11 October 1998). It was reported that ministers were going to embark on a new round of consultation based on a draft bill.

Once a compromise was reached on House of Lords reform, there appeared to be some prospect that a bill might be introduced in the 1998–9 session. Draft legislation was published in January 1999. The dispute between the Ministry of Agriculture and the Treasury over the agency's funding with the ministry sharing the food industry's view that it should be financed out of general taxation was resolved in favour of the Treasury with a standard levy of £90 on retail outlets. This proposal, however, raised a new political controversy about a so-called food 'poll tax' with convenience stores promising a campaign against it.

A number of general lessons can be drawn from this case study:

- A long running problem about food safety arising from the intensification and industrialization of the agency was highlighted by the BSE crisis.
- This raised the political salience of the issue and produced a new elite consensus about the need for an independent food agency which farming interests were not able to resist.
- The debate about the form and functions of the agency produced many opportunities for the use of traditional executive lobbying tactics. In particular, divisions among ministers provided opportunities for the food industry lobby.
- The government placed a very strong emphasis on consulting affected interests throughout all stages of a lengthy decision-making process. This slowed the decision making process down and the industry lobby was able to obtain some concessions. The introduction of the agency was at least significantly delayed.

Policy Implementation and Enforcement

A whole literature in political science is devoted to the way in which the process of policy implementation leads to outcomes very different from those which were originally intended. In the case of the Food Standards Agency, there will be considerable interest in how it actually operates once it is established. The white paper emphasizes the independence of the agency, but also stresses the need to consult with affected interests. Even in the Thatcher period, 'The traditional process of consultation and negotiation tended to reassert itself with regard to practical issues of implementation' (Baggott, 1995a, p.492).

The consideration of policy implementation and enforcement really belongs to a discussion of relationships between pressure groups and the executive branch of government, even though Parliament has a role in the passage of delegated legislation. Many Acts of Parliament are largely put into effect through secondary legislation referred to as Statutory Instruments (laws made by ministers under powers given to them by an Act of Parliament). In particular, there has been a 'growth of Enabling Legislation, which outlines the parameters of a Statute's authority and delegates to Ministers the power to pass Regulations on specific matters within that authority' (Miller, 1990, p.58). Parliamentary scrutiny of such regulations is limited in its effect. Less than a quarter of the

2 500 or so statutory instruments made each year are referred to a Select Committee, 'whose duty is to scrutinize them under very restricted terms of reference' (Taylor, 1979, p.131). Pressure groups are understandably very interested in the contents of statutory instruments. They 'play a major part in crucial political issues, such as the government reaction to BSE, the regulation of telecommunications and the creation of a National Curriculum' (Page, 1998, p.3). Detailed variations may influence considerably the activities and financial rewards of their members. Moreover, there are more opportunities to exert influence than in the passage of primary legislation. A clear majority of Page's respondents (p.9) agreed with the statement that 'consultation on statutory instruments offers groups like ours a better chance to shape legislation than consultation on parliamentary bills'.

Once again, there is an extensive process of consultation with potentially affected groups: for example, in the case of the Control of Pollution (Waste Disposal) Regulations 1987, 11 local authority associations, plus 52 'other interested bodies' ranging from Friends of the Earth to the British Insurance Brokers Association (Norton, 1990, p.206). In dealing with delegated legislation, the executive reveals the extent of its reliance on the consent and expertise of pressure groups:

> Most instruments are only laid after consultation with affected interests. More so than primary legislation, delegated legislation is the product of negotiation within small policy communities of civil servants and affected groups. (In what has been termed quasi-legislation, notes of guidance and circulars drawn up under the authority of primary legislation, group representatives may perform the drafting.)
>
> (p.205)

Even when secondary legislation has been put into effect, and codes of conduct distributed, there is still a gap between implementation and enforcement. Passing a law offers the means of tackling a particular problem, but resources may not allow effective enforcement activity. Since the first anti-litter legislation was passed in Britain in the 1950s, the amount of litter on the streets has increased. The enforcement of environmental legislation is often constrained by the limited staff resources available to the relevant inspectorate or other enforcing body. Many environmental groups consider that prosecutions are still not initiated in enough cases where environmental laws have been breached, although there is less reliance on persuading polluters to remedy their

behaviour than in the past. In some cases, a pressure group is also responsible for enforcement, as in the case of the RSPCA and anti-cruelty
laws:

> The biggest disadvantage for the RSPCA in its enforcement role is a lack of
> statutory power. Only the police have the power to arrest a person suspected
> of cruelty to animals and not even they ... have the power to search the premises
> of a suspect since animal cruelty is not considered to be a serious enough
> offence ... This is not the case in America [where RSPCA equivalents] are
> incorporated as law-enforcement agencies.
>
> (Garner, 1993, p.189)

The Benefits of Being on the Inside Track

It is apparent from the evidence reviewed in this chapter that there are
extensive contacts between pressure groups and the executive branches
of government during the development of policy and its implementation. The growing importance of EU decisions, often highly technical in
character, has increased the importance of such contacts. Many decisions are clearly taken within relatively closed policy networks in which
the complexity of the problems being discussed often constitutes a significant entry barrier. Thus, in his discussion of food standards, Coates
(1984, p.157) observes that:

> Possible changes are widely canvassed, thoroughly discussed, considered in
> detail and, if broadly acceptable to all who show an interest, put into effect ...
> This continuous process of consultation tends to commit the whole policy
> community not only to the policy process but also the decisions it brings forth
> ... almost all members of the policy community have an interest in the smooth
> functioning of the system.

Consider the values that are embedded in that statement. The first is that
of extensive and detailed consultation. The second is that of acceptability to affected interests. A third is the commitment of pressure groups to
decisions arrived at through the process of consultation. A fourth is the
assumption that both government and groups have an interest in continuity and stability in the policy process. These values might be
summarised as the four Cs of insider pressure group politics:

* *consultation* with recognized interests

- *consent* by the interest groups consulted to the decisions taken by government
- *co-operation* by the groups in the implementation of the decisions
- *continuity* in the contours of the policy-making process.

Such a policy process tends to benefit insider groups. Alternative channels are available to groups lacking insider status, through using the media to establish their concerns on the policy agenda, through the courts, or through the passage of private members' bills in Parliament. These methods will be considered in later chapters. Miller (1990, pp.53–6), from his vantage point as chief executive of Public Policy Consultants, assigns influence scores to various components of the political system. The prime minister receives a score of ten out of ten; officials eight; and ministers seven. Apart from the whips, the highest score given to a parliamentary body is six for backbench (not select) committees of MPs and the House of Lords committee which scrutinizes the activities of the EU. MPs/peers as a group receive four, rising to six if there is a small majority or a very public or political issue. Access to decision-makers in the executive branch clearly has its advantages and those advantages are more readily available to some groups than others.

5

The Organization of Representation at the EU Level

This chapter examines the range of groups that operate at the EU level, reviewing the nature of the pressure groups that are in the game and discusses some of the factors that influence the extent to which they are effective. It makes the argument that, notwithstanding some advances by environmental and other 'diffuse' groups (Pollack, 1998) it is business groups that are most effective in exerting influence. There is a review of the different categories and types of pressure group operating at the EU level, starting with business groups and considering why some business interests are less successful than others. Agriculture is examined as a case of a producer group which has lost some ground. The other principal categories of group are then examined with an emphasis on environmental groups which are seen as the main countervailing force to that of business.

The late 1990s has seen a rapid growth in studies about interest repesentation at the European Union level. As decision making has shifted to Brussels, it is understandable that analysts should switch their attention to where power and influence has apparently flowed. The Department of Trade and Industry claims that 'some 70% of legislation affecting British business now emanates from Brussels' (*The Economist*, 2 May 1998, p.25). The impact is much less significant in areas such as health, education and crime policy than it is in relationship to the economic and environmental issues that concern business. Nevertheless, the political centre of gravity is shifting.

Many of the available analyses of pressure group activity at the EU level are case studies or studies of particular sectors of the economy or arenas of representation such as the environment. Such an approach is understandable when relatively little is known about a new arena of interest group activity. However, if case studies are not located firmly within an analytical framework, it is easy to slip into basing a generalisation on what may be an untypical particular example. In many respects the overall research picture remains unsatisfactory:

> forty years of scientific research on the subject ... does not add up to a coherent picture of the nature of interest organization in the EC. There is little consensus about the importance of the different types of interest groups, about the influence they can exert on the politics and policies of the EC, and the effect their activities have on the development of the integration process.
>
> (Kohler-Koch, 1994, p.166)

Although there has been a concern with whether groups have been able to play the positive role in the integration process assigned to them by integration theorists, and debates about the relative merits of pluralist and corporatist models, the debate has generally been atheoretical. It is, of course, difficult to theorize about a political process that is characterized by its particular complexity and unpredictability and which is continually evolving. Nevertheless, the time may have arrived for some new efforts at theory building. The next stage of work must to be see what, if any, generalizations can be made about the forms of representation at the European level and above the influence exerted by different interests.

The Predominance of Business?

The general view taken in this chapter is that business is the predominant influence at the European Union level. This does not mean that other interests cannot win significant victories. Nor does it mean that all business interests are equally effective: in this chapter, examples will be given of production interests that are weakly represented or have lost ground. Business interests are sometimes divided on particular issues for commercial or other reasons. Nevertheless, what is being argued is that on major decisions, such as the establishment of the single market or blocking the carbon tax, business has been very influential, as it has on many technical matters.

An alternative perspective is put forward by Richardson who argues that the EU provides 'a set of opportunity structures and venues which have generally been favourable towards interest groups of all kinds'

(1998, p.2). He argues that the EU group process is 'much more competitive, fluid and unpredictable than the "business rules OK" thesis might imply' (p.22). The degree of competition means that no one interest can dominate the lobbying process over any length of time.

It is certainly not argued here that business always wins, any more than Manchester United has to win all its games or the Premiership title every year in order to be the predominant club in English football. What is being argued is that big business is on the winning side more often than not, so that even if multinational companies do not control the policy game, it produces outcomes which are acceptable to business interests most of the time. If nothing else, business interests are numerically dominant. Aspinwall and Greenwood (1998, p.3) found that European level business groups formed 63 per cent of all the groups surveyed. Green Cowles has been one of the most astute and thorough observers of developments in European level business representation as multinational companies have engaged in political mobilization. She considers that the European Round Table of Industrialists (representing chief executives of 45 leading European companies 'is arguably the most influential interest group in Brussels' (1998, p.108).

The Organization of Business Interests in the EU

General Business Associations

Business interests are represented in a number of different ways in relation to the European Union. First, there are organizations which seek to represent the interests of business as a whole. Second, there are organizations which represent particular sectors or products. Third, there are the lobbying activities of individual firms which have become an increasingly important component of the process. Of the 265 business associations surveyed by Aspinwall and Greenwood (1998, p.5), 66 per cent were associations of other associations, 30 per cent had firms in direct membership and 4 per cent represented individuals or a combination of individuals and firms.

At the level of general business interests there are three organizations which Cowles (1997, p.130) characterizes as the 'big business troika'. They are the European Round Table (ERT); the European Committee of the American Chamber of Commerce; and the Union of Industrial and Employers' Confederations of Europe (UNICE). Each of them has complementary functions and a different emphasis in its work. The three are informally linked together by the European Enterprise Group which is a network made up of the government relations officers of leading multinational companies located in Brussels. It serves as the '"invisible" core for the big business troika' (p.133). In terms of influence on crucial issues, the most important of the three organizations is ERT. Representing the chief executives of leading European companies, it is an interesting example of a lean organization with a focus on major strategic policy issues dealt with through contacts at the highest political levels. As their then general secretary has commented, 'This was agenda-setting of a high order, driven by the strong personalities of individual members, but without being drawn into the detail that other organizations could better supply' (Richardson, 1997, pp.xviii–xix).

Perhaps their single most important achievement was 'relaunching and setting the agenda of the single market programme in the early 1980s' (Green Cowles, 1995, p.503). The ERT had privileged access to top French officials, including President Mitterrand, and France played a key role in initiating the single market programme. The ERT had a series of meetings with the incoming Delors Commission in 1985, including a private preparatory meeting between Delors and the head of the ERT. The ERT also carefully followed through the implementation of the single market programme. These discussions initiated 'a permanent practice of the ERT – namely, meeting with senior government officials of the current Presidency, usually including the head of state or government, to discuss the ERT's suggestions and concerns regarding developments and overall strategies of the European Community' (ibid., p.519).

The ERT has carved out a role for itself as an agenda setter in the EU:

> The close relationship between the ERT and the Commission has been maintained beyond the completion of the single market programme and ... continued under the presidency of Jacques Santer. Officials credit the ERT with introducing new policy ideas and prompting the Commission to re-evaluate policy directions.
>
> (Green Cowles, 1997, p.131)

American multinationals lack the intimate insider status that can be secured by major European companies and they have built up their own highly effective organization, the EU Committee of AmCham which is made up of around 140 companies. The EU Committee has developed a reputation as a very well informed organization which 'has developed a rather elaborate process of "issue management". The process is designed to ensure that EU legislation is identified early on, contacts with the appropriate officials are made, and position papers are written in a timely manner' (Green Cowles, 1996, p.349). Learning from the experience of the ERT, from whom they sought advice, the EU Committee established in 1993 the European-American Industrial Council (EAIC). 'The EAIC is, in effect, an American-style ERT, composed of CEOs from the firms' European operations' (Green Cowles, 1997, p.133.)

American companies have been able to offset the disadvantages they faced as 'outsiders' in the EU by setting up a very effective collective action structure which has enabled them to present themselves as 'European' in orientation and become policy insiders. In doing so, they have been able to draw on the sophistication and maturity that American firms have developed in their lobbying operations in their own country. Washington and Brussels have both developed the dubious reputation of being a '"paradise" for lobbyists' (Graziano, 1998, p.6). One must not push the analogy too far, as the government stuctures are in some respects polar opposites, but there are some similarities in lobbying between Brussels and Washington, in particular the fluidity and unpredictability of the policy making process and the existence of numerous points of access.

The big difference is that power lies primarily with a bureaucratic executive which acts as the initiator of legislation rather than with an elected legislature which is the reverse of the situation in Washington. In terms of the 'day-to-day conduct of government, the Union is "government by committees" probably to a greater extent than any other system' (Graziano, 1998, p.7). Donations to the campaign funds of politicians do not play any role in Europe, because there are no Europe wide election campaigns, while in Washington Political Action Committees are a central part of the lobbying process. The awareness of the staff of the American companies of the particular features of the American and European political settings may give the EU Committee a special set of advantages:

> As subsidiaries of *American* companies they are familiar with the practice of legislative advocacy in its Washington DC form. As *European* subsidiaries, managed and staffed primarily by Europeans, they have been able to adopt lobbying techniques to the very different culture of legislative advocacy in Europe. The EC Committee has been remarkably successful in creating a hy-

brid form of lobbying – clear, unambiguous fact-based presentations – with
the low key, accommodating style favored by Europeans.

(Gardner, 1991, p.43)

Given the economic importance of the interests it represents, and the
sophistication of its representative strategies, most analysts would agree
that the EU Committee is 'one of the most powerful interest groups in
the EU today' (Green Cowles, 1995, p.355).
Both the ERT and the EU Committee are company driven organizations. This has certain advantages both in terms of relations with the EU
and the functioning of the organization. Commissioners like to meet the
heads of major companies whom they see as decision-makers of a similar stature compared with a staff member from a business organization.
A partnership with big business is seen as conferring an aura of legitimacy on the EU's operations. In terms of their internal organization, the
company driven associations represent a relatively small number of decision makers rather than a cumbersome system of national federations.
An interesting issue is whether their influence indicates that the EU has
many of the characteristics of a 'company state' rather than an 'associative state', an issue that will be returned to when the representative efforts
of individual firms are discussed.

The third organization, UNICE, is a federation of federations and is
seen as 'the workhorse of business groups, responding to each EU piece
of legislation of general relevance to business' (Green Cowles, 1997,
p.132). UNICE thus has to carve out a representative space between
ERT dealing with the strategic issues on the one hand, and the associations representing particular sectors which may have more knowledge
of specific technical issues on the other. Indeed, these associations may
often concern themselves with horizontal issues such as competitiveness, energy policy and environmental policy. It is interesting that one
of the specific objectives of the European Chemical Industry Council
(CEFIC) reorganization in 1997 was to allow the development of better
common advocacy on horizontal issues. This is not perhaps surprising
when one considers that there is 'just one person in UNICE even now
working less than half time on environmental matters' (Thairs, 1998,
p.154). In contrast, CEFIC has a whole department devoted to such questions. The representative space of UNICE therefore becomes a contested
arena, not through any rivalry, but through associations pursuing matters
which they see as being within their domain of interest.

Even if it can define a representative space, UNICE has so many national interests to reconcile, compared with the European (or even global) focus of the two company driven groups, there is a risk of producing lowest common denominator policies. Such policies may avoid giving offence but also fail to impress policy makers. It is therefore not surprising that UNICE has faced some operational problems:

> The great breadth of business interests clustered under UNICE's capacious umbrella ... results in a somewhat bureaucratized decision making process and an unfortunate softening of focus in the EC legislative area. Eurocrats frequently complain about bland consensus statements from UNICE which fail to address the specifics of proposed legislation.
>
> (Gardner, 1991, p.40)

Discontent among leading multinationals about the effectiveness of UNICE led to a number of reforms in the late 1980s. A new secretary-general was brought in and UNICE began to streamline its decision making structures. In 1990 UNICE set up an Advisory and Support Group (ASAG) made up of multinational companies. Although partly a device to raise money, this grouping was also seen as a way of building closer links between UNICE and major companies.

Nevertheless, problems persist. There is a view in the Commission that UNICE has not made all the use that it could have done of its status as a social partner. The new director-general appointed in 1998, Dirk Hudig, the former head of ICI's relations with EU governments, wants the organization to concentrate its energies on fewer issues. There is also pressure for a change in the consensual way that UNICE makes decisions, 'a tradition that requires virtual unanimity for any initiative it takes and sometimes thwarts the will of the majority' (*Financial Times*, 25 August 1998). Thus, UNICE rejected negotiations on worker consultation in 1998, even though associations from eleven of the fifteen member states were in favour of holding them.

Small and Medium-Sized Businesses

As many as eleven EU level associations representing small and medium-sized enterprises have been recognized by DG XXIII, the directorate-general of the Commission responsible for small enterprises (Grote, 1992, p.158). Among them is UNICE which has a small firms working party. Although DG XXIII is happy to speak to any organization that appears to represent small firms, concerns have been expressed elsewhere in the Commission (notably in DGV, the social affairs directorate) about the representativeness of small business organizations. Indeed, the Commission has sponsored research on this subject. There was also an attempt to offset fragmentation by the formation of two 'contact groups', a somewhat weaker grouping representing middle-class and craft interests and a second grouping containing the more effective organizations (Grote, 1992, p.159).

The European Association of Craft, Small and Medium-Sized Enterprises (UEAPME) 'tends to be the lead SME organization in the domain' (Greenwood, 1997, p.120). It benefits from substantial financial support from the Italian and German chambers of commerce. The other leading organization is the European Committee for Small and Medium-Sized Independent Companies (EUROPMI). The emphasis in the title is on the form of ownership and this organization tends to represent fewer craft undertakings than UEAPME. This fragmentation does little to offset the general weakness of small and medium-sized business representation compared with that of big business. Smaller firms may in fact be hit harder by EU regulations than larger firms as they may be less able to pass on the additional costs to customers, and have fewer specialized staff to cope with the regulations.

UEAPME particularly resents the representation of small business organizations by UNICE when social partner organizations enter into framework agreements under the Maastricht treaty. UEAPME brought a legal action against the Council of Ministers challenging the two adopted directives. The first of these was rejected in June 1998. The Court of First Instance ruled that the fact that UEAPME was entitled to participate in the social dialogue for consultation purposes did not give it a right to participate in proceedings leading to the conclusion of a binding agreement (Case T-135/96, *UEAPME* v. *Council of EU*, judgment of the CFI, 17 June 1998). In other words, the status of small business associations as second-grade social partners has been formally confirmed, a decision which reflects the realities of the distribution of power.

Sectoral Business Associations

The organizations which represent particular sectors of the economy or even particular products vary considerably in their effectiveness. It should be noted that a product association which has tightly defined goals can be very effective in relation to its particular area of concern. (For an example see Box 5.1 below.) Dealing with a wider span of interest poses more difficulties. Despite the preference of the Commission for dealing with Europe-wide groups that can represent a sector or interest across the whole union, Euro-groups 'have tended to be rather ineffective bodies unable to engage in constructive policy dialogue with the Commission' (McLaughlin, Jordan and Maloney, 1993, p.192). Nevertheless, there are examples of federations which 'can act coherently and decisively' (Greenwood, Grote and Ronit, 1992, p.6). In his research on British business associations, Bennett found (1997, p.87) that 'the major role played by European associations is notable. It is also something of a surprise given the rather negative view of the extent and effectiveness of these bodies in previous analysis'.

Box 5.1 European Wax Federation

Wax encompasses natural and synthetic materials used in a variety of ways in such sectors as packaging, motor vehicles and domestic industries, as well as in foodstuffs. The European Wax Federation, which is a sector organization of CEFIC, brings together 35 European companies manufacturing or blending waxes. Its work in relation to the EU and other interational bodies emphasises the following tasks:

- Regulatory affairs in the EU (Technical, Statistics, Customs)
- Monitoring evolution of EU legislation on Mineral Hydrocarbons
- Health and safety issues related to waxes
- Issue of specifications at the EU level through the Scientific Committee for Food and at the international level through the Joint Expert Committee of Food Additives

---

It is evident from the case study literature that there is considerable variation in the effectiveness of European level federations. What distinguishes those groups that are relatively effective from those that are not? Relevant theoretical perspectives and the various case studies that have been conducted permit some tentative generalizations.

First, it is helpful if the industry contains a relatively small number of prosperous companies. One then has a situation which in Olsonian terms approximates to that of a 'privileged' group where all the members may be prepared to contribute to the provision of the collective good as they all benefit to a significant extent and the withdrawal of any one member would make the collective good more difficult to provide. If companies are generally prosperous, they are more likely to be able to afford to sustain a well resourced association. If the companies are closely linked together through the production process, as in the chemical industry, this may also assist the formation and maintenance of an effective organization.

Second, the industry needs to be one which is seen by the Commission as an important part of European industry, and is hence likely to be listened to. The industry also needs to be significantly affected by EU policy in order to induce its firms to allocate sufficient resources in terms of money and personnel to make the association a success. Starting up a new organization, or reviving a moribund one, when a sector's activities are suddenly impacted by the EU involves considerable start up costs and a steep learning curve to climb. An organization which has been in existence for twenty-five years or more can draw on considerable accumulated experience when it meets new challenges.

Third, an organization is likely to be more effective if it directly organizes firms rather than operating through national federations, or at least if its structure embodies an element of direct firm representation. Such an organization is less likely to be inhibited by particular national preoccupations as it will be driven by firms with a Europe wide perspective. It also does not face the problem of having to extract resources from the often limited budgets of national associations.

Fourth, an association can derive benefits from organizational maturity. Clearly, one danger of maturity is ossification. Therefore, a successful association needs the capacity to think reflectively about its own role and to make adjustments to new challenges, whether they arise from changes in the structure of the industry or a shift in the priorities of the EU. One problem in the courier industry discussed below is that 'Most industry executives were former operations supervisors who were too busy inventing and building a new industry to waste time on subtle policy questions' (Campbell, 1993, p.129).

If one wanted to select one association as an example of an effective sectoral association, the European Chemical Industry Council (CEFIC) would be a prime candidate. With a staff of around 80, and 4 000 experts from companies involved in its committee, CEFIC enjoys a reputation based on expertise and the effective selection of priority issues. One Commission official commented, 'Supposing that I wanted to find something out about biotechnology. I could ring CEFIC and they would have the leading expert in Europe at my desk by the end of the week.'

In the case of CEFIC, all four conditions outlined above are met. A relatively small number of companies produce the basic 'building blocks' of the petrochemical industry. These 40 companies (the number current in the summer of 1998) make up the individual membership of CEFIC and include such 'household names' as ICI and Shell. Although there are small companies engaged in forms of niche production, there is an absence of tension between large and small firms. However, the industry is dominated by a relatively small number of capital intensive firms who have been participants in it over a long period of time and who provide the main support for CEFIC. The industry is an important one in the EU and its activities are considerably affected by EU decisions in areas such as environmental policy, trade policy and competition policy.

CEFIC has evolved a sophisticated structure which allows direct firm membership alongside the participation of national associations. In 1991 CEFIC gave full membership to leading firms and developed a bicameral structure which created a shared balance of power between the historic national association members and the individual chemical companies. A sign of CEFIC's organizational maturity is that it always seeks to develop its organizational structure in response to a constantly changing world, just as companies have to make similar adaptations. As the chemical industry became more specialized, CEFIC decided in 1997 to adopt a 'three pillar' structure made up of member companies, member federations and the associations representing specific product sectors.

CEFIC tries to identify strategic priorities and to pursue these in a way that can be related to current Commission priorities. For example, at its strategy meeting in November 1993, CEFIC decided to give a high priority to the issue of competitiveness. The significance of this issue to the industry is that it provides a paradigm in which it is possible to argue that energy prices should not be forced up and health and environmental regulations should take account of their potential economic impact. In other words, it provides a set of arguments which can be used against policies that are seen as threatening to the industry. The organization wrote what became known as the 'Green Book', a presentation of some chemical industry initiatives within the framework of an EU policy document on industrial competitiveness policy. This led to a Commission document on competitiveness policy specific to the chemical industry and a high level forum reviewed the follow up process in April 1997.

The courier industry offers an example of an industry which has found it difficult to organize at European level as part of its efforts to reform postal policy and defend and enlarge its competitive space. Unlike the chemical industry, where companies are linked to one another (often physically by pipelines) through the production process and senior managers meet each other in a variety of settings, the courier industry is characterized by a lack of solidarity. The industry was led by highly individualistic entrepreneurs. 'In this fiercely competitive industry, the principals rarely spoke and hardly knew each other. Previous industry cooperation had been limited to short, single-issue, national-level policy campaigns' (Campbell, 1993, p.125). Entrepreneurs had to learn how to shift from a personal management style towards the sophistication that is required by government relations as a corporate function.

An organization known as the International Express Carriers Conference (IECC) was set up in 1983 (a much later date than in many other industries) largely at the initiative of DHL who provided much of the funds and guidance. This was a worldwide oganisation, and in 1989 DHL and Securicor pulled out to form a European level organization called the European Express Organization (EEO). The worst possible situation is where one has competing organizations seeking to represent an industry. However, IEEC came to an agreement whereby EEO would manage its public affairs activities.

The IEEC/EEO faced the problem of being an outsider with the Commission relatively slow to appreciate the economic significance of courier services. The existing postal administrations had considerable influence with member state governments. The IEEC/EEO evolved the following strategy which emphasized a restrained approach based on demonstrable facts to enhance the industry's credibility with the Commission:

> The couriers could not hope to compete with the postal administrations in the number of manhours devoted to working with or influencing the Commission in the preparation of the Postal Green Paper. The only road open to us was to make an extraordinarily persuasive case. But first we had to try to dissuade the Commission from adopting a hastily conceived postal policy that reflected only input from postal administrations. For both reasons, we decided to encourage and participate in a series of public and academic decisions of the fundamental public policy issues presented by a Postal Green Paper.
>
> (Campbell, 1993, p.138)

The couriers made some headway, the head of Unipost, the organization of the postal administrations complaining that IEEC/EEO were 'succeeding in creating the perception among legislators in Europe, at any rate, that the wings of the post offices should be clipped' (quoted in

Campbell, p.144). Despite this success, which showed how a well conceived strategic plan could help to achieve insider group status, the IEEC/
CEO faced a number of fundamental problems. These included the difficulty of relating the aspirations of a coalition of entrepreneurs to the
slow pace of EU decision making; limited resources compared with those
of the postal administrations; and 'a tendency for entrepreneurs to un-
derestimate the importance of professional expertise, particularly in the
public affairs area' (Campbell, p.147). Despite being told that the policy
changes they sought were impossible, 'While changing policy is more
difficult than it should be, it is also less impossible than generally
thought' (p.148).

Lobbying Firms

There has been an 'explosion in the number of professional lobbyists,
financial consultants and law firms operating in Brussels' (Mazey and
Richardson, 1992a, p.95). It has proved a fruitful field of operation for
that American creation, the lawyer-lobbyist, and it is estimated that at
least twenty American law firms have Brussels offices. One of the old-
est lobbying firms was established by a British corporate lawyer, Stanley
Crossick, in 1970. By 1987 it had grown to a staff of 50 professionals,
15 of them lawyers. 'Of the ten biggest "public-affairs consultancies" in
Brussels, five have arrived since 1990' (*The Economist*, 15 August 1998,
p.37).

In an effort to make the lobbyists more professional, the European
Institute of Public Affairs and Lobbying runs regular training courses.
A typical course runs twice a week in the evenings in Brussels for twelve
weeks. The first three modules cover how the EU works, many of the
lecturers being Commission officials. The fourth and fifth modules cover
working methods, including examples of specific cases, and are mainly
delivered by lobbyists. Finally, there is a module covering ethical issues.

Lobbying intermediaries are not always well regarded in the Commission, as officials would prefer to deal direct with the interest
concerned. As a Commission official has commented, 'In principle, the
European Commission makes a distinction between people representing
the interests of non-profit-making associations and profit-making organizations such as legal advisers, public relations companies and
consultants' (Mulfinger, 1997, p.69). Another Commission official has

commented, 'the future, I suspect, lies with the professional lobbying firm … This kind of lobbyist is perceived by Commission officials as more professional and is in a position to build up permanent relationships with the Commission' (Hull, 1993, p.86).

In any event, there is an extensive market for their services. One type of client is the institution that wants a presence in Brussels but cannot justify a full time presence there, for example, a local authority. Business interests have often subcontracted their work with the European Parliament, or a portion of it, to lobbying firms. They should not just be seen, however, as simply providing a 'fetching and carrying' service for those who cannot afford their own representation or want to contract out of the less important aspects of their operation. Stanley Crossick is reported to have got a paragraph appended to the Maastricht treaty which qualified the article about equal pay for men and women in relation to pension funds. A European Court judgment might have obliged pension funds to equalize the pension payments they had made to men and women since the signing of the Treaty of Rome in 1957. 'By one calculation, the protocol added to the Maastricht treaty was worth $1 billion to $2 billion a word in savings to the European pension industry' (*The Economist*, 15 August 1998, p.37). Cost-effective influence indeed, but not everyone can afford to pay for it.

Direct Firm Representation

Firms are not pressure groups in the conventional sense of the term. However, because there are conflicting interests within firms, political aggregation sometimes has to take place within them. For example, 'BP is a large producer of both ethanol and fossil fuels and each has a separate profit centre. However, faced with the possibility of the EU environmental legislation that gave tax concessions to synthetic fuel, the firm had to decide whether to lobby for fossil fuels or environmentally friendlier ethanol base products' (Coen, 1998, p.9).

Government relations or public affairs has developed as a speciality within firms in the last quarter of the twentieth century. At the European level, the interest of firms in direct representation was stimulated 'in the late 1970s by the activities of policy approach of Etienne Davignon, then commissioner for industry. Unlike his predecessors, Davignon gave multinational firms direct access to the Commission and worked closely with leaders of firms to negotiate agreements designed to improve their competitiveness' (Green Cowles, 1997, p.119).

By the end of the 1970s about fifty multinationals 'had established relatively sophisticated public affairs departments for managing European policy issues' (p.120). Many of these companies were British or American, coming from a strong 'company state' tradition. With their country's stronger associative tradition, many German companies preferred to work through their national associations and government and some leading companies did not establish an effective government relations presence in Brussels until the 1990s. (Coen, 1998, pp.19–20). However, company culture was also a relevant variable. Philips has been one of the leading companies involved in government relations in Brussels and it is clear that direct interactions with top decision makers suited its style:

> It is a visible power and it prefers to do business with visible power. Philips doesn't feel at home in environments that can not be controlled one hundred per cent, like consumer organizations, public opinion and flanking interest groups. Within the European Commission, contacts were mostly sought at higher levels.

> (Verwey, 1994, p.38)

Philips had an agenda to pursue in relation to the EU which centred around protection from intensifying Japanese competition and assistance from the EU to develop new products. What was referred to as its 'Ambassador in Brussels' operated from an office there, although its head offices were within commuting distance of the European capital. 'This office is far more than a lobbying organization or a listening-post, although it is both of these. It is a means through which the intimate and intense relationship between company managers and European officials can constantly be renewed' (Cawson, 1997, pp.198–9.) It was evident that 'Philips was able to exercise an influence on policy for the electronics sector well ahead of its power in the market-place, especially in the late 1980s and early 1990s' (p.200). This privileged position was reflected in Commission support for a European high definition television (HDTV) system developed by Philips and another company.

Government relations divisions are worthwhile for large firms because they may permit the development of a commercially privileged relationship with the Commission. Government relations divisions in Brussels lead to 'the establishment of an organizational capacity to co-ordinate potential *ad hoc* political alliances and to develop and reinforce existing political channels' (Coen, 1998, p.4). The divisions can give the political work of firms a strategic focus, as well as a sense of what constitutes good tactics. This can produce what seems to be the optimal blend at any one time and for any particular issue of direct representation in Brussels, work through European federations, and the use of national government contacts. It should also be noted that government relations managers have been important actors in the formation, revitalization and operation of Europe wide general business associations. In many ways, these government relations managers are the key actors in the representation of business interests in Brussels.

Their significance raises the question of how far the EU conforms to a 'company state' model. 'In a company state, the most important form of business–state contact is the direct one between company and government. Government prioritizes such forms of contact over associative intermediation' (Grant, 1993a, p.14.) In the associative state, 'business associations play a key role as intermediaries between business and the state' (p.15).

It is evident that the Commission has dealt directly with companies on major issues of policy, not least the internal market project. There is no doubt that large firms 'enjoy privileged access to many national and European policy-makers' (Green Cowles, 1997, p.134). The Commission also has a predisposition to deal with associations. As one senior Commission official has commented, 'it helps to have a single point of access. For that reason trade associations that really do represent their wide range of members are enormously useful to us' (White, 1997, p.74). However, in some sectors, truly effective associations do not exist. For example, the organization representing consumer electronics 'operates as a fig-leaf to conceal from casual inspection the substantial influence of the major European firms' (Cawson, 1997, p.193). Weeks of patient lobbying may count very little when balanced against a conversation between the president of the Commission and the chief executive officer of a major company on the latter's corporate jet. What is visible in the Commission may not be what is most significant.

There are emergent company state tendencies in the EU, but there are also countervailing factors. The Commission is not a monolithic organization and some of its officials may wish to balance a partnership with big business with contacts with other organizations. For example, small and medium-sized businesses can only effectively be represented through an association and the Commission may wish to ensure that their views are heard in policy debates. The Commission has funded environmental and other public interest organizations to help them to work effectively. There is both a neo liberal, big business, company state orientation in the EU and a social partnership tradition. While neo-liberalism has 'for some time ... been the most powerful force in the European political economy' (Crouch and Streeck, 1997, p.12), this situation is by no means irreversible. For the time being what one has is a rather complex picture of an associative order at the base, and a 'company state' at the peak of the pyramid represented by the 'big business troika' and the government relations divisions.

The Decline of a Producer Group: the Case of COPA

It should not be assumed that all producer groups maintain their influence or even increase it as they become more effectively organized. The organization representing farmers, the Comité des Organizations Professionelles Agricoles (COPA) has seen its position change from being possibly the most influential pressure group in Europe to becoming a much more marginal actor. At one time farmers 'were envied by other European lobbies as the most influential special interest group at the Community level' (Phillips, 1990, p.50). 'There is a consensus among authors that the influence of COPA ... is somewhat on the wane' (Greenwood, 1997, p.124).

This contrasts with the major role that COPA played in devising and shaping the Common Agricultural Policy (CAP):

> ... many of the current considerable shortcomings of the CAP can be blamed squarely upon COPA, since it was closely consulted on the measures and mechanisms needed to support farmers when the agriculture policy was first established in the late 1950s and early 1960s. Subsequently, evidence from EU officials and working papers of the EU Commission and Council of Ministers shows that a great deal of the blame for the inadequate action taken by the Council to deal with surpluses and over-spending in the 1980s could be attributed to COPA's role in the decision making process.
>
> (Gardner, 1996, pp.6–7)

This influence was reflected in the establishment of the so-called 'objective method' to fix farm prices in the 1970s. What can be said about the 'objective method' is that there was nothing particularly objective about it as it was a device to protect farm incomes from market forces. The farm lobby dominated the system until 1979 (Phillips, 1990, p.73), but the closed nature of the agricultural policy community came under challenge from a number of external forces. The budgetary strains of the CAP, which at one time was absorbing two-thirds of the EU budget, became too great to bear, leading to the introduction of dairy quotas in 1984. Trade negotiations in the Uruguay Round in the late 1980s and early 1990s set up a situation in which manufacturing exports were threatened by the perpetuation of agricultural protection and led to the MacSharry reforms, essentially a reform of the cereals regime. The budgetary implications of eastern enlargement, and continued trade pressures, triggered off a new round of reform discussions in the late 1990s under the Agenda 2000 banner.

These changes in the policy context produced new strains in COPA, which were both a cause and effect of its decline in influence:

> Beginning in the mid-1970s, COPA lost cohesion and by the 1980s was no longer at the centre of the policy process. When the Commission dropped the objective method and began to address more divisive issues, COPA faced dissension within its ranks as individual commodity groups and national organizations clashed over demands from the Community. The needs of individual members of COPA diverged and in some cases conflicted. The national farm organizations moved into the vacuum with greater consultation with their national governments in an effort to maintain control of the farm policy.
>
> (Phillips, 1990, p.73)

One of the difficulties that COPA has faced is that in order to reassure its constituents it has taken increasingly extreme positions which do not take account of the changed character of the policy debate. For example, COPA has demanded that eastern enlargement 'must in no way put the current level of agricultural support in the EU in question, or adversely affect the competitive position of EU agriculture' (*Agra Europe*, 21 April 1995, p.P/5). COPA has also maintained its opposition to all reductions in farm earnings caused by currency movements. Arguments that other industrial sectors have to live with the vagaries of the currency markets are refuted on the spurious grounds that the price-cutting effect is more immediate for farmers than for other sectors (*Agra Europe*, 13 April 1995, p.E/6).

At policy seminars in Brussels, COPA has often seemed removed from the current debate which is emphasizing a move towards more market-based solutions and transparency for those subsidies that remain. At one such seminar, the leading agricultural economist, Stefan Tangermann,

put forward the interesting argument that COPA and other farm organizations were pursuing a strategy that actually harmed the interests of
their own members because they were not preparing them for the extent
of the changes that were going to be required.

These tensions have produced upheavals at the top of the organization. Andre Herlitska was director general of COPA from its formation
in 1958 until 1994. He was succeeded by Daniel Gueguen who resigned
unexpectedly in March 1996. An internal report in November 1996
warned that unless COPA was modernised its 'future will at best be a
decline into ineffectiveness, at worst a fall to the very bottom of the
downward spiral and extinction'. Means had become an end with the
resources of the organization absorbed in servicing meetings and leaving very little spare for the actual exertion of influence. Attempts to
find a common position on which to lobby were obstructed by 'so many
compromises, so many delays in a complex machinery'. When a position is agreed, the national offices of farm organizations and the COPA
secretariat 'are more often acting in competition with one another' (*Agra
Europe*, 8 November 1996, p.P/5).

In 1997 a Finn, Rito Volanen, was appointed director-general of COPA.
His strategy has been to advance a paradigm that he calls the 'European
model of agriculture' which has entered into the language used by the
Commission. This model 'meant ensuring that farmers' incomes kept
pace with incomes in the rest of society and emphasising the "multi-
functional" role of farming by recognising how agriculture preserved
the rural landscape and maintained employment in the countryside' (*Agra
Europe*, 10 October 1997, p.E/5).

At one level, this is the old call for more public funds for farmers, but
it is being presented in a more subtle way that is more attuned to the
current debate. First, it emphasizes the way in which farmers maintain a
particular kind of landscape that may be valued by urban residents.
Volanen presents two slides at policy seminars: one of a European family farm, in which cows can be seen grazing on a verdant landscape in
front of a lake with the traditional farm buildings glimpsed in the distance; the other of an American 'industrial farm' in a semi-arid landscape
with a cluster of ugly concrete buildings. This links into the second
aspect of the argument which maintains that American agribusiness interests are trying to change the face of European farming to pursue their
own commercial interests. There is a grain of truth in this argument and
it also plays to anti-American sentiment.

COPA has thus devised quite a clever strategy. However, it does very much identify COPA with Europe's more marginal farmers. More competitive farmers might favour greater liberalization and their views could be expressed through national organizations such as the British NFU and its counterparts in other 'reform countries' such as the Netherlands, Sweden and Denmark. The national strains within COPA might thus be exacerbated.

COPA's stance has also led to strains with its affiliated organization, COGECA, which represents farm co-operatives and which has responded more constructively to the Agenda 2000 proposals:

> COGECA said it recognised that farm co-operatives were operating in a much changed economic environment where markets were more international and competitive and consumers made even greater demands on producers. Instead of looking for compensation for changes, COGECA called on the EU to develop a dynamic export policy for agri-food products which would allow EU to take advantage of opportunities offered by more open markets.
>
> (*Agra Europe*, 18 July 1997, p.E/5)

Despite all the problems faced by the farm lobby, EU farmers still received, on average, 42 per cent of their income from subsidies of various kinds in 1997 according to OECD figures (*Agra Europe*, 3 July 1998, p.EP/4). However, COPA's own internal evaluation 'suggests that the generous deals on farm policy frequently obtained by the EU's nine million farmers is despite, rather than because of, the activities of the farm lobby' (*Agra Europe*, 8 November 1996, p.P/5). The activities of national farm lobbies, their influence on their agriculture ministries, and the way in which farm ministers consequently behave in the Council of Agriculture Ministers suggests that in agriculture lobbying at the national level remains an important means of influencing EU policy.

Trade Unions

The 'countervailing' groups which represent different interests or outlooks to those of big business are all politically weaker. Although it was classified by the 1972 Paris Summit as one of the 'social partner' organizations, the trade union movement, represented by the European Trade Union Confederation (ETUC) has been relatively weak at the European level. 'The ETUC is run by a small staff of around thirty-five officials – a ratio of less than 1 per 1 million members – its financial base is weak and it does not have a bargaining mandate or strike resources' (Wendon, 1994, p.247).

Streeck and Schmitter argue (1991, p.139) 'there is no doubt that as a European actor labour is afflicted by *specific disabilities* that are not usually present at the national level and that do not in the same way affect business'. The member organizations, which have been to some extent divided on ideological lines, have generally been domestically oriented with a strong desire to preserve their own autonomy. 'While for unions from advanced countries a joint European strategy is unlikely to offer improvements over what they have already gained on their own, to unions from weaker countries common demands tend to appear unrealistically ambitious and remote from their everyday practical concerns' (Streeck and Schmitter, p.140).

Perhaps because of a recognition of the importance of greater unity if EU policies are to be influenced, there has been an effort to build a policy consensus in recent years. A working group established in 1989 advocated substantial internal reforms within the ETUC, and in 1991 a two-thirds majority voting procedure was adopted. As one trade union leader commented, however, these reforms did not transform the ETUC from '"a coordination body between national centres" into a "transnational organization". Clearly, not all ETUC affiliates, especially the largest among them, are ready to make this move' (Visser and Ebbinghaus, 1992, p. 223). While the labour movement weakens at the national level, conditions at the European level do not favour more effective forms of union organization there (p. 236). The ETUC faces the classic problem of the federation of federations: 'for the present, some national confederations are unwilling to see ETUC develop beyond its present role into a more powerful supranational actor, and will not, or cannot, commit the resources to enable it to so develop'.

It may be that the social dialogue creates new opportunities for influence for the ETUC. 'To date, two major collective agreements signed between labour and management have formulated specific social minimum standards for the entire European Economic Area' (Falkner, 1998, p.3). One consequence of the Maastricht treaty is the development of regular informal meetings of the Council of Ministers for social policy (labour policy in British terms) which involve the ETUC (p.193). Whilst agreements on matters such as parental leave are significant, the ETUC is not involved in the range of contacts and issues covered by the major business groups.

Environmental Groups

Environmental groups have also faced problems in organizing at the European level. Some 59 per cent of public interest groups in Brussels, a category which includes environmental groups, receive funding from the Commission (Aspinwall and Greenwood, 1998, p.3). Despite 6.5 million ECU spent in 1992 on non-governmental environmental groups by DG XI (Rucht, 1993, p. 87) the groups lack adequate resources.

The seven leading environmental groups in Brussels come together in the Group of Seven which 'is an informal arrangement between the NGOs which enables them to coordinate their activities and act sometimes as a single lobby within the European environmental area' (Webster, 1998, p.184). (For membership see Box 5.2 below.) This co-ordinating role was supposed to be fulfilled by the European Environmental Bureau (EEB). It has a staff of eleven and good relations with DG XI. However, its co-ordinating role has been made difficult by divisions over objectives and methods among the environmental groups. Their objectives vary from broad ecological concerns to the protection of a particular species and their methods of achieving them may range from informed and expert lobbying to illegal forms of direct action.

Box 5.2 Members of the 'Group of Seven'

The European Environment Bureau

Friends of the Earth Europe

Greenpeace International

World Wide Fund for Nature

Climate Network Europe

BirdLife International

The European Federation for Transport and the Environment

It may be that a group which can adjust to the elite lobbying style of Brussels can be more successful. Climate Network Europe (CNE) focusses on the issue of global warming. 'CNE has been centrally involved in the EU climate debate from its earliest stages in the late 1980s through to the current day, where it is now regarded as the definitive NGO voice on climate related matter at Brussels level' (Newell and Grant, 1998, p.16). One strategy that it has followed is to build up alliances with business lobbies involved in energy conservation or environmentally friendly generation, such as the European Association for the Conservation of Energy and the European Wind Energy Association. The fact that CNE is a coalition of associations means that it does not have to be sensitive to supporter concerns and can focus on the priorities of policy makers. It has established a reputation with the Commission as the authoritative environmental group dealing with climate change. Their subtle, long term strategy does not, however, bring immediate results and like other environmental groups they are under staffed and under resourced and face many of the most powerful European industrial lobbies.

Although the strategy followed by CNE may be effective in the long run, environmental groups in Brussels face a number of structural problems (Rucht, 1993; Newell and Grant, 1998):

- Too heavy a dependence upon DG XI which is one of the weaker directorates-general and the European Parliament which, although growing in importance, is still unable to deliver significant policy reform. It is often portrayed as a 'green colony' (Pollack, 1998, p.580).
- Lack of resources which enable them to participate in the policy process from initiation through to implementation.
- A consequent dependence on EU subsidies which may threaten their autonomy.
- Environmental issues are particularly subject to the ups and downs of the 'issue attention cycle' and may be displaced on the public agenda by other issues considered to be more important.
- Lack of homogeneity. Structural and ideological diversity makes it difficult to agree on common positions and strategies.
- Their reactive character, responding to an agenda set by the Commission which is not generally dependent on public opinion.
- Strong opponents in a number of industrial sectors with the Commission dependent on their expertise.

Mazey and Richardson (1992b), in contrast, develop an analysis which emphasizes what they see as the strengths of environmental groups operating at a European level. Their strongest argument is that 'The ability of environmental groups to set the political agenda is perceived by the industrialists to whom we have spoken as perhaps the greatest current asset of the environmentalists' (p.120). They claim that 'The European level environmental groups may seem quite well resourced when compared with sectoral business associations at the European level' (p.122). They compare Greenpeace having twelve full-time staff in its Brussels office with the European Association of Textile Polyolefins (EATP) having only four. This is not really a very useful comparison as EATP is a product association, or at best a subsectoral association, rather than a sectoral association such as CEFIC. Indeed, they go on to admit 'that in those areas of environmental policy where industry has a really keen and vital interest, the resources mobilised are very considerable indeed and usually far outweigh those of any of the environmental groups' (p.123). They concede that environmental groups are over reliant on links with DG XI, and they also point out that industrial interests are mobilising more effectively in relation to the environmental issue, although whether being 'proactive' rather than 'reactive' in lobbying style is as big an asset as Mazey and Richardson claim depends on how accurately and how far one can anticipate the future.

The environmental groups which have been most successful at the European level tend to be well-resourced organizations with clear objectives arising from a very specific focus. The best resourced British environmental group, the RSPB, 'was closely involved with the European Commission in the formulation of the EC Directive on the Conservation of Wild Birds and Zoo Check was partly sponsored by the EC to undertake a study of European zoos which has resulted in a proposed directive to impose uniform standards' (Garner, 1993, pp. 190–1). The RSPB is substantially involved in BirdLife International which is one of the Group of Seven.

When it comes to really big issues such as the proposed carbon tax, environmental groups lose out to more powerful business interests:

According to many observers, the proposed carbon/energy tax was made subject to some of the most ferocious lobbying ever seen in Brussels ... business interests fought a tough battle, especially against the tax proposal which, in their opinion, would threaten the competitiveness of EC industries in the world economy.

(Skjaerseth, 1994, pp.28–9)

In the case of the carbon tax, 'The environmental NGOs, which are relatively weakly represented at EC level, could not match this massive bloc' (p.31). The defeat of the carbon tax also made DG XI more cautious and pragmatic in its approach to environmental issues. The adoption of the so-called AutoOil package in the summer of 1998 might be seen as a victory for environmentalists. The package provided for the introduction of tougher tailpipe emissions and fuel quality standards for new cars. However, the package was 'the subject of two years of wrangling between the motor industry and oil producers, with each claiming that the other should shoulder more responsibility for reducing emissions from new cars' (*Air Quality Management*, June 1998, p.5). When business interests are divided, there may be an opening for environmentalists.

Territorial Interests

The only set of interests that is of rival importance to business in terms of resources are the territorial interests, with 135 regions and localities represented in Brussels (Greenwood, 1997, p.128). Territorial interests can be particularly complex 'because the territorial level can be a channel of influence for private interests, and a set of interests within itself, and because what constitutes a region means different things in different member states' (p.218). Like business, these often have the advantage of organizing instititutions rather than individuals (Salisbury, 1984), often regional governments. One of the issues that will face the new Scottish Parliament is that whether it will be able to open a 'Scotland House' which will function as a 'mini-embassy' in Brussels on the model of the office operated by the land of Bavaria. National governments often find the opening of a regional Brussels office alarming (Mazey and Mitchell, 1993). It is a tangible representation of the erosion of nation-state power to both the subnational and European levels.

However, the increasing emphasis on regions in the European Union, with the Committee of the Regions being established by the Maastricht treaty, does mean that regional interests are likely to be increasingly emphasized. There is, however, still a long way to go before there is a 'transformation of national into regional economies and of sub-national regions into subunits of a supranational economy [amounting] to a *regionalization of Europe* as well as at the same time a *Europeanization of its regions* (Streeck and Schmitter, 1991, p.153). The regional interests are not really a countervailing force to business interests, in the sense that trade union, consumer or environmental interests could be. Indeed, the regional interests are to some extent competing with each other for a share of foreign direct investment, and for aid to construct infrastructure that will make their regions more attractive to business investors. Their activities are not in competition with those of business, and in some respects are complementary to them.

Diffuse Interests and Business Interests

Pollack reviews the opportunities that the EU provides for what he terms diffuse interests – 'collective interests held by large numbers of individuals, such as environmental protection, consumer protection, equal opportunities between men and women, and civil liberties' (Pollack, 1998, pp.572–3). He argues that the institutional system at the European level offers such groups opportunities as well as risks, in particular through 'the dual opportunities of mutual access points and stable, ratchet-like policies' (p. 576).

There is no doubt, as Pollack claims, that many Commission officials are responsive to the concerns expressed by such interests. In particular, 'As interpeted and enforced by the ECJ, the EC's equal opportunities policies have forced member states to make numerous adjustments to national policies, and are widely perceived to have improved the lot of women in member states such as the UK and Ireland' (p.584). Social Europe is a reality which can produce outcomes that would not occur if it did not exist and much the same can be said of many aspects of European environmental policy.

Nevertheless, it is important not to confuse specific victories with the big picture. The projects which provide the dynamic of European integration, the single market and EMU, are ones that have been warmly embraced by big business. Business interests have a close and mutually beneficial relationship with EU institutions. There are few environments that are more conducive to the political expression of the structural power of capital. Some organizations may thus feel that they are more disadvantaged than others in seeking to influence the EU. Nevertheless, the EU does provide many opportunities to shape the policy debate and all organizations operating at the EU level have to make choices about how to use the resources available to them most effectively, a subject that is dealt with in the next chapter.

6

How Pressure Groups Exert Influence at the EU Level

This chapter further develops the theme of Chapter 5 which explored the factors that affect the effectiveness of pressure groups operating at the EU level but with a greater emphasis on the structure of the policy process that the groups are trying to influence. Greenwood (1997, p.31) observes:

> The multi-level character of the European policy process means that actors seeking to participate in European public affairs therefore have a number of so-called 'routes' of influence ... they are seldom mutually exclusive. In practice, interests tend to use a combination of routes simultaneously as a means of accessing European public affairs.

That does not mean, however, that each of the routes is equally important or that one route may not be more attractive than another. In practice, much of the lobbying directed at the EU either takes place at the national level, with the objective of influencing discussions in the Council of Ministers and policy implementation or in Brussels with the intention of influencing the Commission and, increasingly, the Parliament (wherever it is sitting).

The Decline of the National Route?

One means of exerting influence at the EU level has always been for a national pressure group to persuade its government to adopt its policy position on a particular issue and to press for it in the Council of Ministers. This lobbying may not occur not just in the national capital, but often through the national official in the permanent representation in

Brussels responsible for the particular issue. However, even if it is conducted in Brussels, it is still predominantly national in character and content.

It is worth remembering that the European Union's decision-making procedures 'are still prescribed by the final say of the member states in the Council. Intergovernmental negotiations and compromises, be it under unanimity or qualified majority voting rules, are at the core of Community politics' (Arp, 1993, p. 163). 'Often the national route to lobbying is the most effective' (Hayes-Renshaw and Wallace, 1997, p.229).

Greenwood suggests that 'Representation at the national level is more available to those interests lacking the resources to take the Brussels strategy' (Greenwood, 1997, p.33). This view receives support from Bennett's research on business associations where he found (1997, p.85) that the national route was the most common one 'for the smallest and least well resourced bodies'. However, even quite powerful interests such as the water industry may prefer to make considerable use of the national route: 'the main lobbying target for the British business community in general and the water industry in particular continues to be the UK Government, even on European matters' (Thairs, 1998, p.166).

Greenwood and Jordan suggest a number of reasons 'which support our contention of the national level being the most important overall for political action aimed at the EC' (1993, p.76). These include conflicts of national interest, the fact that national political parties are more accessible than European ones and networks that may exist between national governments and their citizens working inside the Commission. Perhaps one of the most influential factors is, however, familiarity, which can be eroded as personnel change and new methods of working are adopted:

> National levels in Britain represent very familiar territory, where established policy communities and networks exist between government and representatives of interests expressed through peak and sector associations, individual firm lobbying, consultants and professional lobbyists and contacts with political parties.
>
> (p.78)

Any group that relied solely on its tried and tested links with the national government has always been taking a substantial risk. First, the national government has to be convinced of the desirability of adopting the lobby's position. Persuading 'the UK Government to identify with a particular interest is potentially dependent on political considerations going beyond the specific issue concerned' (Spence 1993, p.52). Second, 'Positions are watered down during the domestic co-ordination process and in negotiation with the Commission and other member states,' (p.49). In the final stage of bargaining in long and exhausting negotiating sessions in the Council of Ministers, the group's position may be suddenly abandoned by the national government in order to resolve a problem elsewhere. Domestic sheep farmers may find themselves abandoned in the interests of New Zealand lamb imports, or vice versa. Third, if the matter is a relatively technical one, the national government representatives may not appreciate its full significance. For example, 'a British minister disappointed national groups when he inadvertently agreed to unacceptable technical proposals during bargaining over emissions regulations' (McLaughlin, Jordan and Maloney, 1993, pp.197–8).

Greenwood, Grote and Ronit (1992, pp.23–4) have argued that, 'The importance of the national route appears in fact to have been somewhat overstated ... there is an increasing confidence and familiarity with the European level, and ... the "Brussels strategy" ... is increasingly being taken.' Similarly, Mazey and Richardson argue that an exclusive reliance on a national level strategy is no longer a viable option. 'With qualified majority voting, a *European* lobbying strategy becomes essential for a group *in addition* to the maintenance and strengthening of links with national officials' (1993a, p.15).

The threshold required to succeed under the qualified majority voting arrangements (which do not apply to all decisions) is still relatively high, and there is still a prediposition in the Council of Ministers to reach a bargained compromise whenever possible. 'No effort was made to outvote, by use of QMV, the French on their problem with the Blair house agreement in the Uruguay Round, even though this was technically possible' (Hayes-Renshaw and Wallace, 1997, p.262). Some of the votes take place when the losers know that the matter has effectively been settled, but wish to record their position for national audiences. Even so, the existence of qualified majority voting provides an additional incentive to abandon rigid national positions and reach a bargained compromise. This may lead to special arrangements such as opt outs and derogations to take account of particular national circumstances which have been pressed by national level interests.

One increasingly hears statements that, for example, 80 per cent of environmental policy decisions are now made in Brussels. It is important to remember, however, that (leaving aside areas such as competition policy) the EU has very little in the way of implementation and enforcement capability. It is dependent on the member states to implement directives. The author recalls an example given at a policy making seminar in Brussels about the mayor of a major Italian city who was faced with the problem of implementing a national regulation which sought to bring into force a new EU directive on air pollution. The task was a difficult one politically as his citizens were very fond of their motor cars, but he faced an obligation to act. He decided that when air pollution exceeded one level, a state of alert would be declared and he would be informed. If it reached crisis levels, a state of alarm would be declared and the city telephone number that citizens could ring to discuss their concerns about air pollution would be answered 16 hours a day, instead of having an answering machine in operation for 16 hours out of 24.

As far as enforcement is concerned, environmental groups seek to act as 'whistle blowers' by 'warning the Commission of implementation failure at the national level' (Mazey and Richardson, 1992b, p.126). Because translating Union directives into action on the ground is the task of the member states, a range of possibilities is opened up for exemption, delay and modification which can be highly beneficial to particular interests. As Sargent notes (1993, p.235) damage limitation is the speciality of trade associations:

> Damage-limitation activities may involve attempts to limit the scope of a particular piece of legislation, to exempt a category of companies altogether, or to remove from the scope of a proposal some of a company's most sensitive products … At other times, attention focuses on taking action to achieve as late an implementation date as possible, in order to avoid the consequences of being unable to meet the requirements of the original deadline.

The bathing water directive is a classic example of the way in which a national government may frustrate the intentions of a directive by interpreting it in a way which nullifies its purpose. After the directive was ratified in 1976, the British government issued guidelines for the identification of bathing waters which required more than 1500 people in the water per mile for a beach to be defined as bathing water. As a result only 27 bathing waters were identified in the whole country, less than in Luxembourg which has no coast. Following pressure from the Commission, the number of bathing waters was increased to nearly 400 by 1987.

However, complaints about the UK's practical compliance with the directive in places like Blackpool led to the Commission bringing the matter before the European Court. The Court clarified what was meant by bathing water in terms of facilities such as toilets and changing huts. The initial discretion given to Britain and other member states has been considerably restricted by the Court's judgment in 1993, but this was 17 years after the original directive. More generally, this example shows the reactive nature of enforcement powers, the limited resources of the Commission, and the dependence of the monitoring process on information provided by the member states (Somsen, 1994). There are many ways in which the application of a directive can be delayed and diverted over many years.

Effective European lobbying has always depended on using the full range of methods available in whatever mix appears appropriate to the particular case. Strategy and tactics may change as the particular issue evolves. An interest which is not represented at the European level is not going to be able to cope with the unpredictability of the decision making process in Brussels where a draft directive may suddenly be taken from the piles of paper on an official's desk and launched on a new stage of its life. There is no substitute for an effective presence in Brussels.

Coen (1997) asked 54 firms to allocate 100 units of political resources between a number of different channels of representation as they would have done in 1984 and as they did in 1994. In 1984 the three leading channels, with roughly equal levels of response, were: EC; national government; and national association, followed closely by national civil service. By 1994, EC was clearly the leading answer, followed by European federation, with the responses assigned to national government, national association and national civil service all falling.

It should be remembered, however, that one is talking here about multinational firms who find Brussels a particularly congenial setting for lobbying. In his work on business associations, Bennett found (1997, p.95) that 42 per cent selected the national route as the main route for European representation; 27 per cent chose a European federation; 17 per cent chose direct lobbying in Brussels; while 11 per cent emphasized the importance of an individual company's own activity. In the case of environmental organizations, Lowe and Ward found (1998, p.4) that 28 per cent of such groups were untouched by Europe; 20 per cent could be classified as 'administrative reactive'; 17 per cent focused on domestic lobbying on European matters; 21 per cent were 'limited proactive in Europe'; and only 14 per cent were integrated into transnational structures. The level of Europeanization was therefore relatively limited, with just over a third of groups engaged in effective action at the EU level.

Even so, it is important to remember how far Brussels politics is still coloured by the pursuit of national interest. This is evident in the manoeuvring that accompanies the allocation of Commission portfolios, or the selection of a new Commission president. It is not confined, however, to major decisions at the highest level. The author represented the UK for four years on a minor EU management committee where national interests frequently surfaced when decisions had to be made. On those more important bodies which have professional rather than amateur members, 'where a lobby can persuade government of its cause, the efficiency and the strength of the machinery of UK European policy-making makes UK officialdom a very strong ally' (Spence, 1993, p.71).

National groups still recognize that 'they must be careful not to alienate their own ministries by pursuing a contrary line to Brussels' (Mazey and Richardson, 1993b, p.247). National associations arrive at their European level meetings with their national baggage in tow. It is only where European-wide multinationals are directly represented that these national perspectives can be cast aside.

The national route is most important in the evolving European Union once a directive has been issued and has to be implemented and enforced. Implementation studies in political science over the last twenty years have revealed the gap between legislation and what actually happens on the ground. These problems are compounded when one has a political system that is a confederation of nation states with different interests and administrative systems that vary in their capacities and forms of organization. Indeed, it is sometimes complained that Britain is too effective in implementing EU decisions.

Even in a long established federal system like that of the United States, pressure groups use state governments to put pressure on the federal authorities (Grant, 1995b). At the policy formation stage, the national route is likely to remain one of a number of important routes used by pressure groups in the EU, while its use at the implementation stage may ease the pain of decisions that threaten particular interests. The position in the mid 1990s is well summarised by Greenwood and Jordan (1993) who argue that in a changing kaleidoscope the national level is the most important overall for political action aimed at the EC, but that the significance of European level channels must not be underestimated, particularly in relation to policy formulation.

The Commission

The European Commission is the principal target of pressure groups operating at the European level. This is because of its importance in the decision making process as the initiator of legislation and because of its receptiveness to interest groups. As a Commission official explained:

> Why do we need the trade associations? I believe we need them for advice on the problems of industry, help in technical understanding, and help in assessing impact. Most of us are not technical experts in product technology. Our expertise is in making the Community system work, in drafting and adopting directives. So we depend on specialists in industry to give us their time and energy to explain the industrial and technical issues to us. From the Commission's side, we have to be listeners.
>
> (White, 1997, p.74)

More generally, the Commission derives legitimacy from the endorsement (or at least the acquiescence) of affected interests for its proposals. Commissioners may seek to mobilize one interest to counterbalance another. Facing opposition from the farming lobby to his Agenda 2000 reforms, agriculture commissioner Franz Fischler complained about the 'conspicuous absence of public comment by the EU's food industry and traders' on reforms which might save them from having to move their manufacturing base outside Europe (1998, p.8).

Although the leading groups do have meetings with individual Commissioners, for most of them the target is Commission services, with 3500 or so senior administrators (10 000 counting middle rank officials involved in policy work) who work in the 23 directorates-general dealing with particular aspects of the work of the European Union such as internal market and industrial affairs or environmental policy. There is also contact with the cabinets, or teams of personal advisers, that assist each commissioner. Despite the increasing use of 'Inter Service' groups, co-ordination between different directorates-general is not as well developed as between government departments in Britain, and often conflicts between different spheres of responsibility have to be settled between cabinets. The author's interviews in Brussels indicate that access to cabinets is available to leading companies and groups. 'This is a real opportunity, since a considerable amount of political horse-trading takes place between Commissioners. It is, however, a fairly unreliable way of influencing a proposal and can never guarantee results' (Hull, 1993, p. 84).

Lobbying activity is focused on particular directorates-general within the Commission. For some interests, their influence is closely bound up with one directorate-general: DG V (social affairs) for trade unions; DG VI (agriculture) for farmers; DG XI (environment) for environmental groups. Hence, their influence is substantially dependent on the influence of the particular directorate-general, substantial for DG VI, less so for DG XI. Business interests have contacts right across the Commission, but tend to concentrate on particular directorates-general. Bennett's research found that DG III (industry) was the most important point of contact with 28.9 per cent of the business associations surveyed selecting it as their main point of contact. However, it is interesting that the second most popular choice was DG XI (environment) selected by 14.5 per cent of respondents, emphasizing the extent and significance of countervailing activity by business against environmental groups. The importance of contacts with DG III is confirmed by Page's research (1997, p.96).

If the decision making process in the Commission is highly political at the highest levels, it is generally relatively technical at the lower levels, giving pressure groups opportunities to press for their definition of the problem being considered to be incorporated in the Commission working document which forms the basis of the decision making process. The average Commission official has a wide range of matters to deal with, and insufficient time and expertise to cope with them adequately on his or her own. A Commission official commented:

> We are terribly understaffed and overstressed. My division is responsible for 44 directives and 89 regulations; monthly mail which requires a substantial answer numbers about 350 pieces. And I have about nine staff to deal with all of this. The corresponding administration in the [United] States has 600 people.
>
> (Quoted in Burston-Marsteller, 1991, p.22)

The combination of a high workload and often relatively young officials with little outside experience provides an opportunity for the pressure group that can offer information and expertise at an early stage of the process of policy formation:

At the beginning he or she is a very lonely official with a blank piece of paper, wondering what to put on it. Lobbying at this very early stage offers the greatest opportunity to shape thinking and ultimately to shape policy. The drafter is usually in need of ideas and information and a lobbyist who is recognized as being trustworthy and a provider of good information can have an important impact at this stage. Thereafter, once the Commission itself has agreed a proposal and sent it to the Parliament and Council, scope for changing the proposal exists only at the margin, involving about 20 per cent of the total proposal.

(Hull, 1993, p.83)

Within a particular directorate-general, one individual may be more responsive to outside representations than another. Informal links may develop with Commission officials from the country of a pressure group, or between staff in a Euro level group and their fellow nationals in the Commission. For Germans, 'A particular way of thinking along certain cultural lines – quite apart from language problems – explains the preference for communication with German Commission staff' (Kohler-Koch, 1993, p. 39). A Flemish government relations manager commented in interview, 'UK people are easier to lobby than anyone else. Maybe this is because the UK is more influenced by the US where lobbying is a qualified profession'.

There may be greater variations than in a national bureaucracy in terms of the approaches to their job of individual Commission officials. In interviews with lobbyists in Brussels, particular individuals in the Commission have often been referred to as easier to deal with than others. The European Union 'has not yet created a unified bureaucratic ideology or operational style ... the Commission does not at present practice anything like the "standard operating procedures" which are usual in Britain and Scandinavia ... for the managing of the interface between groups and government' (Mazey and Richardson, 1993c, p.117).

It must be emphasized, however, that for all their apparent dependence on groups, Commission officials retain considerable discretion and autonomy. 'The evidence that EU officials listen to interests is certainly vast, yet there is also plenty of evidence that they are prepared to stand up to them by, say, taking them to court or passing legislation that directly harms their material interests' (Page, 1997, p.110).

COREPER – Europe's Managing Board

Before policy proposals are considered by the relevant Council of Ministers, they will be considered by the Committee of Permanent Representatives (COREPER) made up of each member state's representative in Brussels. Agriculture has its own committee called the Special Committee on Agriculture, another indicator of the insulation of the agricultural policy community. Proposals are first examined by a working party of experts from the relevant government departments of the member states, along with a Commission representative.

COREPER 'and the working parties below them resolve nine-tenths of the issues before ministers even meet, leaving only the most politically sensitive points to be decided' (*The Economist*, 8 August 1998, p.37). 'In this stage of decision-making the national administration is again the main target of interest representation' (Kohler-Koch, 1993, p.39). Through the work of these bodies, the areas of disagreement between member states can be narrowed, and issues sifted into those which are relatively non-contentious, and those which will have to be the subject of ministerial discussion. If the working party can agree, the proposal goes to COREPER for its assent, and is passed to the Council under the 'A' list procedure. If the working group cannot agree, and COREPER cannot resolve the problem, it goes to the Council for discussion as a 'B' list item.

Members of COREPER do not, however, wait until items appear on the agenda in front of them before deciding how to deal with them. The officials in the UK permanent representation 'maintain close contacts with their opposite numbers in the Commission, forming a kind of permanent UK lobby with the aim of influencing the Commission's forward thinking and obtaining early warning of proposals and modifications to the Commission's negotiating position' (Spence, 1993, pp.66–7). The permanent representation 'is thus a prime focus for the private-sector lobby' (p.66). As well as being another route through which developments in Commission thinking may be influenced at an early stage, 'there is evidence of private exchanges with national permanent delegations at COREPER resulting in influence being exerted through the European Council' (Greenwood, Grote and Ronit, 1992, p.19).

The Council of Ministers

'As the final decision maker in most areas, [the Council of Ministers] is the most obvious, but also the most difficult target, except for the most powerful interests. The Council meets behind closed doors, and does not allow for easy access' (Hayes-Renshaw and Wallace, 1997, p.227). National pressure groups will, of course, already have lobbied their governments to persuade them to adopt a particular position and some of the top level business groups place considerable emphasis on briefing the country holding the presidency of the Council at any given time.

Although the actual meeting of a Council is conducted in the absence of lobbyists, and is therefore insulated from any direct pressure, 'it is not uncommon to see Ministers hurry downstairs during breaks in Ministerial level discussions ... to brief waiting lobbies in the Council ante rooms' (Greenwood, 1997, p.32). Particularly in the case of Council of Agricultural Ministers, the ministers themselves may be embedded in a policy community which ties them closely to particular client groups. In the case of agriculture, however, the imperatives of the EU's budgetary problems, and the need to reach a successful conclusion to the international trade negotiations known as the Uruguay Round, meant that agricultural ministers pressed ahead with significant reforms to the CAP. When ministers enter the council chamber, intergovernmental bargaining becomes paramount, and there is a sense in which even the most influential interest groups become outsiders.

It is important to emphasize that each individual Council has its own particular atmosphere. Those Councils which meet more frequently may develop their own 'club like' atmosphere and a common set of working assumptions, although these can be disrupted by national ministerial changes. Virtually the whole composition of the Agriculture Council changed in 1998. Each Council may approach its task in a particular way which may make it more sympathetic to some lobbies and less so to others. For example, a friend of a minister in the Blair Government told the author that the minister (who attended three different Councils) had found the Council of Environment Ministers to be a particularly strange one as its business was conducted in an absence of an almost complete disregard of factors affecting the competitiveness of European industry.

The European Parliament

The Maastricht and Amsterdam treaties have substantially enhanced the powers of the European Parliament (EP). Article 189b of the Maastricht treaty introduced the co-decision procedure which means 'the Parliament can negotiate with the Council of Ministers on demands for changes to legislation endorsed by an absolute majority of MEPs' (Collins and Burns, 1998, p.3). Once ratified, the Amsterdam treaty will extend co-decision from 15 to 38 (later 40) legislative areas including social policy, the environment and the European social and regional funds.

It is, nevertheless, something of an exaggeration to talk, as some MEPs do, about the completion of the transformation of the EP's role to create a system of joint decision-making with the Council. Its influence over so-called 'compulsory' expenditure on the CAP, some 50 per cent of the total budget, remains limited. The EP is not an exclusive legislature and cannot create new legislation, even if the co-decision procedure allows it to revise and even block legislation emanating from the Commission and the Council of Ministers where the conciliation procedure has failed. In practice what is happening is that a series of informal meetings involving the Parliament, the Commission and the Council takes place before the conciliation committee, as defined by the treaties and the Parliament's rules of procedure, actually meets. This informal process is naturally of great interest to lobbyists, both in terms of intelligence gathering and exerting influence.

The EP is seen by lobbyists as 'a place where you can get your wording into play relatively easily' (*The Economist*, 15 August 1998, p.37). However, arguments that 'it is now arguably a far more powerful assembly than can be found in many member states' (Page, 1997, p.91) perhaps says more about the national legislatures than about the EP. Moreover, they do not have to contend with another body (the Council of Ministers) which can still be argued to be the predominant legislative power. As long as member states want to defend their own particular interests, they will not allow the Council of Ministers to lose too much power to the EP.

The committees of the EP, particularly the more influential ones such as the Environment Committee, have become key lobbying targets. 'Although its legislative burden is amongst the heaviest of any committee, it draws up more own initiative reports than almost any other committee' (Bomberg, 1998, p.140). Its activities are of keen interest to both business and environmental lobbies.

The unofficial groupings of MEPs from different parties and member states known as Intergroups have also become lobbying targets. There are around sixty of these groups covering subjects such as financial services, pharmaceuticals, defence industries and small and medium-sized enterprises. Several have been set up very recently 'and may herald a trend for more sectoral interest to seek sponsoring MEPs to address issues of concern to them' (Porter, 1998, p.4). However, if they come to be seen as too easily influenced by outside interests, their role may be limited.

There has been plenty of lobbying activity at the EP, to the extent that its regulation has been a topical subject for several years, yet for most groups it has until recently been a secondary rather than a primary focus of lobbying activity. It has been particularly used by groups that might have difficulty in pressing their case elsewhere in the Union's institutions and that have some public support which can be mobilized to exert pressure on MEPs. It would appear 'that the EP attracts a disproportionate amount of lobbying from certain types of group (environmentalists, women, consumers, animal rights), who may not enjoy such easy access to the Commission and/or national governments' (Richardson, 1998, p.11).

For example, the lobby to stop testing cosmetics on animals 'knew that it had little chance of successfully lobbying the most influential institutions directly, particularly as the (opposing) views of industry were already well represented at this level'. It therefore adopted an 'approach of lobbying the Commission through the Parliament' (Fisher, 1994, p.233). The limitations of this approach were revealed when 'the Council rejected the Parliament's amendments without any further discussion' (p. 237). Fisher reached the conclusion that his study of this particular lobbying effort showed the extent to which the EU was still driven predominantly by economic forces and 'the ingrained institutional reluctance to accept the European Parliament, with its more socially oriented agenda, as an equal and respected partner when shaping European policy' (p.239).

Business groups have often subcontracted European Parliament representation to a lobbying firm, although CEFIC appointed a full-time liaison officer in 1990. This decision reflects an increasing realization that business interests will have to pay more systematic attention to the Parliament, particularly to its committees. Higher calibre individuals are being elected, although the benefits of this are to some extent offset by higher turnover than in the Commission. Bennett's research on British business associations found that over 50 per cent of them had met with UK MEPs, and nearly 30 per cent had met with European MEPs. Some of this contact may be seen rather cynically as a long-term investment, one lobbyist commenting:

> [MEPs] are flattered when you take an interest in them. You give them information about an issue that helps them look and sound good. But they are still trivial in terms of decision-making power. Cultivating them is an investment in the future.
>
> (*The Economist*, 15 August 1998, p.37)

There is evidence that as the Parliament has become more important 'business interests are ... learning how to engage the Parliament, such that the special relationship between public interest groups and the EP has been disrupted' (Greenwood, 1997, p.48). Thus, while the Parliament was relatively weak, public interest groups flocked to it, but winning its support had little practical effect. Now that it has more influence in the decision-making process, the influence of the public interest groups is being offset.

The European Court of Justice

The European Court of Justice (ECJ) offers an alternative route for groups that have not been successful elsewhere. 'When groups have failed to gain satisfaction in the national venue, the Commission, EP or Council of Ministers, they have the option of bringing cases (usually in the name of individuals) before the Court, or of persuading the Commission to bring a case before the Court' (Richardson, 1998, p.13.) The drawback with this approach is that while the Court may be useful in establishing particular decisions which may have far reaching implications, 'access to the European Court is very restricted. Moreover, it is difficult to control the implementation of the decisions of the Court' (Rucht, 1993, p.88).

For women's groups, the ECJ has been an important venue for forcing change at the national level, constructing new agendas and requiring policy makers to focus on new areas of activity. 'The ECJ over the years has been a powerful institutional catalyst of change. Landmark ECJ judgments have been important both in clarifying – and in most cases – extending the scope of the directives' (Mazey, 1998, p.144.) Some of these achievements have, however, been undermined by the development of a neo-liberal climate of deregulation within the EU (pp.147–8).

Even for weaker business interests, legal action may be a less attractive venue. The courier industry was reluctant to file a complaint against the postal administrations under EU law even though it was legally feasible. 'We concluded that a formal complaint at that time would unite all the postal administrations against the courier industry before we had a recognized commercial role in the Union economy' (Campbell, 1993, p.133). With a relevant Commission decision under appeal, 'We did not want to launch a massive legal case until the law was clear' (p.134). This reminds us that the law can be a very slow, as well as a very uncertain, means of securing policy change.

It is therefore not surprising that only 5 per cent of the British business associations surveyed by Bennett had made approaches to the ECJ, only fractionally more than those who had contacted the Committee of the Regions. The interventionism of the ECJ, and the fact that it acts as a counterweight to intergovernmentalism, is not something particularly welcomed by business interests.

The Economic and Social Committee

The Economic and Social Committee (ESC) was the body specifically set up to represent interests under the Treaty of Rome, but it is of marginal importance. 'It is a measure of the present lack of significance of the [ESC] that some Brussels commentators suggested that 'it would be a waste of valuable InterGovernmental Conference (IGC) time to even discuss the question of whether it should be abolished' (Greenwood, 1997, p.48).

Even when the European Union has moved in the direction of more corporatist arrangements, it has preferred to work through less cumbersome arrangements such as the Tripartite Conferences of the 1970s. Streeck and Schmitter (1991, p.138) note, 'there is general agreement that it has, in fact, accomplished very little. In particular, it was never able to serve as a privileged access point for organized interests to European-level decision making'. It is the Commission that remains the key access point for pressure groups 'because the Commission is the only EC institution which is involved in each of the different stages of the policy cycle, from agenda-setting to the formulation and implementation of a policy' (Kohler-Koch, 1993, p. 39).

Making Sense of EU Level Pressure Group Activity

Trying to make overall sense of pressure group activity at the EU level is not easy because it also involves trying to take a view about the emerging European polity, a complex system of multi-level governance. It is evident that the way in which EU institutions are structured, the activities they carry out, and the symbolism they embody, all have a significant effect on collective action at the EU level (Cram, 1998). However, although the EU has acquired many state-like characteristics in terms of a capacity to make (although more rarely to implement) authoritative decisions, 'it is unlikely that Euro politics will lead to a breakdown of the national model of state–society relations in favour of a new European polity' (Aspinwall, 1998, p.212). Or, to put it another way, whatever happens in 'Euroland', Britain may be a more peripheral part of an increasingly differentiated Europe.

The EU level adds a new level of political activity, complicated by the emergence of new subnational levels (in Wales and Scotland). These new levels have had a profound impact on the national level of political activity, but they have not replaced it. Are there any models that can help us to understand what is happening at the EU level?

Corporatism

There has always been something of an ideological predisposition towards corporatism in the European Commission. In part, this is because many of the member states have Christian and social democratic traditions which have made them well disposed to corporatism. It is also because corporatist arrangements have been perceived as one way of assisting the integration process. In the jargon of the Union, the terms used have been 'social partnership' and 'social dialogue'. In the 1970s there was a Bureau of Social Partners which was not a marriage agency, but an attempt to involve the trade unions more effectively in the work of the European institutions.

In the 1970s social partnership was promoted through a series of 'Tripartite Conferences' which came to an end in 1978 after the ETUC withdrew because so little was being achieved. They were revived in 1985 through meetings at the Val Duchesse castle near Brussels involving members of the commission headed by Jacques Delors, UNICE, the ETUC, and the European Centre for Public Enterprises (CEEP). In 1989, a political level steering group was set up to develop the social dialogue with priority being given to education and training and labour market issues. The employers gave rather reluctant assent to this process. According to the head of the CBI Brussels office:

> It is worth stressing that we see UNICE as our lobby and no more than our lobby. Three years ago we stretched a point and agreed that it should become our social partner, i.e. that it should meet in joint session with the European TUC, under Commission chairmanship and should develop the social dialogue.

> (Eberlie, 1993, p.204)

Article 118b of the Single European Act gave a formal status to the notion of social dialogue stating, 'The Commission shall endeavour to develop the dialogue between management and labour at European level which could, if the two sides consider it desirable, lead to relations based on agreement'. This idea was extended in the agreement on social policy in the Maastricht treaty which was not signed by Britain until Labour took office. The CBI had initially agreed to support the proposal when it found itself in a minority of one in UNICE, but backed down after opposition from within its membership to any notion of binding implementation (Grant, 1993a, p.190).

The agreement on social policy in the Maastricht treaty establishes 'dialogue between managment and labour' as one of the objectives to be pursued in the implementation of the 1989 Social Charter. The implementation of directives in areas such as social security, redundancy protection and employee representation may be entrusted by a member state to management and labour at their joint request, a classic neo-corporatist provision. Article 4 of the agreement provides for management and labour to arrive at agreements which can then be implemented by a Council decision.

Having analysed these processes, Falkner (1998, p.189) comes to the conclusion that 'against frequent expectation, current EC social policy-making is not in principle different from corporatist policy styles prevailing in some member states'. However, she admits 'that the contemporary version of corporatism is comparatively restricted in functional scope and belongs to the sectoral or area-specific level' (pp.187–8). Some EU policy networks may be expected to turn into corporatist policy communities as a means of removing the burden of particular tasks from the state at a national or EU level. 'From an aggregate perspective, the EU can be expected to stay a mixed system whose public-private interaction patterns vary according to sectoral or policy-specific regimes' (p.188).

Pluralism or Technostructure?

The problem remains, what is the nature of the mix? Although corporatist elements are certainly present, to many analysts it looks predominantly pluralist. Streeck and Schmitter (1991, p.157) saw Europe developing an American style of 'disjointed pluralism'. Page (1997, p.94) prefers a model of consultative pluralism 'in which a variety of groups with weak or no potential veto power compete for influence within the executive'. He sees Europe-wide groups as having 'limited powers to shape Commission policy directly' with 'a potential for diversity among individual, sectoral or national interest organizations, not only in the views they represent but also in the strategies they choose to represent them' (p.102).

Page emphasizes that he is focusing on the Commission rather than on what happens at national level or in the Council of Ministers. One might question whether there is in fact an asymmetrical relationship between groups and government with a potentially strong role for bureaucrats as a major source of professional expertise as this model is seen by Page (p.94) to imply. As has been discussed, middle level bureaucrats in the Commission see themselves as quite dependent on pressure groups for information and expertise, while some business groups are capable of making strategic interventions at the highest levels of decision making.

As we saw in the case of CNE, the most successful groups are those which can adapt to an elitist, technocratic style of decision-making. It may therefore be useful to deploy Pross's adaptation of Galbraith's notion of the technostructure, the technostructure being defined as 'a sophisticated communications network of technically proficient specialists that cuts across the lines dividing government and business and in which technical knowledge is the currency of power' (Pross, 1986, p.49). The increasing dominance of technical competence in the policy process had, according to Pross (p.49) important implications for democracy:

First ... it 'short-circuited' traditional institutions of political representation. Second, it changed the language of policy-making in a fashion that excluded lay people, including politicians. Third, in promoting neutral competence, it denigrated political participation in both administration and policy-making and substituted for it technical expertise.

In some ways the situation is worse at the European rather than the national level because there are no traditional institutions of representation. Political parties are relatively marginal actors in the European policy process. Their absence gives great scope for pressure groups. Although the influence of the European Parliament in the policy process has increased, its views can still be disregarded with the Council of Ministers, reflecting the balance of views among member states, remaining the leading legislator. The view that EU citizens apparently take of the EP is reflected in an average turnout in its elections that fell from 63 per cent in 1979 to 56 per cent in 1994, with UK turnout the lowest in the EU at 36.2 per cent in both 1989 and 1994.

There is concern among European Commission officials about the distance between the European decision-making process and European citizens. The author has co-ordinated a European research project designed to see how socially excluded groups of citizens might be empowered to participate in environmental decision-making, an arena where environmental groups remain relatively marginalized and, in any case, largely represent more affluent citizens.

Business does not always get what it wants at the European level, and it may be that the agenda of women's groups or the concerns of environmentalists get more attention than they would if the EU did not exist. Nevertheless, the multinationals wield considerable structural and political power and there is a sense in which the EU is 'their' project, however much it may be presented as a social vision. There is the progressive Europe of the centre-left heads of government who predominate in the late 1990s, but there is also the Europe in which Volkswagen chauffeurs the chair of an influential emissions committee around Brussels (Page, 1997, p.89) or in which Jacques Delors flew on corporate jets as the guest of the chief executives of major European companies (Green Cowles, 1997, p.134). The expertise of business does need to be tapped and utilized, and the EU should avoid policies which damage competitiveness, but these priorities need to be balanced by broader social and environmental considerations. It is open to question whether the present system of interest representation at the EU level achieves such a balance.

7
Agenda Setting: the Media and Direct Action

An important part of the political process is getting an issue on the political agenda and defining it in a way which is helpful to your particular point of view. In a fragmented society one of the ways of doing this is through the media. A survey conducted in 1992 found that 13 per cent of pressure groups regarded the media as their most important target. Four out of five groups 'claimed that they were in contact with the media at least once a week; half had daily contact with the media' (Baggott, 1995b, p.183).

One of the objectives of direct action, discussed later in the chapter, is to gain media attention, although it may also be designed to inflict financial losses on targets to discourage them from their activities. As Robinson comments:

... the direct action movement has opened up new institutional venues (the media and construction sites) which are not dominated by the institutional bias of the road lobby. The act of protest has become news in, and of, itself.

(Robinson, 1998, pp.157–8).

One must not, however, fall into the trap of equating politics with what is in the media at any point in time. The media can mould the political agenda, but 'there is no simple correlation between the political agenda and the media agenda. There are complex interactions between the political, public, scientific and media agendas' (Anderson, 1997, p.142). Applying a model of source–media relations 'tends to result in an exaggerated focus upon the media in relative isolation from broader structures of power that incorporate pressure politics' (p.72).

Getting Issues on the Political Agenda

The political agenda is crowded, and there are limits to the number of
issues which can be processed at any one time. This is reflected in the
pressures on Parliamentary time. Even under the Thatcher Government,
which was supposedly committed to rolling back the influence of the
state, each Queen's Speech contained a substantial amount of new legislation. The Cabinet and its Legislative Committee have to discuss which
possible measures are to have priority in a particular session. During the
year, there will have to be discussions about whether to offer minor concessions to speed up the passage of a particular piece of legislation, and
when and where the guillotine should be applied.

However, important though the legislative agenda is, the political
agenda is a somewhat broader concept. It refers to those issues which
arouse public concern at a particular period of time. There may be short-
run variations in response to particular events, but there may also be
longer-term shifts in public opinion. The media undoubtedly plays an
important role, if not in creating public opinion then at least in reinforc-
ing it. The rise in the importance of the environment as a political issue
undoubtedly owed something to increased media attention. In part, this
reflected the growth of television as a communications medium, particularly the introduction of colour television. Pollution disasters offer
powerful visual images: a spreading oil slick; stunted trees; dying seals.

Some groups, particularly cause groups, may be seeking to establish
'their' issue on the political agenda or to give it a higher priority as a
prelude to obtaining effective political action. Indeed, the emergence of
a new issue may often involve the formation of new cause groups or
coalitions of such groups. Some sectional groups may also wish to obtain public attention for their problems, for example teachers'
organizations may wish to draw attention to problems of violence against
teachers, or of increasing stress levels being experienced by school heads.
Very often, however, sectional groups will want to keep issues away
from public attention as much as possible, so that they can be processed
through familiar consultative channels.

Once an issue has been placed on the political agenda it 'passes into the
relatively closed world of the executive departments of state and, to a
lesser extent, interdepartmental and cabinet committees, where the consideration given to issues and possible responses by politicians and officials
is still largely shielded from public gaze' (Solesbury, 1976, p.392). Media
attention may soon switch elsewhere and, as Solesbury points out, there

are a variety of 'partial responses' open to government which may reassure the public without eradicating the original problem (p.394). Interest groups can use the media to move an item up the political agenda. In general, however:

> The combination of national mood and election is a more potent agenda setter than organized interests ... [Interest groups] less often initiate considerations or set agendas of their own. And when organized interests come into conflict with the combination of national mood and elected politicians, the latter combination is likely to prevail, at least as far as setting the agenda is concerned.
>
> (Kingdon, 1984, p.208)

A decreased ability to influence the content of the political agenda may reveal a weakening of a group's position. Smith notes that 'The farmers failed to keep the salmonella in eggs issue off the agenda' and sees this as 'indicative of a general weakening of the position of farmers' (1991, p.244).

Even when a pressure group has the national mood on its side, it will find it difficult to overcome government resistance. The RSPCA had widespread popular and legislative support, as well as the backing of other key groups such as the Police Federation, for its dog registration scheme. The Conservative government defined the problem in terms of a scheme for a restricted range of dangerous breeds, being motivated not by animal welfare considerations, as the RSPCA was, 'but by a concern for human victims of the attacks' (Garner, 1993, p.82). Even though the government's majority was reduced to three on a three-line whip, the RSPCA still lost (p.194).

Some issues are more amenable to a campaign based on the media. It has been suggested that 'media exposure can be particularly effective when the issue concerns a clear cut decision' (Anderson, 1997, p.41). The Snowdrop campaign was one of the most successful single-issue campaigns in British pressure group history. Started by people with little political experience and with no more equipment than a decorator's table and a petition after the Dunblane massacre, they secured a handgun ban in less than a year. The media quickly took up the campaign, giving it a prominence it would otherwise have lacked. Media involvement 'not only made the Snowdrop petition difficult for the government to ignore, it also forced the gun lobby to seek legitimacy in the public arena' (Thomson, Stancich and Dickson, 1998, p.339). There were many factors that contributed to the success of the Snowdrop campaign, not least the ineptness of the gun lobby and the combination of reason and emotion in Snowdrop's own appeal, but the concerted campaign by the tabloids and the broadsheets helped to keep the issue on the political agenda until it was resolved.

The Importance of the Media to Pressure Groups

The effective management of relations with the media has become a crucial skill for pressure groups. Whiteley and Winyard note (1987, p.10) that a number of changes in the political environment have produced a situation in which 'Ministers and officials who might have reacted with hostility to the publicity associated with lobbying activity in the 1980s now regard it as a more normal aspect of campaign strategy'.

One indication of the increased importance of the media is the greater attention they have been given from the 1970s onwards by established insider groups. Groups which in the past have relied largely on behind-the-scenes contacts in Whitehall found that such a strategy was no longer adequate; it was also necessary to try and create a favourable image to reinforce their contacts with civil servants and politicians. For example, in 1977 the CBI initiated an annual conference to help to raise its public profile.

It is not just sectional groups that have been giving a higher priority to media relations. Established cause groups have also revised their strategies to give a new emphasis to contacts with the press. For example, the Council for the Preservation of Rural England (CPRE) was run for nearly forty years by a general secretary 'whose style of operation was through personal contact in the corridors of power. He fastidiously avoided embarrassing those he influenced or sought to influence' (Lowe and Goyder, 1983, p.75). The CPRE subsequently became more media conscious, with an increasingly sophisticated approach to the use of the media. Thus, when a new director was appointed in 1980, he 'had experience in advertising and freelance writing for television and radio' (p.75).

Probably no group has used the media more than Greenpeace, both to attract members and to publicize its causes. Greenpeace has applied considerable professionalisation and sophistication to its media operations. It provides pre-packaged video news releases in a form which takes account of the deadlines of news organizations. Anderson (1997, p.85) outlines the scale and scope of Greenpeace's media operations:

Greenpeace Communications ... has a full in-house film, video and photo-graphic capability incorporating a small television studio, three editing suites, a digital sound studio and a commercial film and television archive. These facilities also include compressed digital satellite encoders and decoders and three-dimensional computer graphics. The Greenpeace press desk operates on a 24-hour basis to accommodate the deadlines of media organizations around the world.

The Different Forms of Media

The term 'media' covers a variety of forms of dissemination – television, radio, press and the internet – and, within each of those forms, material that is targeted at a variety of audiences. Television thus carries mass-audience programmes and also programmes likely to be watched by a very small audience interested in a particular issue. As the number of providers increases, a trend that will be accelerated by digital television, the audience is increasingly fragmenting. This may make it easier for pressure groups to reach audiences likely to be well disposed to them, but harder to use television as a means to influence decision makers. We are hardly likely to see a pressure group founded again as a result of a television programme, as in the case of Shelter and the tel-evised play *Cathy Come Home*. Nevertheless, the major current affairs programmes still carry enough weight with decision makers to have some influence on the political agenda:

Specialist programmes such as BBC 2's 'Nature' provide analysis on the full range of environmental issues, whilst the investigative journalism of pro-grammes such as 'Panorama' ... has increasingly been used to 'expose' na-tional and international environmental problems ... Following the broadcast of such programmes, MPs can find themselves under pressure from an en-quiring public with regard to issues they have previously given little consid-eration.

(Robinson, 1992, p.110)

Sometimes it will be advantageous for pressure groups to try and reach the largest possible audience through a medium such as the television news or a mass circulation newspaper. On other occasions, however, a more targeted approach may be desirable. It may be more appropriate to influence informed opinion through the broadsheet newspapers which are read by large numbers of decision-makers. Current affairs radio pro-grammes have a significant audience among politicians, who are said to compete with each other to get on the *Today* programme broadcast in the mornings on Radio 4, which can also help to set the day's political agenda. Its influence may have been diminished, however, by the fall in Radio 4's ratings following reorganization of the schedule.

Each policy community will also tend to support its own specialist press. For example, some idea of the scale of the specialist press in agriculture is given by the fact that the Guild of Agricultural Journalists has more than five hundred members. Specialist journalists sometimes become too close to the sources they rely on and reflect too readily the views of the policy community they are reporting:

> From the late 1960s until the mid-1980s most writers on social security were sympathetic to the views of the Child Poverty Action Group ... just as defence correspondents have tended always to see the viewpoint of the chiefs of staff and the Ministry of Defence.
>
> (Riddell, 1996, p.6)

Important interventions may come from unexpected sections of the media. Marsh and Chambers note that the Corrie abortion bill was attacked by the whole range of women's magazines. Most surprising was the 'strong attack on the bill which came from *Woman's Own*, a magazine not known for its radical views and with a largely conservative readership' (Marsh and Chambers, 1981, p.133). Indeed, *Woman's Own* paid for an opinion poll which provided evidence of widespread public opposition to the Corrie bill and was sent by the magazine to all MPs just before the debate at report stage. One MP listed it as one of the reasons why the bill eventually failed (p.146). More generally, 'The women's magazines carried the pro-abortion lobby's message far more widely than ever before, and not just to the more radical women. The anti-abortion groups lacked this kind of publicity' (p. 133). Greenpeace retains a features writer who specifically targets women's magazines that appear to be in need of copy and well disposed to environmental issues (Anderson, 1997, p.174).

The Internet

The internet provides a new and important medium for pressure groups. There has been a somewhat surprising variation in the response of pressure groups to this new opportunity. (See Box 7.1 for websites from a

Box 7.1   Selected pressure group web sites

Royal Society for the Prevention of Cruelty to Animals
http://www.rspca.org.uk/
A very attractively designed site with animal pictures and moving
graphics on the home page. Details of campaigns on such subjects as
puppy farms and cosmetic testing on animals. Offers advice on '10
ways to make an impact when writing to a politician or newspaper
editor on an issue you feel strongly about.'

Greenpeace
http://www.greenpeace.org.uk
Home page offers links into press releases, photo gallery, priority
campaign, section for younger surfers etc.

Compassion in World Farming
http://www.ciwf.co.uk/
Site had not been updated for two months when visited, but offered
press releases, campaign leaflets, reports, a manifesto and details
of items for sale.

CEFIC
http://www.cefic.org/
One of the most comprehensive sites offered by a European level
organization providing full information about the wide ranging
activities of CEFIC and its affiliates.

Confederation of British Industry
http://www.cbi.org.uk
Provides news and press releases and information on how to join the
CBI. A little dull, but it is understood that the site is to be redesigned.

National Farmers' Union
http://www.nfu.org.uk/
Key items of news and press releases highlighted, along with a
search facility for the press release archive. Site of more use to
someone with knowledge about the industry than the casual surfer.

Website addresses can change. A search engine like Yahoo can be used to
identify other sites.

cross-section of pressure groups.) The RSPB, the cause group with the largest membership, 'was a late starter' (Lawson, 1997: p.69). It did not set up a strategic development team to examine computer services until November 1997 and no website could be traced in the autumn of 1998. The potential audience for a website is illustrated by the fact that the regularly updated World Wildlife Fund site receives 40 000 hits a week. (p.69). Among business interest associations, a third were reported to have websites by late 1998 (*Forum News*, November 1998, p.1). Websites can perform a number of functions. They can publicize the pressure group's activities and policy positions and act as a recruitment mechanism. Making current policy papers available for downloading over the web should be much cheaper than sending bulky packages through the post. The website may also be used to get the group's message across when it is facing difficulties in its relationship with the media. After encountering 'a period of intense scepticism within the news media', Greenpeace increasingly relied 'on their own Web site ... to get the message across' (Anderson, 1997, p.113).

More important, websites and associated e-mail lists can be used as a means of mobilization. For example, the Independent Manchester United Supporters' Association (IMUSA) made extensive use of electronic media, including the e-mail lists of supporters of other clubs, to rally support for their lobby of Parliament in opposition to the proposed BSkyB takeover of the club in the autumn of 1998. Rick Everitt has commented, 'I'd go so far as to say that had the Charlton list existed in 1985 it would have been the crucial factor which, by allowing fans to organize themselves in time, would have made it possible to stop the move from The Valley' (Everitt, 1997).

Building society 'carpetbaggers' who seek to demutualize building societies were making extensive use of websites and e-mail lists at the end of the 1990s to exchange information and views on tactics. This led a spokesperson for the Building Societies Association to observe:

> What concerns us about the internet is the ease of communication and how much easier it is for them to get 50 members together [the number of backers needed for a conversion resolution]. In the age of e-mail communication, it has to be questioned whether that threshold is high enough.
>
> (*Independent on Sunday*, 16 January 1999)

Media Channels at the EU Level

Using the media at the EU level faces the problem of the relatively limited number of outlets with a specifically EU focus. There is extensive representation of press agencies, newspapers and television channels, but their reporting is often directed towards national concerns. The Europe wide market for news about the EU is a relatively limited and specialized one. 'Public discourses on Europe and the EU are still mainly national, as is reporting by the media. Thus it does not play the role in the policy cycle of the EU that has been commonplace in the political life of Western political systems at the end of the twentieth century' (Wessels, 1997, p.34).

Hence from the perspective of the pressure group:

> The European level is generally lacking in the media opportunity structures familiar at the national level. However, there are now a few genuinely European level media outlets and there are signs that some of these are perceived by groups as worthwhile channels for communicating to European policy makers.
>
> (Richardson, 1998, p.18)

Richardson notes that pressure groups do make quite considerable use of advertisements in publications such as *European Voice*. They may take out full page advertisements 'often over a period of months when controversial issues, such as control of genetically engineered products, is passing through a key phase of the legislative cycle (particularly in the EP)' (p.19). Leading business groups such as the ERT and AmCham have sought media publicity for their policies, but largely in the papers read by key influentials such as the *Financial Times, Economist, International Herald Tribune* and *Le Figaro*. Unlike the national strategies of pressure groups, which have a considerable focus on popular media including television and the tabloid press, EU strategies are often rather elitist in character and principally use print media. This emphasis reflects the nature of the EU.

How Pressure Groups Use the Media

Pressure groups use the media in a variety of ways, but is it possible to offer a categorization of the various forms of use? It is suggested that six distinct uses can be identified: visibility, information, climate, reactive response, influence and content.

Visibility refers to the use of the media to establish a presence, and to recruit and retain members. The Aberdeen group's data shows that of the members of Friends of the Earth surveyed 23.6 per cent joined after seeing a press/media campaign. The groups are commercial clients of the press, as well as providers of news:

> Greenpeace, for example, is regularly contacted by newspapers alerting them to advertising possibilities when an environmental story is being published. Thus, on a page with a lead story and a picture of environmental damage or stricken wildlife, the group will have a membership advertisement.
>
> (Jordan, Maloney and McLaughlin, 1994b, p.551)

The sinking of the Braer oil tanker off the Shetlands in 1993 provoked a wave of group advertising, and by joining or sending money to the group concerned, readers could feel they were doing something to help the afflicted animals and birds. Some publicity comes free, however, and is not linked to a disaster. For example, a television programme called *The Animals Film* 'was an important moment in the growth of public awareness of animal exploitation' (Porritt and Winner, 1988, p.52). Retaining members is a problem for many cause groups and constant exposure for the group in the media reassures its membership that it is active, and helps in the retention of members. There is little point in recruiting a large number of new members as a result of a blitz of media publicity if their interest cannot be engaged and their support retained.

The media can be an important source of *information* for pressure groups. The trade press can unwittingly reveal clues about what a particular firm or industry is doing. 'Lobbyists scan the papers in the search for stories, data, opinions and letters related to themselves' (Davies, 1985, p.181). Frank Field recalls how the Child Poverty Action Group (CPAG) carefully read the court page to produce a list of individuals who had access to the then prime minister (1982, p.54).

Climate refers to the long-term efforts of pressure groups to change the climate of opinion on an issue in a way that is favourable to their objectives. This may involve seeking to influence informed opinion and decision makers, but it is also important to seek long-run changes in public values which set the context within which policy is made. 'Through their background campaigns, environmental groups in general have enhanced their public image and generated a climate of opinion sympathetic to environmental protection.' (Lowe and Goyder, 1983, p.79).

Reactive response is necessary when a news story emerges that is potentially threatening to a group's concerns or activities. Sometimes an organization may have to react very quickly to an unfavourable story: for example, the egg industry was obliged to react in December 1988 to a statement by a junior minister, Edwina Currie, about allegedly extensive contamination of eggs by salmonella. In such circumstances, a group may be forced into a defensive stance. However, properly managed, such situations can be used to create favourable publicity, particularly for cause groups. The group may be invited on a television programme to explain its position, or can at least write to the press in response to editorials or letters from others.

Using the media as a means of exerting *influence* on government is clearly particularly important. Of course, ministers are not usually going to change their policies because of a newspaper editorial or a critical television programme. However, the sudden development of a campaign in the media may catch them off guard and oblige them to respond, as in the case of the Snowdrop campaign discussed earlier. Media coverage may reinforce a case being made to civil servants by demonstrating that the matter is one of public concern. Direct action by the anti-roads lobby changed 'the perception of the transport issue from that of a technical and specialist issue to an emotive and public one' (Robinson, 1998, p. 191). If an existing policy network loses control over the public perception of the issue in this way, it may also start to lose its control over the policy process itself. Media attention may help to move a problem up the political agenda. Field recalls that one way of getting the CPAG's correspondence 'onto the top of the pile and read by ministers was to ensure publicity for the letters in the media ... ministers would then request an internal briefing, thereby getting the department's attention onto the issue being raised by the Group' (1982, pp.53–4).

Publicity to exert influence requires a rather different strategy from that used by a group seeking visibility to get established. At that stage, a variety of stunts may be a justifiable means of launching the group and attracting members. However, Whiteley and Winyard's research (1987, p.130) makes it clear that groups can be damaged by irresponsible publicity. Civil servants do not like groups who appear to be more interested in television publicity than in serious negotiations. Explaining the difference between responsible and irresponsible publicity, Whiteley and Winyard (p.120) comment:

Responsible publicity meant coverage in the quality press about the group's activities and the needs of its clients. Primarily it involved a reasoned presentation of the group's case. It did not involve attacks on the character and motives of ministers and officials, or illegal demonstrations such as sit-ins in supplementary benefits offices. These were seen as counterproductive.

Finally, pressure groups may lobby the media directly and attempt to influence the *content* of its output. An organization representing rural local authorities, the Rural Services Partnership, announced that it would ask editors of television and radio series such as *Emmerdale*, *The Archers* and *Peak Practice* to 'highlight real problems country people face in getting access to public services' (*Financial Times*, 2 June 1998). The producers of *The Archers* 'are heavily lobbied by all and sundry' (quoted in Porritt and Winner, 1988, p.127). In a postmodernist world, the line between image and reality is often blurred and when one of the characters, Susan Carter, was sent to prison, a 'Free the Ambridge One' campaign led to a debate about sentencing policy and a statement from the home secretary.

Another aspect of the content of the media which attracts attention from pressure groups is advertising. The Advertising Standards Authority (ASA), which regulates print and poster advertising, has found itself receiving an increasing number of objections to adverts for particular causes. It has upheld complaints from the British Fur Trade Association against a leaflet from Respect for Animals, while the NFU successfully objected to a press advertisement placed by the League Against Cruel Sports. The Vegetarian Society, which has placed some controversial advertisements, has complained that the ASA 'treats campaigning groups as if they were selling products like baked beans. Different criteria should be applied' (*Financial Times*, 16 June 1998). As it finds itself increasingly caught in the crossfire between pressure groups, the ASA has made it clear that it will not be bullied into changing its mind despite 'a readiness among some organizations to challenge its competence to decide the validity of some claims' (*Financial Times*, 16 June 1998).

The Limits of Using the Media

The relationship between pressure groups and the media has come under increasing strain. There has been a growing suspicion on the part of television journalists that they have been manipulated by pressure groups to put across a slanted message. In a speech to the Edinburgh TV Festival in

August 1995, Mr Richard Sambrook, a BBC news editor drew attention to Greenpeace's ability to outspend television companies in shooting footage of its own protests and commented, 'this particular David isn't armed with a slingshot as much as an AK47' (*Financial Times*, 6 September 1995). Shortly afterwards, Greenpeace admitted that they had disseminated inaccurate information about the quantity of oil on board the Brent Spar oil rig. As a consequence, 'The press in Britain adopted a line that Greenpeace had been trying to win at any cost, had been inventing scare stories that had been found out' (Jordan, 1998b: p.17).

In February 1996 the *Sea Empress* spilled oil and killed wildlife along the Pembrokeshire coastline. A media circus descended on Pembrokeshire with environmentalists and journalists who knew each other staying in the same hotels waiting for 'the sound bite ... that would capture public attention'. A study of the incident concluded that 'Big voluntary bodies with environmental conservation interests which are used to playing the media game can also cause serious damage to public confidence and local relationships when they parachute into an incident' (Caldwell and Morgan, 1997, p.5).

Food scares have been another area in which pressure groups have relied on capturing media attention. A senior BBC food programme producer attacked campaigning groups for causing 'unholy confusion' about food safety. He quoted the case of a pesticide used on apples which was found to cause cancer in rats when given to them in large quantities. Entertainment stars launched a campaign against the pesticide which was eventually withdrawn. It was later pointed out that mushrooms contained exactly the same carcinogen in far greater quantities (*The Guardian*, 30 December 1997).

Incidents of this kind have led to a new scepticism among broadcasters about the claims of pressure groups. The BBC commented on Greenpeace's admission of issuing mistaken data that it demonstrated 'how important it is for the media to test the veracity of what any organization declares or states' (*Financial Times*, 6 September 1995). One might have thought that was standard journalistic practice, but it is evident that the media have been willing to accept statements from pressure groups at face value without further checking because they have been seen as 'the good guys'. In a sense, they were reflecting public attitudes because survey data 'on whom the public rely for information on the environment shows environmental groups (including Greenpeace) as being trusted by 81–85% of the public whereas the oil industry is trusted by only 32–36% and spokespeople for the oil industry by only 25%' (Jordan, 1998, p.9).

Even if pressure groups can convince the media that they have a credible case, media attention is essentially ephemeral in character (this is particularly true of television). The attention span of the media is necessarily limited. In the case of the *Sea Princess* incident:

> Someone who lived in Birmingham, fed on a diet of popular press and television, might be forgiven for thinking after two weeks that the whole episode was over. Yet the graft of cleaning up the mess was only just beginning, as were the necessary studies that would demonstrate or refute what the long term environmental impacts will be. Neither of these were sexy subjects for a media driven to seeking the sensational.
>
> (Caldwell and Morgan, 1997, p. 5)

There is a danger of confusing a television programme with effective political action. As Porritt and Winner (1988, p.86) comment, 'If a nation's ecological wisdom were measured by the number of television programmes it makes about the environment, Britain would have little to worry about.' The drama of a dramatic media event staged on television may mislead public sympathizers into thinking that policy has already been changed:

> For example, watching a handful of heroic Greenpeace 'rainbow warriors' ... on television, the audience may think that effective action has already taken place ... Coping with the many persistent environmental problems ... requires a steadier engagement at the international level, and changes in personal behaviour, instead of merely spectacular, predominantly symbolic, actions which may simply soothe the broader public.
>
> (Rucht, 1993, p.93)

Robinson's careful study of anti-roads protests found that the anti-road groups were able to impact on the 'public' perception of the issue but not on the 'private' perception which occurs in a policy making process 'characterised by frequent contact between government bureaucrats and the pro-roads group in a core policy community' (Robinson, 1998, p.194). Although the protests 'influenced the news agenda and through that public perception of the transport issue, they have had much less effect on the private perception of the transport issue which remains dominated by the interaction between government and erstwhile insider groups' (Robinson, 1998, p.205).

Sophisticated groups realise that using the media is one part of an overall strategy of exerting influence. The media may be particularly important in getting an issue established on the public agenda. However, at a later stage of the decision making process, different strategies and the tactics may be necessary as the group encounters the forces which produce inertia and continuity in political decision making.

The Use of Direct Action

The continuing strength of the forces resisting change is one explanation of the increasing use of 'direct action'. Indeed, it is possible to talk of a new 'protest culture' (Brass and Koziell, 1997, p.7) that cuts across a number of issue areas including animal rights, roads and civil liberties.

Direct action is perhaps easier to define in terms of what it is not rather than what it is. Conventional forms of politics like holding meetings with ministers or civil servants, writing letters to MPs or delivering petitions to Downing Street does not constitute direct action. Garner (1996, p.83) notes that direct action 'covers a huge variety of actions and should not be thought of as synonymous with illegality'. Direct action may be violent or non-violent, illegal or legal, but it can be conceived of in terms of a gradation of activities, starting with lawful demonstrations and culminating in criminal acts such as violence against individuals. Although it may be seen as a means of exerting pressure on government through the publicity generated, it may be more directly targeted at those carrying out the activity, whether it is those out hunting or a multinational company trying to dump an oil rig at sea.

How are we to explain the apparent growth of direct action? Brass and Koziell suggest (1997, p.7):

There is a common link between the animal lovers and the anti-road activists … many of them have tried conventional channels for change, but have got so fed up with the lack of response that they have decided to take matters into their own hands. And it's not just a question of having to wait too long for things to get better, increasing numbers of people are coming to the conclusion that their needs will never be addressed by those in power.

Thus, when the Labour government was seen by animal rights activists not to act quickly enough to introduce legislation banning fur farming, an Animal Liberation Front spokesman talked about the 'bitter disappointment of activists … It leads to suspicion and distrust of parliament and the

certain escalation of extra-parliamentary activity' (*Financial Times*, 19 August 1998).
  Each of the forms of direct action referred to in Table 7.1 below will be considered in turn with reference to relevant examples. As Garner notes (1996, p.84), 'It is often difficult to draw a hard-and-fast distinction between direct action and more traditional pressure group activity since it is at least partly aimed at generating publicity which puts pressure on decision-makers.' Securing publicity is one of the main objectives of protest marches which almost count as a conventional form of politics. However, 'demonstrations can backfire. A poorly organized or badly attended demonstration reflects adversely on the campaign and can undermine its cause' (Baggott, 1995b, p.180). Even a successful march is

Table 7.1 A typology of direct action

Form of action	Legality	Main objectives
Protest marches	Usually legal	To demonstrate to decision-makers scale of support and concern on an issue
Boycotts	Legal	To inflict a commercial punishment on a firm
Stunts	May be marginally illegal	To focus attention on an issue through publicity
Blockades, occupations, other disruption	Open to civil action, increasingly criminalised	Exertion of direct pressure or target to inhibit or prevent activities
Destruction of property	Illegal	Bringing activity to an end
Violence against individuals	Criminal	Punishing those seen as responsible for 'immoral' acts

open to the criticism that 'Popular protests tend to reflect political impotence' (*The Economist*, 28 February 1998). Organizers also have to remember that 'There is a bewildering array of statute law covering public protest ... The picture is further complicated by the extremely variable way in which these provisions are enforced' (Day, 1998, p.219). Most protest marches are, however, allowed to go ahead and do so without anyone being arrested.

A classic example of a peaceful but influential event was the biggest march in Britain for fifteen years organized in March 1998 by the Countryside Alliance, ostensibly concerned with a range of countryside issues, but focused on threats to hunting. A quarter of a million people turned up and the Blair government was evidently badly rattled. A private members' bill on hunting was effectively killed off by lack of government support and the government appeared to be back tracking on its support for legislation on the 'right to roam' in the countryside.

Boycotts can be difficult to organize on a scale that makes them effective: a few committed activists refusing to buy a product will have little practical effect. One of the most successful boycotts in recent years was when motorists in Germany were called on to not to buy their petrol at Shell garages in protest against its plans to dump the Brent Spar oil platform at sea. The Shell companies in Germany and other countries affected 'saw the boycott as pain with no gain. There was little reason for them to dig their heels in against the consumer power' (Jordan, 1998, p.23). Pressure was brought within the Shell organization on Shell UK to dispose of the platform in a different way that would be seen as more environmentally friendly.

'Stunts' were important in the early days of the environmental movement when empty bottles were dumped at the offices of soft drinks companies or whales were towed up the Thames. The publicity attracted helped to kickstart the environmental movement, but inevitably 'stunt fatigue' set in and the stunts started to become more daring and more likely to place activists in conflict with the law. In 1987 Greenpeace activists ignored injunctions to block the outlet pipe from the Sellafield Nuclear Reprocessing Plant. In the resulting contempt proceedings, two of those involved were jailed. In 1994 anti-road activists managed to attract attention without being prosecuted by draping anti-motorway banners over the home of the then transport minister who telephoned the home secretary to complain about the breach of his security (*The Independent*, 27 April 1994).

Blockades, occupations and disruptions are really at the heart of modern direct action. They are intended not only to attract publicity for a cause, but also to prevent a particular activity taking place, or at least to make it more expensive, more difficult or less enjoyable. Thus hunt saboteurs use a variety of techniques to try and disrupt hunts and prevent a 'kill' taking place. The Campaign for the Abolition of Angling used frogmen to empty keep nets at a competition and dragged ropes across the river to create waves. Protesters against exports of live farm animals try and stop the vehicles reaching the ports.

Anti-roads protesters occupy the routes of roads and dig themselves in elaborate tunnels to make it difficult for them to be cleared from the site, thus adding significantly to the cost of building the road (most contracts set a fixed price for security above which the contractor bears the cost). A security adviser to the construction industry commented that protests had become more sophisticated and hence costly to deal with over time:

> The first anti-road demonstrators simply occupied the route. They then moved into the trees to avoid eviction and when we became experts at removing them from the trees they moved underground. Evicting them used to involve some local muscle, now you have to hire specialist climbers and cavers.
>
> (*Investors Chronicle*, 12 September 1997)

Farmers have learnt how to blockade key retailer distribution depots in their campaigns to halt sales of Irish beef, claiming that 'We've got to the stage where we can pick up the phone and within three hours have the supermarket distribution network completely shut down' (*The Guardian*, 17 January 1998). Such actions clearly create substantial economic damage.

Destruction of property is clearly illegal, although it also inflicts considerable commercial damage. Opponents of genetically engineered crops such as the 'Lincolnshire Lollards' or the 'Wardens of Wiltshire' have destroyed plants at test sites, terminating the experiment which cannot then be repeated in the growing season. By midsummer 1998 at least 27 of the 163 test sites in the UK had been vandalized (*Financial Times*, 23 July 1998).

Some anti-road protesters have sabotaged equipment at road construction sites, while the destruction of thousands of pounds worth of computer equipment at the Department of Transport was attributed to them. In December 1995 a demonstration lasting one day by 250 people opposing the extension of a Somerset quarry cost the quarrying company

£100 000 in damage to equipment and £200 000 in disruption (*Investors Chronicle*, 12 September 1997). Mink have been released from farms which, because of the difficulty of recapturing them, amounts to a form of destruction of property, although the protesters themselves would object to the caged animals being described as 'property'. Transport fleets used for moving meat or even milk have been the target of arson attacks. The most criminal form of direct action is violence against the individual. Bombings of abortion clinics and shootings of doctors working in them have occurred quite often in the United States. In Britain, it is animal scientists who have most frequently been the target of violence, including bombings. A lorry driver who was not connected with the transport of animals was killed when his windscreen was smashed by protesters near Dover.

The Effectiveness of Direct Action

Many supporters of direct action are not concerned with the effectiveness of their actions in the sense of whether they win or lose the sympathy of public opinion or decision makers. Because they are driven by a sense of moral outrage, the action almost becomes more important than its effects. They see it as an end in itself rather than a means to an end. Thus members of the militant gay rights group OutRage! 'denied they had scored a public relations own goal by invading the pulpit during the Archbishop of Canterbury's Easter sermon' (*The Guardian*, 13 April 1998). One member of the congregation commented that 'I have sympathy with what they are saying. But tactics like this merely set the cause back'. OutRage responded that the congregation were bound to take a negative attitude, but they were appealing to a wider audience outside the Church. It is open to question, however, whether what OutRage! describes as 'in your face action' increases public support for gay rights.

The firebombing of milk tankers at two depots in Cheshire was seen by moderate animal rights activists as signalling 'another advance for "militant veganism", a philosophy so puritanical that its advocates want the abolition of all animal husbandry, the closure of the meat, dairy, fishing and egg industries ... To them, a truly caring society would be one without milk, cheese, butter and eggs' (*The Observer*, 4 June 1995). Such an objective is unlikely to be achieved by conventional political methods, given the likely extent of popular opposition. Indeed, many vegetarians would argue that being a vegetarian involves a moral choice which is debased if it is made compulsory.

Clearly the approach of the animal rights movement and that of organizations like the Royal Society for the Prevention of Cruelty to Animals (RSPCA) are poles apart. When mink were released in the New Forest, the RSPCA expressed concern about the threat to native birds and endangered species:

> As a law-abiding organization we utterly condemn these actions. As an animal welfare organization we would also condemn these actions because they are not in the interests of mink or wildlife.
>
> (*Financial Times*, 19 August 1998)

The ALF would not, of course, be concerned about breaking the law and would claim that its actions were in the interests of the mink. The RSPCA, which wants to outlaw fur farming by conventional political methods, was placed in the position of feeling obliged to help capture the mink released by the ALF.

Sometimes there may be a combination of direct action by experienced protesters who have participated in campaigns elsewhere alongside more conventional forms of action by local residents. One might think that this would lead to irreconcilable tensions, but the evidence is rather mixed. The 'campaign against the expansion of Manchester Airport was the first airport protest in Britain in which the mobilisation of largely middle-class residents was accompanied by the presence of a committed group of direct action protesters' (Griggs, Howarth and Jacobs, 1998, p.358). As the campaign progressed, the two groups came closer together with a group of local women forming a practical support group for the eco-warriors. 'As the direct action campaign developed [local residents] originally hostile to direct action campaigners, their lifestyles, but also their methods, came to identify with the environmental cause that the green activists championed' (pp. 367–8).

The experience at the road protest at Solsbury Hill near Bath was rather different. 'Over time, the Donga presence on the hill became more and more contentious for the mainstream SOS [Save Our Solsbury] group.' (North, 1998, p.6.) There seem to have been a number of particular reasons for the alliance in Cheshire, including the nature of the pro-runway campaign. 'Tarring middle-class residents, their legitimate interests and forms of protest, with the same brush as the eco-warriors resulted in the creation of solidarity and a degree of identity between widely divergent forms of campaigning' (Griggs, Howarth and Jacobs, 1998, p.368.) Also in Manchester there were key figures who were able to act as 'policy brokers' between the two different campaigns. It would seem, however, that the Solsbury case points to some of the limits of a 'twin track' approach which combines conventional pressure group methods with direct action. Those operating 'in political society, with their articulation on public opinion and use of the media, became increasingly intolerant of what they perceived to be the un-media friendly Dongas' (North, 1998, p.21).

Many direct action campaigners would, of course, not see their campaigns as being intended to reinforce conventional forms of activity, but to halt or disrupt activities which they find morally reprehensible. Earth First! comments on its website:

> Conventional 'green' campaigning is not enough to stop the destruction that is happening. Politicians and companies ignore letters, petitions and public enquiries; they reject overwhelming evidence because it goes against their interests ... the only solution is for people to take their future in their hands and physically halt further destruction of nature.

What is evident is that direct action can have a substantial impact on the fortunes of targeted companies. The cost of protecting staff and buildings against animal rights protesters following a critical Channel 4 documentary helped push Britain's largest animal testing company, Huntingdon Life Sciences, £3.5 million into the red in the third quarter of 1997 (*Financial Times*, 22 November 1997). As a result of pressure on customers, Glaxo Wellcome, Zeneca and Astra all announced that they would stop placing new contracts with Huntingdon (*Investors Chronicle*, 12 September 1997). The company was investigated by the Home Office after the documentary and its shares were down to 12.5p in mid-January 1999 compared with 124p in early 1997 Campaigners have threatened to extend their 'economic sabotage' to institutional investors unless the company stops all animal experiments, planning a march on the Co-op Wholesale Society's Manchester headquarters, and claiming its investment breaches the Co-op's ethical investment criteria (*Independent on Sunday*, 14 June 1998).

It should be pointed out that the direct effectiveness of such protests has been limited. For example, no road has been stopped once construction has begun. (The project for the construction of a road through Oxleas Wood in South-East London was dropped, but many other factors were influential and there was no direct action on the site of the type that has occurred elsewhere.) There may, however, be substantial indirect effects. Some investment analysts think that anti-road protests, by reducing overall road spending, have had an impact on the valuation of the whole construction sector in the medium term, although the effect is very difficult to quantify (*Investors Chronicle*, 12 September 1997). With environmental protests seen as an increasing problem, 'the easiest solution for investors is to avoid companies that carry a risk of environmental protest' (*Investors Chronicle*, 12 September 1997). If that advice was widely followed, companies operating in environmentally sensitive areas would find it more difficult to raise capital.

Direct action is very sensitive to discretionary action by the police and civil action or private prosecutions by affected companies. The 1994 Criminal Justice and Public Order Act introduced the new offence of 'aggravated trespass'. There are, however, limitations in the extent to which this legislation can be applied and in practice much depends on the attitude of the police on the ground. As was evident from the course of the farmers' protests, the attitude of the police was highly variable with, for example, senior police officers sitting in while the protesters negotiated agreements with the owners or managers of distribution depots. However, when farmers picketed Tesco distribution depots in April 1998, they found the police there in full riot gear with dogs. When the police chose to do so, they were able to stop blockades as at Fishguard in June 1998. A planned 48-hour blockade was stopped after 15 hours when the police set up road blocks to stop more protesters arriving and warned that tractors used in the blockade could be impounded (*Farmers Weekly*, 19 June 1998).

Civil actions or private prosecutions can be a significant deterrent to direct action. The fur campaign group, Lynx, was forced to dissolve after losing a libel action. It has been suggested that during the Brent Spar episode 'Something of the reluctance to call openly for consumer action may have reflected fears in Greenpeace that they might be sued by Shell for harming their sales' (Jordan, 1998b, p.23). A tactic widely used in the United States is called the strategic action against public participation (Slapp) which has the effect of frightening protest groups into silence. This tactic is even more effective when groups like Greenpeace accumulate large funds and have staff on substantial salaries who might be placed at risk (indeed one of the objections of Earth First! to more conventional green groups is their corporate structure and hierarchical character). The animal testing company, Huntingdon, spent £719000 taking legal action, including suing People for the Ethical Treatment of Animals in the United States.

Threats of civil action and private prosecution may have little impact on roads protesters who have no private property or on animal rights activists who may regard being imprisoned for their cause as a form of martyrdom. However, these tactics may have more impact on more conventional individuals who have been attracted to a particular protest. 'The Department of Transport used Slapp successfully at Twyford Down, suing anti-road protesters for £1.9 million and thus scaring the middle classes away' (*Independent on Sunday*, 24 August 1997). Farmers leading dock and supermarket pickets have been warned that they could face private prosecutions for unlawful disruption of trade. Attempts to criminalize protest can, however, backfire. Dudley and Richardson argue (1998, p.741) in relation to the 1994 Criminal Justice and Public Order Act:

> Current evidence suggests ... that this new legislation, far from constraining the issue, has simply facilitated its further expansion by adding a new dimension to the protesters' portfolio of arguments ... the issue of civil liberties and the rights of the 'unorganized' to participate in the formulation of public policy have now been drawn into the once simple 'roads' issue.

Part of the 'new politics' has been a cultural shift which means that direct action has become a more accepted part of the repertoire of pressure group action. But if it is here to stay, is that a good thing for democracy?

Direct Action and Democracy

The growth of 'single issue' pressure groups which often use direct action tactics is often criticized on the grounds that, unlike political parties, they do not have to balance out a range of issues and come to difficult decisions about priorities. They can 'demand' action on a particular issue without having to take account of the wider consequences for the economy or society as a whole. Expectations rise, but the financial or enforcement resources are not necessarily there to meet them. One person interviewed by Brass and Koziell (1997, p.18) commented, 'I think that people are different now, people demand more of authorities ... nowadays people will ask for more.' At its worst, this can become a kind of infantilist politics in which people think that their demands are superior and should be met now, regardless of the preferences of others.

Instant gratification is sought:

> They want direct action and take it. They are much more impatient than some
> past generations of political activists who put up with all the layers and the
> time lag that exist between going to a meeting or march and any positive
> result that might be achieved.   (p.8)

The result can often be a kind of lifestyle politics which trivializes
important political issues: 'In DIY culture the lifestyle comes before
politics. A percentage of the people are highly political: the rest are
subscribing to the politics as part of the lifestyle' (p.10). Politics becomes another form of consumption, rather than participation in a
political dialogue, in which one takes part in an action simply as an
experience. Campaigning organizations become protest businesses which
market a particular identity and lifestyle choice to consumers (Jordan
and Maloney, 1997).

It is, however, important to be aware of the real forces that underpin
the growth of direct action. One response to globalization is to take direct action at a local level where one may see a tangible impact in an
otherwise alienating world and thereby gain a sense of personal empowerment. People 'feel that public institutions and the Government
are too busy trying to compete in the global market economy to actually
listen to the needs and ideas of … individuals and communities' (Brass
and Koziell, 1997, p.7).

Trade unions were one traditional channel through which people expressed their opposition to dominant forces in society. However, as they
have become weakened, new channels have been sought out to express
opposition. Opposition, and the generation of new ideas, are part of a
healthy democracy. 'Unless you have [a] healthy flow of demands coming through, the political system will just fossilise' (p.11). The more
inclusiveness is stressed as a central value in society, the more some
members of society will feel the need to dissent in an unorthodox fashion.

8

Pressure Politics Outside Whitehall: Parliament, the Courts and Local Government

This chapter reviews a number of routes which pressure groups may use other than seeking to influence the national executive or EU bodies, or agenda setting activities through the media and direct action. Using Parliament, working through political parties, taking action in the courts or operating at the local level are secondary forms of activity for most groups. As Maloney and Jordan note (1998, p.21), 'the bureaucratic arena will almost always hold more appeal for groups'. Nevertheless, there is sufficient activity through these channels to mean that a comprehensive account of pressure group politics in Britain cannot ignore them.

The visibility of Parliament in the political process can lead to a perception that it is more influential than it actually is. However, when one has a government like the Labour government elected in 1997 which enjoys a very large majority in the House of Commons and has enforced strict party discipline, the opportunities for exerting influence are very limited. Even private members' bills which do not enjoy government backing are unlikely to prosper, as opponents of hunting found in 1997–8. Garner notes (1998, pp.109–10), 'the system of animal welfare interest group politics has increasingly been focused on the executive ... parliament plays, with the exception of the hunting issue, a peripheral role'. Maloney and Jordan (1998) argue that taking the policy making process as a whole, Parliament is not a major point of contact. Nevertheless, there is quite a lot of lobbying activity focused on Parliament, even if its style and character were affected by a number of scandals during the 1992 Parliament and the consequent introduction of stricter codes of conduct for MPs.

Parliament has conventionally been regarded as a route used to influence the decision making process by outsider groups who lack good contacts with civil servants, but insider groups would appear to be even more active in terms of a range of different types of contact with Parliament than outsider groups (Judge, 1990a, p.36). 'This suggests that, apart from their closer governmental links, insider groups are generally more active than outsider groups' (p.35). The 1974/9 Parliament, when the government lacked a working majority for the greater part of the Parliamentary term, encouraged more sectional groups to become involved with Parliament. Although cause groups can sometimes attain their objectives through the passage of a private member's bill, sectional groups can also make effective use of Parliamentary contacts. Bruce-Gardyne (1986, pp.152–3) recalls what happened when, as a minister, he was presented with a complex scheme designed to enable horse traders to escape VAT:

> I was vastly unimpressed, until I was accosted by one of my senior colleagues in the corridors of Westminster. 'I hear', he told me in a voice full of menace, that 'you're being bloody-minded about our horse-trading scheme. Well forget it. It was all fixed up with your predecessor, and I can assure you that if you muck it around, we'll make your life a misery.' I had second thoughts.

Most associations representing particular industries will either have their own small staff dealing with Parliament, or retain a firm of Parliamentary lobbyists to assist them with Parliamentary representation. For example, the Chemical Industries Association employs a Parliamentary Adviser, and administers the All Party Parliamentary Group for the Chemical Industry with a membership of some seventy MPs together with members of the House of Lords. The group meets to hear about developments in the industry and to discuss relevant legislation, and its members are also individually briefed on a large number of subjects. A piece of legislation which is particularly important to the CIA may involve the Parliamentary Adviser attending every debate and committee session in the Commons and Lords; briefing individual committee members, civil servants and ministers; and commenting on large numbers of amendments put down by MPs.

Ways of Using Parliament

Parliament is made up of two houses; a variety of mechanisms for processing legislation and discussing current political issues; and (counting active peers) over a thousand individuals with a wide variety of political interests and priorities. How can pressure groups go about influencing a very complex institution which is understandably protective of its traditions and privileges?

One possibility is to organize a letter-writing campaign. Certainly, MPs are receiving more and more letters. Many of these letters will, of course, be concerned with problems faced by individual constituents, and MPs will give consideration of such letters a high priority. Circulars from pressure groups are likely to receive little, if any, attention unless the MP or peer has a special interest in the issue. 'Perhaps half the mail sent to an MP is consigned to the bin by his secretary' (Miller, 1990, p.99.)

One tactic that a pressure group may use to avoid the waste-paper basket is to get its members to write to their MP on an issue which concerns it. A letter from a constituent has to be given some attention and the RSPCA persuaded 30 000 of its members to write to their MPs when the Foster hunting abolition bill was under consideration. Such a stratagem can backfire if it is not well managed. Bruce-Gardyne recalls that MPs received a larger number of letters from Catholic constituents complaining about a plan to charge for school transport. 'On closer inspection most of these communications had fairly obviously been signed, not by Catholic voters at all, but by their children scribbling under the vigilant eye of their local parish priests' (Bruce-Gardyne, 1986, p.155.)

An alternative is to telephone or e-mail MPs. When it appeared that a Commons Select Committee might reject a ban on handguns, the *Sun* 'printed the telephone numbers of its Conservative members and suggested that readers might like to ring them to complain about its conclusions' (Thomson, Stancich and Dickson, 1998, pp.334–5).

Although paid advocacy by MPs is now banned, they may continue to act as paid advisers to pressure groups. By amending a resolution of 1947, the House of Commons has prohibited members who have received any kind of payment from advancing a cause 'by means of any speech, Question, Motion, introduction of a Bill or amendment to a Motion or Bill' (Rush, 1997, p.19). Nor may they participate 'in delegations to ministers or civil servants affecting only the body from which they have paid interests' (p.14). Following these changes, there has been a drop of about two thirds in the Parliamentary consultancies held by MPs (Gronbech, 1998, p.115).

That many ambiguities remain is illustrated by the role of the all-party subject groups which organize members of all parties, sometimes having peers as members as well. These groups are not without significance:

> They have a liaison function with ministers and can exert pressure to modify policy proposals or influence legislation. They are part of the consultation process which seeks views[s] from both inside and outside of Parliament.
>
> (Maloney and Jordan, 1998, p.14)

The number of such groups has risen from 80 to about 160 over the last 15 years, leaving aside 100 groups set up to improve contacts with particular countries. A new register of such groups shows that the most prosperous is the Beer Club which receives £40 000 a year from the brewing and pub interests. A number of the groups provide hospitality and trips for MPs, although some are run on a shoestring to further particular causes, such as the health risks associated with organophosphates. The Transport Forum is funded by 11 outside organizations and is run by a lobbying firm. According to the lobbyist concerned, 'It allows sponsoring bodies to get to know a group of parliamentarians interested in transport matters. How they use that afterwards is their business, not mine' (*The Independent*, 10 November 1998).

Convivial discussions between MPs and outside interests tend to arouse suspicions, but there is a particular danger of equating activity with effectiveness in the case of Parliament, and it should be remembered that it is very unusual for a government with a working majority to be defeated on the floor of the House of Commons on one of its bills. Ultimately, the government can make the matter one of confidence.

A pressure group cannot realistically expect to defeat legislation to which a government is committed. A more successful strategy may be to change the detailed provisions of a bill in a way which is of benefit to a pressure groups members. An attempt can be made to do this at standing committee stage when the bill is considered line by line – although, of course, standing committees are whipped. There is, however, always the possibility of government backbenchers siding with the opposition to defeat a particular clause which concerns a pressure group. That stratagem is less likely in the 1997 Parliament, but even a government with a big majority may consider from time to time that the best course of action is to make concessions. Thus, at standing committee stage 'The toing and froing between members and groups, either in person or through correspondence, is often continuous and extensive' (Norton, 1990, p.186).

Private Members' Bills

Private members' bills offer one route by which pressure groups, particularly cause groups, can hope to attain their objectives. However, it is a hazardous route, even for relatively uncontentious proposals, and has probably become more so as opponents of such bills have made more use of consulting firms to advise on blocking tactics. Relatively few private members measures ever become law:

> The scales are heavily weighted against them. In the first place the Government takes up most of the time of the House for its own business, so that a Private Member has to be more than fortunate to get enough time to take a Bill through all its stages before the end of the Session. In the second place it is difficult for a Private Member to organize a majority favourable towards his Bill – or, as is more usually the case, to prevent a majority of unfavourable Members voting against it.
>
> (Taylor, 1979, p.89)

Capital punishment was abolished, abortion legalized, divorce liberalized and theatre censorship ended through private members''legislation, but the period between 1964 and 1970 was exceptional. Major changes were brought about through private members' legislation during this period 'because the Labour Government granted time to the various bills' (Marsh and Read, 1988, p.64). Far more typical of the successful use of private members' legislation by pressure groups is the relatively technical measure which offends no important countervailing interest. A member who wins a high place on the ballot for private members' bills will receive many approaches from groups who would like him to introduce their proposals as bills. Marsh and Read (pp.63–4) cite the case of a Conservative MP who having specified 'no animals, no sex' was offered a bill by the British Insurance Brokers Association who wanted to establish a register for legitimate insurance brokers. 'The bill was passed without a vote although there was considerable debate and the Government granted time for the consideration of Lords amendments' (p.64).

Having public opinion on your side is certainly not sufficient to ensure the passage of a private member's bill. Polls conducted since the late 1950s have shown that a growing majority of the population favour the abolition of hunting. Over the 1970s and 1980s polls 'showed a hardening of opinion against fox hunting ... and by the early 1980s some polls were indicating 80 per cent support for a ban' (Garner, 1993, p.47). Attempts to ban blood sports through private members' legislation have, however, failed. This was partly because of the political skills of a group of pro-hunting Conservative MPs, and partly because of the 'vagaries of the procedures for Private Members' bills in the House of Commons' (Thomas, 1983, p.268). In addition, 'Blood sports enthusiasts have increasingly (and cleverly) turned their attention to conservation justifications' (Garner, 1993, p.173).

The League Against Cruel Sports decided that, rather than trying to pursue the fruitless route of private members' legislation, it would be better to use evidence of public opinion to persuade the Labour Party to adopt a manifesto commitment to abolish hunting. It was argued that 'only a government bill would succeed in passing all the parliamentary stages and only a manifesto commitment would be likely to get sufficient parliamentary time and attention to get the bill through the Lords' (Thomas, 1983, p.222). This decision represents a significant recognition of the limitations of private members' bills as a means for cause groups to attain their objectives. The Labour Party manifesto commitment was diluted between 1983 and 1992 (Garner, 1993, pp.201–2). By 1997 it had become a promise to support a private members' bill on the issue, although Tony Blair subsequently claimed that the only commitment was to allow a free vote (which has always been permitted on such measures).

A bill was introduced by a Labour MP, Mike Foster, in the 1997–8 session but, despite receiving a second reading vote of 411 to 151 in favour, failed because the Government did not give it any of its own time. A government minister claimed that even if time had been provided, 'members opposite will use the procedures of this house to thwart it' (*Financial Times*, 24 November 1997). Even if it had got through the Commons, it would have faced serious opposition in the Lords, facing the government with the dilemma of whether to use the 1949 Parliament Act to override any veto. The government appeared to have been shaken by the scale of support for the pro-hunting Countryside March and did not want to jeopardize its other legislation by supporting a controversial measure. The government may in the future be prepared to consider dealing with the matter through the more secure route of a backbench amendment to a criminal justice bill, or by allowing local authorities to decide whether to ban hunting in their areas. Private members' bills arc too fragile a device to secure controversial reforms.

Private Bills

Private bills as distinct from private *members'* bills constitute a form of legislation which is often of particular interest to sectional pressure groups. Without going into all the complexities of this particular type of legislation (there are also hybrid bills), these are largely bills promoted by local authorities or other public bodies to acquire land or undertake some new activity. In 1994 a private bill brought forward by British Rail to construct a new railway across London (Cross Rail) was defeated in committee. Proposals put forward by Labour-controlled local authorities have sometimes attracted the opposition of bodies such as the CBI. As many as seventy bills of this type may be passed in a Parliamentary session, with much of the work being undertaken in the Lords. The committee stage of such bills has a quasi-judicial character, with counsel representing both sides, and evidence given on oath. Because of the expense involved, promoters of such measures are generally willing to enter into discussions before committee stage to agree amendments. They are sometimes the subject of intensive lobbying. P & O encountered controversy 'after they hosted a party in the House of Commons at the same time a Private Bill they were sponsoring to extend Felixstowe docks was being discussed on the floor of the House' (Grantham and Seymour-Ure, 1990, p.75).

Parliamentary Committees

Executive policies and actions are scrutinized by select committees of both Houses. Pressure groups dutifully prepare memoranda of evidence for such bodies, and the more important ones are asked to present themselves to answer questions from committee members:

> Outside interests ... make a substantial input to the evidence received by select committees and in written evidence make the largest contribution to all except four committees ... [pressure groups] ... are a major source for committees of non-governmental information.
>
> (Rush, 1990, p.145)

Bruce-Gardyne represents the dismissive executive view of select committees when he states that they 'produce a constant flow of reports which are rarely discussed in Parliament, and seldom make a stir ... rarely, in practice, do they make much impact on departmental policies' (Bruce-Gardyne 1986, p.141). Members of the Study of Parliament Group, on the one hand, tend to take a positive view when looking at the role of select committees from the perspective of legislative studies specialists. Thus, Rush argues (1990, p.148):

> In so far as select committees can make recommendations, a significant proportion of which are accepted by the government, it is likely that pressure groups do have some effect from time to time. One of the attractions of select committees for outside interests is that they generally operate in a less partisan atmosphere than other areas of Commons activity ... Many of the recommendations made in committee reports concern the details of policy, rather than the principle, and the details of policy are what many outside organizations are interested in influencing.

Of course, even if government accepts recommendations in a select committee report, it may be because government thinking was moving in that direction anyway, and the committee has absorbed some of the drift of thinking from civil servants who have given evidence. One would also need to ask whether the recommendations, once accepted, were actually implemented in an effective way. The Public Accounts Committee has been the committee that has been most effective in following through earlier investigations, but then it has the resources of the National Audit Office at its disposal.

Peter Riddell has argued that it is the hearings rather than the reports that matter. Extracts are shown on television each morning and are watched by those with a serious interest in politics such as political correspondents (Seminar by Peter Riddell, Oxford, May 1994). There is no doubt that the reputations of ministers and others can be diminished by poor performances. However, pressure groups are more interested in policies than personalities and political careers. While acknowledging their increasing expertise and useful scrutiny of public bodies, Miller lists their weaknesses as 'Executives may ignore their work' and 'Usually work too late to influence policy' (1990, p.55).

In practice, some of the most influential bodies in Parliament are the little-known but important specialist backbench committees of MPs interested in a particular subject. Clearly, it is the backbench committees of the governing party that are of real importance; such committees have been better developed in the Conservative Party. Miller (p.40) notes that particularly 'At a time of large Government majorities they are a powerful focus for backbench opinion on the Government side, with privileged access to Ministers and a representative role enhanced by their regular meetings, at which business, industry and other interest groups are given the opportunity to voice their concerns or be questioned by MPs'.

Ministers have been persuaded to drop contentious proposals because of a backbench revolt in one of these committees, as happened, for example, with the Thatcher Government's first set of proposals to introduce student loans. Lawson recalls that among the bodies he consulted in the Conservative Party while drafting the budget were the executive committee of the 1922 Committee and the backbench Finance Committee with the whole Treasury team going to the latter meeting. 'On occasion, they could influence events: for example, the introduction of cash accounting for VAT for small businesses in my 1987 Budget ... stemmed directly from views expressed at these meetings' (Lawson, 1992, p.320). The backbench specialist committees are therefore an important target for pressure group activity at Westminister. They have, however, tended to be weaker in the Labour Party and are probably of less significance under the Blair Government than they were during the Conservative years.

The House of Lords

The political capital and legislative time which the Blair Government is devoting to removing hereditary peers from the House of Lords suggests that they are concerned about the obstructive potential of a second chamber in which they lack a majority.

Baldwin (1990, p.158) argues that the House of Lords 'has increasingly become a focus for lobbying'. A working peer told the author that he received an almost unmanageable volume of communications from pressure groups. Perhaps the most important reason for this development has been:

> growing assertiveness, making not merely drafting or technical amendments to legislation but in changing it considerably. Between 1979 and 1987 the Conservative Government was defeated on 106 occasions ... The modern

> House of Lords is increasingly prepared to create difficulties for the Government of the day. The fact that a number of these defeats have forced the modification or withdrawal of various proposals, as indeed have pressures from the peers which did not lead to a defeat, has not gone unnoticed by pressure groups. (p.159)

Under the long period of Conservative government, this growing assertiveness could be seen as a response to what often seemed to be the weaknesses of the opposition in the House of Commons, particularly up to 1992. It was relatively easy for the House of Lords to assert that it is the voice of the people, or of disadvantaged groups, when it was facing what was often a very unpopular Conservative government. (Its critics would claim it is the last refuge of the old Establishment displaced by Thatcherism). The House of Lords continued to amend Labour legislation, for example seeking to replace the closed party list system for the European Parliament elections by an open system.

The House of Lords thus offers pressure groups another opportunity to make detailed amendments. In the case of the legislation to ban most categories of handguns, the Lords made a number of amendments which would have had the effect of diluting the legislation. The Conservative government was able to overturn the most significant of them, in face of support for it by nearly a hundred of its own MPs, with votes from the opposition parties. One amendment which created a computerized register of holders of gun licences was retained. 'The amendents voted for by the Lords proved to provide further embarrassment to a government which was seen to be reacting to events rather than shaping them' (Thomson, Stancich and Dickson, 1998, p.338).

As the examples quoted above show, any amendment which is too contentious is likely to be reversed when the measure returns to the Commons. However, the House of Lords offers fruitful ground for inserting relatively technical amendments which may be important to a pressure group's members. Even if the amendment is not pressed to a vote, it may be used to extract further assurances from the government. This is a tactic which has been used with considerable success by the CBI over the years. When the 1966–70 Labour government announced its intention to reform the Lords, the CBI stated that it would 'take any opportunity of advocating the retention of arrangements which would preserve the advantages industry has enjoyed under the present system' (CBI Annual Report 1967, p.22). Indeed, Bruce-Gardyne (1986, p.147) argues that 'Whitehall remains ill-equipped to handle the House of Lords'. It is not easy to find able junior ministers to represent a department in the Lords, and they are then called upon to handle all aspects of its work.

As greater restrictions have been placed on the relationships between MPs and lobbyists, the lobbying firms have increasingly turned to the upper house where peers can still ask Parliamentary questions and speak in debates on their behalf. One public affairs consultant commented, 'They are also cheaper and are better in Europe, where people are still impressed by their titles' (*Sunday Times*, 2 November 1997).

Whether the reformed Lords will be as docile and 'on message' as ministers appear to wish remains to be seen. If it eventually included an elected element, as some reformers advocate, its legitimacy would be enhanced and it would become more of a counterweight to the Commons. It could even become the most important Parliamentary target for lobbyists if it developed a greater capability to change legislation through detailed amendments whose significance was not widely understood. Lords reform may appear to be eminently sensible, but it is also something of a pandora's box with unknown consequences for the influence potential of pressure groups and hence for democracy.

Professional Lobbyists

Mounting concern about the role of professional lobbyists culminated in the so-called 'cash for questions' affair, which was one of the events that led to the Nolan Report on standards in public life and a new set of rules governing the relationships between MPs and lobbyists. There had long been rumours circulating that it was possible to get MPs to put down questions in return for an appropriate consideration. *Sunday Times* reporters posing as businessmen approached a number of MPs to see if they would table Parliamentary questions in return for payment. 'Two Conservatives (Graham Riddick and David Tredinnick) agreed and found themselves at the centre of suggestions that this was merely the tip of an iceberg of parliamentary corruption' (Rush, 1997, p.11).

The Nolan Committee examined the 1995 Register of Members' Interests and found that 26 MPs had agreements with lobbying or public relations firms, while another 142 had consultancies with business associations, making up nearly 30 per cent of backbench members. The Nolan Committee stopped short of recommending a ban on contracts with lobbying firms, but did recommend a ban on multi-client consultancies. Although, as noted above, the House of Commons went further and banned paid advocacy, the position remains somewhat ambiguous:

> The House of Commons has banned paid advocacy, but MPs may continue to act as paid advisers to companies, trade associations, trade unions, pressure groups and other organizations. Yet advice can be just as valuable, sometimes more valuable than advocacy.

(Rush, 1997, p.24)

Certainly the Blair Government has seen no reduction in the activities of the lobbyists or the controversy surrounding their activities. The so-called Cronygate scandal was launched by a report in *The Observer* in July 1998 which made a number of allegations about preferential access and inside information obtained by lobbyists with links with the Labour Party. 'All the lobbyists involved had played a role in modernising Labour prior to office and, more importantly, were close friends of many still playing a key role with the now governing party' (Souza, 1998, p.43). The most serious allegations related to a young man called Derek Draper who had worked for Peter Mandelson. He claimed to be able to gain access to ministers and to Downing Street, having enjoyed 'close connections with Downing Street Adviser Roger Liddle' (p.43).

New lobbying firms continue to be set up by individuals with links with the Labour Government. After being managing director of Market Access (later GPC Market Access after a takeover) Mike Craven became the Labour Party's acting chief press officer. He then left the Labour Party to set up a new political lobbying company and is 'expected to have a number of blue chip companies on his books' (*Financial Times*, 31 October 1998). Souza argues (p.143) that 'Labour need the commercial lobbyist to meet the business world'. However, if this is the case, one wonders what Labour was doing on the 'prawn cocktail circuit' in the City in opposition, or why business associations and government relations departments are falling down on the job. To some extent, the political lobbying industry seems very adept at creating its own demand. As Souza admits (p.149), 'The commercial lobbying industry's appointment of Labour arrivals was not necessarily to access Labour ... but a marketing tool to retain clients and take on new ones.'

Sectional groups and companies are the main users of their services, although well-resourced cause groups may have their own Parliamentary lobbyist. Some firms specialize in monitoring developments, and drawing the attention of clients to emerging issues which should concern them. Given that they have staff reading *Hansard* and other

Parliamentary documents for a number of clients, they are often able to provide such a service more economically than if a pressure group tried to undertake this sifting work for itself. They also build up a body of knowledge about the special interests of MPs, which they can utilize to meet the particular needs of their clients. One consultant explained in interview that the nature of the work:

Depends on the nature of the lobby, depends on what one's objectives are. There are 101 different things – identifying MPs who are personally interested and sympathetic, briefing people before 2nd Readings in public bills, suggesting amendments, a lot of work during standing committees.

Although many consultancy firms are very politically sophisticated and display a high level of professional skill, there has been an element of the 'emperor's clothes' about the work of professional lobbyists. There is never a tangible end product which can be attributed to the efforts of the lobbyist; if the campaign is successful, it may have nothing to do with the lobbyist's efforts. Some less well-informed clients are too easily impressed by lunches being arranged with MPs, or with being escorted to meetings at the Palace of Westminster. However, it is evident from Gronbech's work that clients have been on a learning curve and have become more sophisticated in the specification of their requirements, making the lobbying business more demand led than supply led as was often the case in the 1970s and 1980s:

Almost all lobbyists interviewed felt that their clients had become much more professional, that they were much better at using lobbying services than they had been in the early years of the industry ... The recession of the 1990s made competition among lobbyists much fiercer and compelled many clients to take a hard look at the value they got for money paid to their lobbyists.

(Gronbech, 1998, p.162)

Certainly, money is not being spent for no purpose and 'there are various cases which suggest that consultants have achieved for clients outcomes that otherwise were unlikely to have been achieved' (Grantham and Seymour-Ure, 1990, p.73). Most companies probably have a good idea of what they derive from hiring a lobbyist, seeing them as reinforcements for their existing network of contacts. 'In that sense they are a *corporate accessory* and when hired, a needed and valued one' (Moloney, 1996, p.147).

One of the reasons why MPs are sometimes receptive to professional lobbyists is that they are overworked and poorly provided with support staff and facilities. Improvements in this area might help to offset worries about the susceptibility of MPs to external pressures. Even so, as the House of Commons Select Committee on Members Interests stated in one of its reports on the issue, 'It is the right of any citizen to lobby his Member of Parliament, and if he considers that his case can be better advanced with professional assistance he has every right to avail himself of that assistance' (House of Commons, 1985, p.iii).

An effective pressure group must pay attention to Parliament, but it is unlikely to be its main channel of access to decision makers. The executive remains the arena in which pressure can most usually be applied, before the government has closed its options and committed itself to a particular course of action. 'Ultimately, the point of pressure of party committees, all-party groups and consultants and their clients alike is the executive' (Judge, 1990b, p.222).

Political Parties

As was emphasized in Chapter 1, pressure groups and political parties are essentially different political formations. It is therefore not surprising that links between pressure groups and political parties are not well developed. Except in special cases, such as the anti-hunting lobby, developing overly close links with one political party would be counterproductive, as it would mean that the group would be influential only when that party was in power, and might not be very influential even then because its support was taken for granted. Hence, 'the party channel is seen as a low contribution insurance policy' (Maloney and Jordan, 1998, p.19).

One time when the pressure group and party worlds do come together is at the annual party conferences when the groups rent stalls and sponsor fringe meetings. 'At the Labour Party conference in 1995 there were 165 exhibitors stands, in 1996 there were 209, and in 1997 there were 199, and at all three party conferences well over two hundred organizations were represented' (p.13). If nothing else, this serves as a means of keeping in touch with the pulse of party opinion and may offer a chance for a discreet word with a minister. Looking at the list of exhibitors at the 1995, 1996 and 1997 Labour Party conferences one is struck by the absence of leading insider groups such as the CBI, NFU and BMA, although the RSPB and the RSPCA were there, as were many other animal lobbies. Many companies were present, alongside more obscure trade associations (such as the Multiple Newsagents Association) and cause groups (such as Baby Milk Action). A visible presence at the party conference may be seen as useful, but it is not a significant means of influencing policy.

Pressure Groups and the Courts

Pressure groups are making increasing use of the courts. Using the courts can be expensive, time consuming and uncertain in terms of outcome. Even if a group wins a victory in litigation, government may reverse the decision in subsequent legislation. It is therefore not surprising that Whiteley and Winyard (1987, p.108) found that the great majority of groups 'have not seen the judicial process as a significant focus of their activities in attempting to influence policy making'. This is in contrast to the United States where pressure groups make extensive use of the courts. In part, this it is because it is a more litigious society, but also because the American legal system takes a more generous view of what constitutes 'legal standing'. Hence, there are fewer entry barriers to associations than in the British system.

However, when other channels have failed, it may be the only available means of reversing a government decision. The use of judicial review which reviews the lawfulness of decisions made by public bodies has grown considerably in the last two decades. It is particularly valuable to campaigning groups as it 'is usually aimed at stopping decisions before they are put into effect rather than when it is too late and the harm has already been caused' (Day, 1998, p.185). Admittedly, the courts do not 'replace the decision complained about with a decision the campaigners prefer' (p.166). Frequently the flaws revealed are procedural ones and the decision-maker may simply be ordered to reconsider the decision in a lawful way. However, the associated publicity may make a repetition of the decision unlikely, while the delay imposed can be a death blow to many time sensitive projects.

The incorporation of the European Convention on Human Rights into British statute law may also open up new opportunities for pressure groups to take legal actions. For example, 'gay pressure groups have lined up test cases of discrimination to bring against churches as soon as the European Convention reaches the British statute book' (*The Guardian*, 26 November 1997).

Even when a case is lost, it may bring benefits to campaigners. The libel case brought by the fast food chain, McDonald's, against a small campaigning group called London Greenpeace was the longest of its kind in legal history. 180 witnesses gave evidence on a wide range of aspects of the company's operations, and there was a widely held perception that the case had not been an unqualified success for the company from a public relations standpoint. It demonstrated that 'a libel case can lead to worldwide publicity in a way that would never have been possible otherwise' (Day, 1998, p.79).

Greenpeace is one organization that has made extensive use of the courts alongside their direct action tactics. Although they lost a long battle to halt the commissioning of the Thorp nuclear reprocessing plant:

> Whitehall officials credit the pressure groups with having forced the government to re-examine Thorp's future … Part of that influence, officials made clear, was the pressure group's increasing use of the courts. Officials say Greenpeace's threat of legal action last summer prompted a second public consultation on the plant, delaying the go-ahead by several months.
>
> (Maddox, 1994, p.8)

The law is, however, a double-edged weapon which can be used against pressure groups as well as by them as shown by the example of radical anti-fur campaigning group, Lynx. The adversarial process of the courts may not be the best way to resolve complex public policy issues.

Local Government

In 1998 residents of Shooters Hill in south-east London and Tysoe in Warwickshire fought unsuccessful battles to save their local fire stations. The station in London was a full-time one, that in Tysoe was a retained one whose future had been in do ubt for many years. In Warwickshire the residents were fighting Warwickshire County Council which provided the service. In London they were battling against a quango, the London Fire and Civil Defence Authority. The Shooters Hill residents organized a petition and staged a protest march. They won Greenwich Council over to their side and the Council unsuccessfully sought a judicial review of the decision in the High Court.

As noted in Chapter 3, fire services are provided by local authorities in accordance with Home Office norms which stipulate a minimum level of cover, for example in a rural area like Tysoe the first appliance must reach a fire within 20 minutes. Local authorities have a limited budget for fire fighting which is constrained by the special arrangements for fire fighters' pay that tend to produce relatively large settlements by public sector standards. An unfunded pension scheme represents a further serious problem. Local authorities are thus an agent for the central government, which inspects their work. Their discretion is limited and often amounts to deciding how to reduce services in the light of financial constraints.

The picture in relation to fire services is not untypical of many areas of local authority activity. Successive governments have eroded the autonomy and cut back the resources of local authorities, while often imposing new duties on them. As a result, they are often perceived as the ineffective instruments of central government which may help to explain why turnout in local government elections is so low.

Nevertheless, there is considerable pressure group activity at the local level, although of a different character from that found nationally. A survey of six very different localities found that 16.1 per cent of respondents had participated in informal group activity at the local level and 12.7 per cent in an organized group (Parry, Moyser and Day, 1992, p.319). Local pressure group activity is often organized by 'sporadic interventionists' (Dowse and Hughes, 1977) in which a primarily social or welfare organization becomes mobilized because of a threat to its activities. In other cases, a loose campaigning group is formed to fight on a particular issue such as Shooters Hill Residents Against the Closure and is dissolved once the issue is resolved one way or another.

There are, however, some more permanent primary pressure groups at the local level. A study of local elites found that 'Within the interest group category, the most frequently mentioned were civic societies and residents' associations who, together, formed a fifth of all group contacts' (Parry, Moyser and Day, 1992, p.390). They were also selected by political leaders as the most influential type of group within the organized groups category (p.393). When they are not successful as pressure groups, residents' associations may mutate into local political parties (Grant, 1977).

Economic interest groups are another important category. Particularly in larger cities, chambers of commerce may have substantial full-time staffs and have developed a close insider group relationship with the local authority. In rural areas, farmers and landowners have been influential to the extent that 'the agricultural interest and the "public interest" are synonymous, or are at least seen to be so' (Newby *et al.*, 1978, p.235). However, the influx of middle-class incomers in rural areas with environmental agendas has tended to undermine their power. Environmental groups have considerably increased their activities at the local level. 'Some environmental groups such as the Ancient Monuments Society, the Georgian Society and the Victorian Society have developed insider status to the point where they have to be consulted as a matter of statute by the local authorities before a listed building is altered or demolished' (Robinson, 1992, p.38). Friends of the Earth has attempted to build constructive relationships with a number of local authorities and 'is increasingly involved at the centre of local government forums' (Ward, 1993, p.472).

The voluntary sector (for example Councils of Voluntary Service) is of increasing importance at the local level. It is often responsible for the delivery of services funded by the local authority and may operate out of council premises provided at a peppercorn rent. Stoker (1991, pp.124–8) argues that 'given the rise of self-help organizations within the sector and a more general willingness to engage in campaigning activity, the potential for and likely effectiveness of voluntary sector lobbying of local authorities has been considerably enhanced'. The transformation of local government in the direction of an 'enabling' model (Brooke, 1989), which leads to more emphasis on partnerships with the private and voluntary sectors, creates a new class of 'insider' groups whose involvement in service delivery gives them a special opportunity to influence policy development. However, they are almost 'prisoner' groups whose influence is purchased at the expense of independence and autonomy.

In many ways, the distinction between insider and outsider groups has often seemed to be more marked at the local than the national level. There is not the same tradition of long-term routine consultation at the national level. This is accentuated by the fact that local pressure groups have fewer resources in terms of their own staff than their national counterparts, whilst, as specialists rather than generalists, local authority officers are less dependent on them as a source of information and consent than are civil servants.

Given these circumstances, considerable advantages accrue to the predominantly middle-class community group that can tap various forms of specialist expertise from within its own ranks. An example is the

Central Leamington Residents' Association founded in 1985 which has among its members nearly two hundred households living mainly in larger Regency and Victorian properties. It claims in its well prepared literature to be 'influential and widely respected', enjoying a seat on the Leamington Spa Town Forum.

Thus, 'the interests which succeed are those of the middle class whose wealth and educational resouces give them easier entry to decision-making arenas' (Rallings, Temple and Thrasher, 1994, p.30). Concern has been expressed that the interests covered by local pressure groups are too limited in their range and that pressure group tactics simply reinforce the privileges of those who are already powerful. But then much the same could be said about the national and EU levels as well.

9

The Politics of Production and Consumption

The postwar period has seen a shift from a politics of production to a politics of collective consumption. At a very general level, this could be seen as a shift from modernity towards postmodernity, from a society where the factory was a central icon to one where it has been replaced by the shopping mall. There has been 'a gradual weakening ... of a politics based ... on class interests and class perceptions (Heller and Féher, 1988, p.3). 'What takes its place is more heterodox, so that one sees the creation of brand-new, and highly diverse, social issues'(p.10). Politics becomes a forum in which the construction of identity can take place and be expressed, rather than a means for the articulation of 'objectively' derived economic interests.

A politics of production is centred around a struggle between management and labour over the distribution of the fruits of the productive process. In that sense, it is an inherently adversarial form of politics, but it need not be conflictual. It is perfectly possible for there to be a production coalition between management and labour to maintain protectionist barriers to inhibit the entry of foreign imports, to preserve long established restrictive labour practices, or to obtain investment and research and development subsidies for an industry. There may also be coalitions between government and producers in which the meeting of production targets is rewarded by financial subsidies which in essence was the bargain enshrined in the 1947 Agriculture Act. The nationalized industries represented, for much of the time, a coalition between government, management and labour with the primary objective often seeming to be the retention of jobs in the industry rather than the service of its customers.

Thus, the politics of production centred around such issues as wages and conditions; attempts by government to influence the outcomes of collective bargaining through incomes policies; the rights of trade unions; industrial relations law; arrangements for worker participation in decision making; and the negotiation of subsidies for agriculture through the mechanism of the 'annual review'. It lends itself to a politics of bargaining in which the same partners enter into a series of negotiating exchanges, learning about each other's expectations and responses. It is a politics in which adjustments at the margin are often possible: a slightly higher wages norm or an increase in the subsidy for a particular agricultural product.

The politics of collective consumption is concerned with the outcomes of the production process, rather than what happens within the process itself. It is concerned with the externalities of the production process. It is called a politics of collective consumption because at its core is a concern with collective goods, or at least goods which have some of the characteristics of public goods. Examples would include the quality of the air we breathe or the quality of the sea water we bathe in.

It is a politics that is less amenable to elite bargaining which makes policy adjustments at the margin. In part, this is because new actors enter the policy process with new and less-understood expectations. It is also because more fundamental choices are involved: either air presents a threat to health, or it does not; bathing water is clean or it is not. Moreover, many of the core values of production are called in question: the existence of a car-based economy, or the perpetuation of intensive agriculture.

This new politics raises a number of issues. First, to what extent has the politics of production been displaced, and to what extent is it still thriving? The politics of production has not disappeared and the politics of collective consumption will not necessarily predominate. The extent to which old productionist coalitions are able to resist pressure for change will be discussed in relation to the case of agriculture. There will then be an examination of the extent to which the CBI has enjoyed a revival of its access to government with the election of a Labour government. Second, in this new politics, how does one represent the interests of consumers? How can such a broad and diffuse category be taken into account in the political process? Can even more specific groups of consumers such as football supporters be adequately represented? Is in fact the protection of consumers taking place outside what we would conventionally regard as the political process? Third, is the distinction between production and consumption a false dichotomy? Is there a possibility of new coalitions between producers and consumers?

This chapter, then, represents an attempt to understand changes in the political context within which pressure groups operate. At the onset of the new millennium are we facing a new type of politics in which many of the old certainties and categories have dissolved and lost their relevance? And if this is happening, at least to some extent, what are the implications for the political process and democracy?

The Politics of Production Survives

Agriculture offers in many ways a classic example of the politics of production. Through the Common Agricultural Policy, farmers have continued to receive substantial financial subsidies. A typical farmer might expect to derive half of his or her income, directly or indirectly, from various forms of subsidy and market support. For a marginal farmer, the proportion might be much higher. These subsidies have survived at a time when support for other industries has been removed or substantially reduced.

These financial arrangements have been underwritten by the fact that farming is the only industry which has its own government ministry, the Ministry of Agriculture, Fisheries and Food (MAFF) which has had a close relationship with the NFU. This relationship was challenged to some extent in the 1980s by the emergence of new concerns about the environmental impact of farming. This did lead to some policy changes, although often it meant new forms of support for farmers.

Farmers' representatives have continued to operate within a framework of thinking which suggests the survival of productionist assumptions. When the rise of sterling reduced the value of CAP subsidies, farmers' organizations pressed for this to be offset by compensatory payments. Admittedly, such payments are permitted under CAP rules, but sectors of manufacturing industry whose exports were hit by the rise of sterling would not have expected the government to pay them compensation. The chairman of the Devon NFU complained: 'There appears to be almost anti-farmer, certainly an anti-subsidies, culture in the MAFF civil service nowadays. But the fact is that they are responsible for farming's income' (*Farmers Weekly*, 14 November 1997). It might have been thought that in a supposedly market economy farmers were responsible for earning their own income. However, such is the influence of the old productionism in agriculture that the assumption is that government must negotiate with farmers' representatives about the size of the industry.

As the president of the Scottish NFU commented:

> ... above all, we need a clear statement from government about its view of the future role of agriculture. If government wants fewer farmers then it must come out and say so. Then we can sit down with ministers and plan some orderly approach.

(*Farmers Weekly*, 19 June 1998)

Farmers therefore had a considerable shock when the Blair Government's first agriculture minister, Dr Jack Cunningham, announced that 'my number one priority was to meet the needs of consumers' (*Farmers Weekly*, 1 May 1997). He explained, 'We need to guarantee there is more consumer input to this department and we have to have a pretty fundamental change of emphasis' (*Farmers Weekly*, 9 May 1997). A year later, it was reported that 'Many farmers are still reeling from the shock of a farm minister who puts consumer interests ahead of the producer' (*Farmers Weekly*, 1 May 1998). Within a month Dr Cunningham had abolished the nine regional advisory panels of farmers in England. Farmers complained that this 'would leave ministers vulnerable to single issue pressure groups' (*Farmers Weekly*, 30 May 1997). A more positive way of putting it would be to say that it opened ministers up to a wider range of views.

The problem of falling farm incomes was felt particularly acutely in Scotland where there is a large number of hill farmers with low net incomes. The president of the Scottish NFU, Sandy Mole, nevertheless insisted that the organization must continue to pursue an insider strategy:

> There are some who think our case will be improved by marching around in the streets or by dishing out daily insults to the government. They are wrong headed. We have a government with a majority of 170. We have to build bridges with them. I will put our case with passion and as persuasively as I can, but I will always do so with courtesy. If we want to be respected by government, there is no other way.

(*Farmers Weekly*, 10 October 1997)

Mr Mole was able to head off a threatened rebellion at the SNFU's annual council meeting in October. However, his policy of opposing direct action came under increasing strain and 'led to increasing anger and frustration among members' (*Farmers Weekly*, 12 December 1997). In December 1997 he was pressured into giving some union support to a port blockade at Stranraer and Cairnryan organized by the National Cattle Association's Scottish beef council. Following a meeting of the union's general purposes committee that was reported to be openly critical of his policy, he became the first Scottish NFU president to resign since the union was founded 85 years ago. That this should have happened was a measure of the strains induced by government policy.

However, it quickly became clear that there were limits to the government's radicalism, particularly after the Countryside March in London. Talk of replacing MAFF with a new Ministry of Rural Affairs with a new mission died away, and even the idea of changing the name of MAFF no longer appeared to be discussed. However, when Dr Cunningham was replaced by Nick Brown in the summer 1998 reshuffle, it was evident that policy was reverting to a more conventional productionist form. Mr Brown visited the farm of the NFU president and said that he was 'absolutely determined to work as closely as possible with the NFU and other organizations' to help the industry 'get through the [present] difficulties into a more certain future' (*Financial Times*, 25 September 1998). It emerged that the government was working on a package of short-term aid and longer-term restructuring measures which was announced in November 1998. With Mr Brown being seen as having been moved sideways because of his close association with Gordon Brown, 'the chancellor is determined to help his old friend in his new job and to try to rebuild the government's relations with the rural community' (*Financial Times*, 5 October 1998).

It was evident that farmers were experiencing sharp downturns in their incomes, although it is questionable whether other small businesses in financial trouble would have received financial help. Not only is there a long domestic history of productionist co-operation in agriculture, reinforced by the existence of MAFF, but these productionist assumptions are also embodied in the CAP.

The CBI Resurgent

From its formation in 1965, through the interventionist 1970s, the CBI was involved in a close relationship with government as one of the tripartite 'partners'. The CBI's role in tripartism was viewed with suspicion by the Thatcher Government which relied increasingly on direct contacts with individual business persons or with more ideologically congenial organizations such as the Institute of Directors. It became cus-

tomary to refer to 'the deeply strained relations of the Conservatives
and the CBI' (May, McHugh and Taylor, 1998, p.260). With the return
of the Blair Government, all this changed. As one long serving CBI
official remarked to the author: 'There was a long period when the Conservatives wouldn't even talk to us – and we are an organization that
likes to talk to people. Now it's like the 1970s again and we are at the
heart of things.'
Much of this has to do with the personal values of the prime minister.
'One of the most striking traits of Tony Blair is his reverence for big
companies. His empathy with professional managers – especially the
quasi-American model which throngs the CBI – is infinitely greater than
any fraternal bond with trade unionists' (*Financial Times*, 4 February
1998). He made it clear before being elected that he wanted to have a
closer relationship with business:

> People don't even question for a moment that the Democrats are a pro-busi-
> ness party. They should not be asking that question about New Labour. New
> Labour is pro-business, pro-enterprise and we believe that there is nothing
> inconsistent between that and a just and decent society.
>
> (*Financial Times*, 16 January 1997)

Those to the left of the government felt constrained to ask, 'Has any
government been so besotted by business as this one?' (*New Statesman*,
20 June 1998). For their part, the CBI made it clear that they intended to
build a partnership relationship with the Labour government. In a message to CBI members, the CBI's director general made clear that the
organization would not adopt a confontational strategy against Labour's
employment agenda. Specific proposals would be argued against, but
the government had kept its side of the bargain: 'It has ... lived up well
to its promise to campaign for flexible labour markets across Europe,
working closely with us to oppose unnecessary legislation' (*Financial
Times*, 3 August 1998). This positioning alongside Labour was made
easier by resolute Conservative opposition to entry into the Euro in the
medium term, a stance which isolated the Conservatives from the mainstream of business opinion.

Sectoral Representation of Business Interests

Particular sectors of the economy have their own concerns or issues which traditionally have been dealt with by organizations known as 'trade associations'. The effectiveness of these associations has been a subject of concern ever since the Second World War. Some of them are well resourced and highly regarded (see Table 9.1 below), but others have failed to reach a standard that allows them to interact effectively with government. As one experienced observer of the business association scene commented in interview:

> Trade associations enjoyed a fairly close relationship with members until the beginning of the 1990s. They were social clubs, places for discussion. Great demands were not made on them.

The recession of the 1990s encouraged a new momentum to the scrutiny and review of trade association effectiveness. On the business side, the recession encouraged members to think again about whether they were getting value for money. What made this critical mood more significant than earlier waves of concern about trade association effectiveness was that it was matched by a revival of interest on the government side when Michael Heseltine became President of the Board of Trade. To use the language of the Organization of Business Interests project, the logic of membership and the logic of influence converged.

Table 9.1 Major trade associations in Britain

Name of association	Members	Staff
Association of British Insurers	440	150
British Printing Industries Federation	3 000	120
Electricity Association	27	150
Freight Transport Association	11 600	350
Mechanical and Metal Trades Confederation	34	164
National Farmers' Union	121 454	808
National Farmers' Union of Scotland	12 000	100
National Housing Federation	1 400	115
National Federation of Retail Newsagents	25 000	100
National Pharmaceutical Association	6 000	115
Retail Motor Industry Federation	12 500	170
Society of Motor Manufacturers and Traders	871	105

Note: Major trade associations (excluding 'peak associations') have been defined as those with a staff of 100 or more. Professional associations such as the BMA are excluded.

Source: Derived from data in *Trade Association Forum Directory, 1998.*

A senior member of the government (subsequently deputy prime minister), Heseltine made speeches in 1993 and 1995 critical of trade association performance and effectiveness. In February 1996 the Department of Trade and Industry (DTI) published the *Best Practice Guide for the Model Trade Association* which set out key criteria and established benchmarks for trade associations to aspire to. The main headings covered are set out in Box 9.1 below. From the autumn of 1996 a series of benchmarking clubs was set up to help trade associations identify their strengths and weaknesses and share best practice. These and other initiatives were spearheaded by the Association of British Insurers with support from the DTI from 1995 to 1997. In 1997 the CBI established a Trade Association Council on the same basis as its Smaller Firms Council and also took over responsibility for the Trade Association Forum. From January 1998 this became a self-funding body within the CBI seeking to raise trade association standards. Its activities can be followed on its website: http://www.taforum.org.uk.

These efforts to improve trade association effectiveness are important and worthwhile if one thinks that government needs representative bodies with which it can have a dialogue about competitiveness and innovation issues. Two problems face this initiative. One is the calibre of trade association staff, the other the stance of the Blair Government.

A comprehensive and useful set of core competences for the senior managers of trade associations drawn up by Compass Partnership was made available in 1998 under the auspices of the Trade Association

Box 9.1 Benchmarks for trade associations – main headings

•   Works effectively to represent the sector's interests at all levels of the legislative and regulatory process
•   Works proactively to improve the sector's competitiveness
•   Supplies sound information and advice to members
•   Promotes good public relations and communications
•   Promotes exports and other market oppportunities
•   Promotes training and education
•   Promotes standards and product/service quality
•   Promotes innovation and technology transfer

Source: Department of Trade and Industry, *A Best Practice Guide for the Model Trade Association*.

Forum. However, as one respondent bluntly put it, 'if you pay peanuts, you get monkeys'. Many directors of associations do receive salaries comparable to the higher levels of the civil service, but it is interesting that 39 per cent of those in the Compass Partnership survey did not have a degree or equivalent qualification, although admittedly the proportion increased in the large associations (Compass Partnership, 1998, p.9).

It is also interesting that only just over a quarter of those responding had followed a trade association career route, having been employed previously by the same or another trade association. Indeed, 10 per cent came from a military background, a choice which in the writer's knowledge of associations can sometimes be disastrous. The nature of trade association work is changing and requires different and more sophisticated skills. As Boléat has noted in his handbook on trade associations, the main task used to be servicing committees and 'The skills required were those of a committee clerk' (1996, p.152). By the 1990s, more tasks were being devolved to the secretariat who had to be able to take more responsibility.

Unfortunately, as one interviewee observed, 'For a lot of people, trade association work is a second career and there is not a lot of career development'. The Compass Partnership survey found that fewer than half the associations surveyed had a formal appraisal system in place and the amount spent on training by associations was significantly lower than the average for British industry (1998, p.1).

These problems require action by the trade associations and members which is often slow to occur in the absence of some external stimulus. Apart from exogenous shocks such as recession, government can provide a continuous stimulus for reform. However, the Labour government seems less interested in this issue than its predecessors, one respondent observing that trade associations never came up in ministerial conversations. This may be a mistake as government success is still linked to economic success and that is in turn dependent on an effective working relationship with business.

What the examples of farming and business show is that the politics of production is far from finished and is capable of revival, although problems remain with sectoral business associations. Farmers are more marginal economically, but long standing historical relationships, reflected in specialized structures, are not easily eroded. The story in relation to trade unions is, however, a rather different one.

Trade Unions Contained

There have always been difficulties about accommodating trade unions within traditional forms of pressure group analysis. Their principal function has to be to engage in collective bargaining with employers (which covers less than half of the workforce at the end of the 1990s) and to represent their individual members who may become involved in disputes with employers. Nevertheless, trade unions in general, and the Trades Union Congress (TUC) in particular, came to play a central role in the politics of production. This role was brought to an end by the Thatcher Government and it has not been recovered to any significant extent under 'New Labour'. It has been suggested that 'The prime minister never hides his disdain for the unions ... He does not share their collectivist values nor their wish to exercise a substantial influence over public policy' (*Financial Times*, 31 March 1998).

One of the defining characteristics of the 'New Labour' approach is that its advocates would like, if at all possible, to break away from the traditional relationship between the Labour Party and the trade unions. If such a radical move might be too much for the Labour Party to stomach, then at least the aspiration is to keep the trade unions at arm's length rather than having the close and intimate relationship epitomized by the image of the serving of 'beer and sandwiches' at 10 Downing Street when a major industrial dispute had to be settled under the Wilson Governments.

That is not to say, of course, that the unions themselves wanted to adhere to the old way of doing things. The essentially technocratic secretary of the TUC, John Monks, made an important statement of the unions' perspective on the relationship at a fringe meeting at the 1994 Labour Party conference, the first time a TUC general-secretary had been to the party conference for 50 years. Mr Monks made it clear that the unions did not want to replace beer and sandwiches in a smoke filled room by chablis and canapes in a smoke free zone. The unions wanted 'fairness not favours' from a Labour government rather than a return to the social contract style deals of the 1970s when they demanded influence in managing the economy. The trade unions had got their priorities wrong:

> Despite the social advantages, 1970s style corporatism is now as dated as kaftans and beads – and has eve less chance of a comeback. Much time and effort was spent with ministers, civil servants and employers and their representatives. Too little time was spent in the workplaces.
>
> (*Financial Times*, 5 October 1994)

Such a change of attitude was essential because the unions have lost much of their traditional displacement in the economy and the polity. Much of their legitimacy as an 'estate of the realm' was stripped from them by the Thatcher Government. Because of changes in the structure of the economy, shifts in the relative power of employers and workers, and lingering public perceptions that unions are in some way 'old fashioned', the displacement of the unions has been substantially reduced. Trade union leaders are no longer 'household names' enjoying frequent and extensive media publicity as was the case in the 1970s.

The typical trade unionist is no longer a male manual worker, but rather a white collar employee in the public sector who may be of either gender. Of those working in public administration and in the National Health Service 63 per cent were unionized in 1996–7, along with 58 per cent of those in the public education sector. In contrast, only 7 per cent of those working in hotels and restaurants were unionized and 11 per cent of those working in the wholesale and retail trade (*Investors Chronicle*, 12 June 1998). It is estimated that no more than 20 per cent of private sector employees belong to a trade union. Telephone call centres, which have come to occupy such a substantive and symbolic place in the economy, employ a workforce predominantly made up of women who are often on temporary agency contracts and are generally not unionized.

There have been 18 consecutive years of decline in membership of the TUC, which fell from 12.2 million in 1979 to 6.7 million in late 1998, although admittedly the net fall in members in 1998 was the slowest for a long time. (*Investors Chronicle*, 12 June 1998; *Financial Times*, 9 December 1998). Union membership has declined by about 30 per cent since its peak in 1979, and union density (membership relative to total employment) has declined by about 15 per cent over the same period. While over half of males born in the early 1950s were union members when they entered the labour market, the figure fell to just over a third for males born in the late 1960s (*Financial Times*, 8 January 1999). Faced with a £300 000 deficit, the TUC had to announce a 10 per cent cut in the size of its staff in January 1999.

The unions have themselves gone through a process of modernization, both offering a wider and more attractive range of services to members and also undertaking a number of mergers which have produced a small number of big unions, although not the arrangement of one union per industry found in Germany. Among the most important mergers have been those which produced the Manufacturing Science Union in 1988; the merger of the engineering and electrical unions in 1992; and the creation of a big public sector union, Unison, through the merger of the white collar local government union NALGO, the manual union NUPE and the health service union COHSE. One much heralded merger that has not taken place is between the two general industrial unions, GMB and TGWU. Nevertheless, this general trend towards a smaller number of larger unions has diminished the significance of the TUC's co-ordinating function.

The unions have made some gains under a Labour government which they would not have obtained from the Conservatives, but there are strict limits to their influence. For example, a minimum wage has been established, but at a much lower level than they would like. The dispute over union recognition provides a good case study of the extent of union influence under the Blair Government. Labour committed itself to a recognition law in its election manifesto. The law is of considerable importance to the union movement as it is believed that it will reverse the decline in membership. For the trade unions statutory union recognition was a 'defining moment' described as 'our line in the sand' (*Financial Times*, 31 March 1998).

In September 1997 the prime minister told the TUC at its annual conference that they should try and negotiate a voluntary deal with the CBI that would provide common ground. This effort at social partnership led to a joint document in December 1997 that set out points of agreement and disagreement. Union leaders were 'convinced that what they saw as a subsequent toughening of the CBI's stance was due to encouragement that the employers were receiving from Downing Street' (*Financial Times*, 31 March 1998).

However, in the last few weeks before the 'Fairness at Work' white paper appeared in May 1998 there appears to have been something of a shift towards the union position. In part, this appears to have been due to pressure from the deputy prime minister, John Prescott, although the unions were invited at the end of April to a rare lunchtime meeting with the prime minister. However, the meeting was described as 'cold and formal', registering at the bottom of the culinary scale with only a glass of water served (*Financial Times*, 26 April 1998). Nevertheless, when the white paper, which was intended to provide the framework for workplace legislation for the lifetime of the Parliament, did appear, it included a number of concessions to the unions. Admittedly, it backed the CBI line that recognition in a workplace ballot should only be granted where 40 per cent of those eligible to vote voted in favour rather than a simple majority. However, it also contained a provision for automatic recognition without a ballot for unions where they could prove that they had more than 50 per cent membership in a workplace. While the CBI wanted to exclude enterprises employing fewer than 50 workers, the government cut this figure to 20, bringing 2 million more workers within the proposed legislation.

Subsequent lobbying efforts by the employers to dilute any return of trade union power bore fruit when a detailed outline of the proposed legislation was published in December. It was seen by commentators as representing 'a shift in favour of employers' (*Financial Times*, 18 December 1998) compared with the white paper. In particular, the proposal to allow unions automatic recognition if they could show that they had 50 per cent plus one member in a bargaining unit was dropped. An independent committee with the power to call a ballot will decide whether recognition is acceptable. The draft legislation also contained a number of obstacles making the recognition process more time complex and consuming. When the bill was published at the end of January 1999 it is significant that employer criticisms did not centre on the recognition proposals, but on other aspects of the measure.

What emerges from this case study is that trade union influence on government legislation is now conditional on the support of particular ministers, particularly given that the prime minister and his industrial relations adviser, Geoff Norris, who evidently played a key role throughout the decision making process, are seen as at best lukewarm towards them. The TUC was quite reliant on support from Margaret Beckett, the trade and industry secretary when the white paper was being drafted. Her successor, Peter Mandelson, was clearly in a 'New Labour' mould, as was his replacement, Stephen Byers. 'He is a Blairite moderniser and the trade unions expect no respite from him when it comes to ensuring harsh terms for the promised legislation on trade union recognition' (*Sunday Times*, 3 January 1999.)

The trade unions are very much part of the traditional politics of production. In less than twenty years they were moved from the centre of the political process to a marginal position. Some partial restoration of their influence is possible, but it is unlikely that they will ever again occupy a central place in the economic policy making process, nor necessarily would they want to.

Representing Consumers

The difficulty with representing consumers as a category is that it is one to which potentially everyone belongs. It is larger, even, than the electorate, as it includes those who are below voting age and foreign nationals resident in a country. 'No-one is just a consumer, yet everyone is a consumer in some sense' (National Consumer Council, 1997, p.5.) Different consumers face different financial circumstances, have different preferences and different levels of risk averseness. They do, however, have a common interest in having goods that are safe and in not being misled about the good or service that is being provided.

What is evident is that there is seen to be a distinction between production and consumption, even though most people are simultaneously producers and consumers. 'The doctrine of consumerism, at its simplest, is that there is a highly significant division of society into producers and consumers; and that for one reason or another the consumer deserves support' (Tivey, 1974, p.204.) Tivey points out that a person's purchasing power and status is considerably influenced by the job they occupy. People still ask, 'What do you do?' when they mean 'What is your job?' as if work was the only significant part of a person's life. In contrast, 'an individual's activities as a consumer consist of a multitude of separate purchases, and even if many of these are not satisfactory, this can be rarely satisfactory for him as his productive role' (p.206).

In contemporary terms, Tivey's remarks seem a little dated as shopping is seen as a central leisure activity which yields a significant flow of satisfaction (at least for some people). Nevertheless, there is still something in his argument that 'The need for consumer protection arises, therefore, from an incoherence in the economic system, caused by the greater attention which the rational individual gives to his role as a producer compared with his role as a consumer' (p.206).

How does one start to redress this imbalance? One traditional response was the formation of the co-operative movement, the retail wing of the labour movement which returned the profits made to its members through a 'dividend'. In the years of scarcity and rationing after the war, the co-operative movement had a leading role in the provision of retail services in Britain. But its market share steadily declined as more competitors emerged and consumer tastes became more sophisticated. Without shareholders to answer to, the management was often not very innovative, the quality of the goods often not high, and the prices less than competitive. There was, in any case, always something of a contradiction between its role as a producer and its championship of the consumer. Indeed, in 1967 the Co-operative Union joined the new retail organization, the Retail Consortium. The modern consumer movement is really the product of the postwar period, once the immediate recovery period was over, rationing was removed and consumers started to enjoy a new affluence:

> Its emergence was due to the convergence of two interrelated socioeconomic changes. First, during the 1950s economic relations rapidly became more complicated: the number and complexity of consumer goods available increased dramatically; marketing techniques became more sophisticated; and complicated purchasing transactions, such as hire purchase and consumer credit, began to emerge. Second, prolonged economic growth contributed to both prosperity and greater expectations about the quality of life defined in more than simply economic terms.
>
> (Young, 1998, p.151)

One response to these developments was the Consumers' Association, founded in 1956, which flourished as a testing agency reporting its results on comparative tests on consumer goods. Starting out with relatively modest subjects such as electric kettles, scouring powders, cake mixes and sunglasses, the reports were published in its journal, *Which?* This in turn yielded resources which enabled it to engage in lobbying activity. In the 1960s, the Consumers' Association had a number of prominent members of the Labour Party on its Council, inspired by the motive of 'redressing the imbalances in society' (Roberts, 1966, p.89). Initially, the Consumers' Association attracted well educated people from upper income groups, although 'as time went on, the membership began to spread, though slowly into the skilled working class' (p.81).

There were, however, clear limits to an approach to consumerism which was based on giving improved information to allow the affluent segment of society to make better purchasing decisions. The National Consumer Council was therefore set up in 1975 as a largely government- funded body with 'a special duty to speak up for the inarticulate and disadvantaged consumer' (1997, p.5). This particular innovation came at a time when tripartism was at its height and could be seen as a partial attempt to redress an unequal balance between producer and consumer interests.

From the perspective of consumer representatives, this has not happened. 'Consumer bodies do have the opportunity to influence decisions, but their efforts are easily outweighed by the industry lobby' (p.14).

'Our overwhelming impression is that the DTI often regards consumers' concerns as secondary to business's' (p.15). Business itself, of course, has no interest in trading practices that discredit a whole sector, but rogue traders remain only lightly constrained by the law. The lack of sufficient action at the national level has not generally been offset by any significant activity at the EU level. One problem has been that 'Due to the different ideologies and priorities that stem from their different memberships, the European consumer organizations frequently find it difficult to co-operate' (Young, 1998, p.166). Although one might think that the European Union would have an interest in identifying with its citizens as consumers, it has been left to one of the less influential institutions, the European Parliament, to make much of the running. Institutional and policy pull within the Commission has been relatively weak with a separate directorate-general for consumer affairs only being established in 1995. 'Even then it is still one of the smallest directorates-general and has only recently gained the capacity to monitor adequately developments in other directorates-general that are relevant to consumers' (p.166.)

From the perspective of the consumer organizations, then, the current set of structures is clearly unsatisfactory. The Consumers' Association has commented:

> The massive lobbying efforts of industry, e.g., of farmers, the food processing industry, the car industry, the road-building industry, the pharmaceuticals industry etc, carries far too great an influence. What is good for industry may not always be good for consumers, but the present structure doesn't provide the necessary counterbalance.
>
> (National Consumer Council, 1997, p.28)

Similarly, the National Consumer Council itself takes the view that 'producers and providers carry too much weight' (p.55). The problem is, who is to decide what is a necessary counterbalance, or what the right weight is for different elements in a system of representation. There may be a 'scientific' answer to what constitutes a healthy level of salt in processed food, but there is no such answer to the proper balance of a system of representation.

The National Consumer Council tends to look to rather statist answers. They want to change 'the institutions and procedures through which the consumer perspective is brought into Whitehall's processes' (p.55). It may be, however, that consumers themselves think that the best option open to them is actually a privatized system of retail-led governance. This is a genuinely new form of politics which involves the private representation of 'public interests'.

Retailer-Led Governance

The retailing of food products and fast-moving consumer goods in Britain is dominated by a relatively small number of 'household name' companies such as Sainsbury's and Tesco. There is intense competition between these companies for market share, although it has been suggested that mark-ups for some goods are considerable and that prices generally are higher than those found in similar stores in the United States. Through the use of loyalty schemes, each retailer has sought to build up a relationship with an identifiable group of customers whose spending patterns can be monitored.

Work carried out by Marsden and Flynn suggests these market relationships have been paralleled by the emergence of a private interest style of regulation which may be characterized as 'retailer-led governance'. Retailers have built up relationships of trust with their customers, particularly in relation to issues of food quality and safety which is one of the major areas where they compete with each other. This means that 'retailers have become agents of social legitimation as well as exchange, tending to conflate questions of political citizenship with consumerism' (1997, p.13).

'In stark contrast, consumer groups at a national and European level make only marginal contributions to debates on food safety and quality. This is in despite of increasing opportunities to participate in the policy process' (p.2). Given 'limited resourcing and access to policy makers, consumer groups frequently find it difficult to distinguish their specification of the interests of the consumer from that of the major food retailers' (p.28). One thus finds an apparent convergence of interest between consumer representatives and part of the production and distribution chain, centred around such notions as the informed consumer. Focusing on the freedom of the informed individual to consume is rather different from how the representation of consumer interests was seen in the early postwar period:

> Such a notion of rights is quite different from that which prevailed at the end of the Second World War. Then there was a sense of a collective consumer

interest whose choice was largely determined by government. The role of government was to ensure freedom from want through the provision of affordable and safe food. Now it is the corporate retailers who play a central role in promoting to individualised consumers their vision of quality and diversity of consumption.

(p.28)

The fact that retailers have been able to assume this role in part reflects the fact that their own competitive strategies entail the projection of their own constructions of the consumer. However, it also reflects the existence of something of a vacuum in consumer representation which they have been able to fill. Diffuse and often secondary interests such as those of consumers are often difficult to organize. Hence, one ends up with a paradoxical situation in which there is surrogate representation of consumers by one part of the production chain, albeit it one that is also putting pressure on primary producers and manufacturers to meet defined quality standards, for example through assured quality schemes offering traceability for crop production.

There have been some signs of increasing resistance to the enhanced economic power of retailers, but they have positioned themselves in a very astute way as the consumer's champion. The real beneficiaries of the shift away from an old style politics of production may be the retailers, so that the main consequence of a new politics of collective consumption is a shift of power from one end of the food chain to the other.

The Limits of the Consumer Paradigm: the Case of Football

The example of retailing suggests that the consumer seeking representation may only effectively be able to do so through a construction of his or her identity devised by producers as part of their marketing strategy. The case of the football supporter also gives some cause for concern about the construction of identity as a consumer.

With the floating of many clubs on the stock exchange, and the acquisition of some clubs by leisure or media interests, football has become very much part of big business. Particularly in an era of digitalization, television companies know that securing exclusive rights to football matches is one of the keys to capturing customers. All kinds of product from soft drinks to clothing can be marketed through an association with football.

One must, of course, be careful not to fall prey to a belief of a 'golden age' in football when the players earned a similar wage to a skilled worker and clubs were deeply embedded in their communities. Clubs were usually controlled by business people, and when these were the owners of small scale local businesses, their vision was often a rather narrow and parochial one. Whatever one thinks about the controversy of the merits of terracing, football grounds have become more comfortable and safer places to attend as more money has been pumped into the game. Neverthless, football supporters are very open to exploitation. Their loyalty to the 'brand' (club) is very strong and even if they are dissatisfied with the product, they are unlikely to move elsewhere. 'Customers make choices, supporters do not' (Horton, 1998, p.111). The normal consumer option of 'exiting' to another product is not generally available. 'Exit with voice' does sometimes occur. From time to time one reads of disgruntled fans returning their season tickets, but how many actually do is open to question, and probably even some of those return sheepishly to reclaim them later. There are some signs of consumer resistance to the high prices of football merchandise, and frequent changes of kit. Nevertheless, however much clubs talk of acquiring a 'customer focus', along with other marketing jargon, the perception of many supporters is that 'There is a distance between football and its supporters which is ... getting wider ... Football has marginalised the supporters' (p.183).

What options are open to supporters to make their views known to clubs? A very few clubs, such as Charlton, allow supporters to elect a member of the board. Specific individual complaints can be raised on a club's e-mail list and may be responded to at some clubs where perhaps some unfortunate member of the staff becomes a kind of unofficial 'ombudsman' for fans. There are a number of radio 'phone in' programmes (both nationally and for particular clubs on local stations) where fans can ring in with their grievances. However, the people who run the programmes often have their own agenda and can be very astute in directing the conversation in the way that they want it to go. At most, these programmes act as a kind of 'safety valve' which can promote action on a particular grievance; at worst, they are a whingers' paradise.

In terms of some form of collective action, supporters can join a supporters club, but this is often a classic 'insider' group. In return for 'consultation' rights with the board, an office at the ground and perhaps access to tickets for popular away matches, the supporters club is expected to adhere to a code of 'responsible' conduct. In frustration, some supporters, as at Manchester United, have formed 'independent' supporters' associations. These are classic outsider groups, with no access to the relevant decision-makers, which have to resort to a variety of tactics to attract attention. They are also open to criticisms about how representative they are of the generality of fans.

There is, however, a more fundamental problem. The very idea of being a supporter may be in jeopardy if the fan defines himself or herself as a consumer so that football becomes 'a financial transaction between a seller and a buyer' (Horton, 1997, p.112). The best service is then given to the person who pays the most, and even that person is in a relatively weak position compared to instutional shareholders and sponsors. Horton argues, 'We should talk the language of entitlement, not of the customer' (p.113). The difficulty is that in pursuing such an aim one comes up against 'the generalized bias of the market: to cater to those particular consumer demands that are amenable to commercialization' (Hirsch, 1977, p.91). The genie of market forces is out of the bottle in football and can't be put back in again. However, by defining themselves as consumers who expect a particular standard of service, football fans may be entering into the role that football as a business expects of them. Self-definition as a consumer offers the promise of autonomy, but can facilitate sophisticated forms of manipulation.

The Erosion of Producer Power: the Case of Education

The case of education illustrates some of the danger that may arise from too great an erosion of producer power. Traditionally, education was a relatively closed policy community in which considerable influence was exerted by teachers and educational experts:

> The educational values and policies are thus those of the teachers and their associations, the local education authority administrators, inspectors, and advisers at both central and local levels. The DES officially takes no view on educational matters as such, but will generally support the assumption that authority should rest with the teachers, the schools and the local education authorities in determining educational policies.
>
> (Kogan, 1975, p.59)

The provision of education has now shifted towards a consumer model. In primary and secondary education this does not mean in general the pupils themselves, although in further and higher education they may be more inclined to define themselves as consumers and to expect certain standards of service. Rather the consumers have been seen as parents and business. The former have become more directly involved in the running of schools with the enhanced role of parent governors. The way in which local management of schools (LMS) allocates funds largely on the basis of pupil numbers creates competition between schools which in turn encourages parents to 'shop around' for the best provider. League tables provide further comparative information to the prospective 'purchaser'. Business has long been dissatisfied with the standards of literacy and numeracy achieved by school leavers. With Britain showing up poorly in some international comparisons of attainment, and with an increasing emphasis being placed on 'human capital' as a key factor in international competitiveness, successive governments, starting with the Callaghan Government in the 1970s, have taken up the question of the performance of education and introduced a succession of policy initiatives.

There has been a clear weakening of the influence of producer organizations:

> The ideologically loaded management concepts of quality and efficiency have been mobilized to weaken the influence of teachers and their organizations on educational standards. Instead of being participants, through centralized negotiation and LEA-level consultation, in the management of the school system, the aim is that teacher unions are to be excluded from all areas of decision making.

(Sinclair, Seifert and Ironside, 1995, p.254)

Like the European farmers' organization discussed in Chapter 4, it may be that the teaching unions have not always served their own members well. They may have been too willing to defend teachers who fell below acceptable professional standards. Their annual conferences often seem to be one of the last outposts of a form of militant trade unionism that was prevalent in the 1970s.

As an influential Labour MP commented:

> Sadly the teachers themselves – or at least their representatives – are not much help in improving the profession's image. Much of the profession seems stuck in a 1970s time warp. When the public think of teachers, they think of militant unions, resistance to change and long holidays.

(Hodge, 1998, p.10)

Transparency about the performance of schools is arguably justified, although there has been perhaps an over-eagerness to stigmatize 'failing' schools that are often located in areas of severe economic and social deprivation. The Conservates in particular were inclined to blame 'the nation's economic and moral decline upon teachers and their collective organizations' (Sinclair, Seifert and Ironside, 1995, p.254).

From a world in which the expert providers knew best, and the consumers were expected to accept gratefully what they were offered, the pendulum has swung in the opposite direction. The producers are required to deliver the expected changes in performance, and if they are badly demoralized by continuous criticism and increased paperwork, they may not be well placed to do so. By 1998 there were serious problems of teacher recruitment, exacerbated by the fact that many older and experienced teachers had taken early retirement. These were in part due to pay problems which were unlikely to be resolved by altering the career structure to create a small number of highly paid posts for teachers judged to be high performers. The continual denigration of the profession had created a situation in which a teaching career was seen as a much less attractive option than in the past. This is not helped by the centrality given to business values in society, not least by the Blair Government.

Educational performance was unsatisfactory in many respects, and a closed policy community did need to be opened up. However, the consumer is not necessarily well served by undermining the status and morale of the producer. 'Vested interests' do at least have a concern for what they are protecting and know something about it. The consumer's demand for rising expectations to be fulfilled may ultimately be self-defeating.

A False Dichotomy?

The preceding discussion has illustrated many of the problems that arise in the representation of the 'consumer', along with the risks that may arise from pushing the erosion of producer power so far. As in the case of education (and health), it is often government (after listening to business) that defines what the 'needs' of the consumer are. For all the emphasis on the sovereignty of the consumer, and the language of customer care and focus and quality management, the outcome has often been weak and relatively ineffective forms of representation and the manipulation of the individual purchaser of goods and services by business through his or her adoption of a particular definition and role as a consumer. There is a paradoxical sense in which some sets of producers (such as teachers) have lost ground, but consumers are often not that much better served. The privatization of the railways offer another example where, although certain individuals may have made windfall gains, the consumer perceives that the service offered has not improved.

However, it is also necessary to examine the consumption of collective goods as it is here that new social movements have been more influential. It may be that to think of 'producers' and 'consumers' in the search for solutions to such collective good problems is a false dichotomy. In this respect the theory of ecological modernization has been influential.

This perspective 'challenged the fundamental assumption of the conventional wisdom, namely that there was a zero-sum trade-off between economic prosperity and environmental concern' (Weale, 1992, p.31). Commitment to a high level of environmental protection was 'actually a precondition of successful economic development. Pollution represents wastefully used resources, while cleaning it up can absorb an expanding share of national income. The development and production of environmental protection equipment and technologies can open up new export markets and highly skilled job opportunities. Efforts to internalize externalities open up not a cleavage 'between businesses and environmentalists, but between progressive, environmentally aware business on the one hand and short-term profit takers on the other' (p.31).

Similarly, one might argue that the dichotomy between farmers and environmentalists is a false one. Both farmers and the environment could be portrayed as victims of a global food system, led by multinational companies, which encourages intensive forms of production which in turn reduce the proportion of added value that is returned to rural communities. Whereas half a century ago at least half of the money spent on food found its way back into the rural community, now the share received by farmers is typically 10–20 per cent. Value has been concentrated 'on the input side by agrochemical, feed and seed companies and on the output side by those who move, transform and sell the food' (Pretty, 1998, p.10).

These are attractive arguments which seem to offer an approach to solving old dilemmas, but how much have things changed? It is perhaps easier to secure a shift in opinion than it is in action, particularly by regulatory authorities. As one of the leading theorists of ecological modernization, Hajer, has noted in relation to the environment-friendly setting of the Netherlands, 'ecological modernization discourse won in the "chamber of concern" but did not prevail in the "chamber of regulation" in which policies are formulated and implemented' (Dryzek, 1996, p.121). It is relatively easy for business representatives to say that they are committed to sustainable development, but what changes in their behaviour follow? Might it be that most businesses are still short term profit takers, or at least environmentally aware to the extent that it is prudent to be seen to comply with regulatory requirements and burnish their image?

For some commentators, ecological modernization is based on 'comfortable assumptions', claims 'to get the best of all worlds' and 'is too good to be true' (Giddens, 1998, pp.57–8). 'It isn't really convincing to suppose that environmental protection and economic development fit together comfortably – the one is bound to come into conflict with the other' (p.58).

The old certainties are still there: they have not dissolved or lost their relevance. The representation of the individual consumer remains weak, but the politics of collective consumption has grown in importance. There is thus a new politics in uneasy coexistence with the old politics of production, dealing with issues 'outside traditional social democratic politics – ecology, animal rights, sexuality, consumers' rights and many others' (p.48).

As far as the environment is concerned, it can plausibly be argued that there has been a recasting of the policy debate which 'may be the enduring legacy of the last 25 years of environmental activism' (Dryzek, 1996, p.121). As Dryzek notes, one can win debates and 'lose in power play'. When the politics of collective consumption comes into conflict with the politics of production, economic imperatives may prevail. In many ways, it is a battle of interests with ideas, and the ideas often win in the long run if they are strong enough. An interesting period of transformation is under way in interest politics and the long-run outcome cannot yet be predicted with any certainty.

10

The Effectiveness of Pressure Groups

As was emphasized in the introduction, any study of pressure groups must be concerned not only with how they operate, but also with what they are able to achieve. Questions about who gains and who loses should be at the core of any political analysis. Difficult methodological problems arise, however, in the analysis of effectiveness. What is the pattern of cause and effect? Do groups become more effective because government policy changes in a way that makes them of central importance? Fo example, in relation to overseas aid policy, 'the relative success enjoyed by business interests in winning concessions from the government owes as much to the reorientation of aid policy as to the skill and influence of the lobby itself' (Bose, 1991, p.143). Recent writing has challenged accounts of pressure group capture of government and argued that 'State actors have incorporated groups in order to achieve their own goals' (Smith, 1993, p.228). Are groups responding to an agenda and policy opportunities created by government, or do groups themselves bring about changes in government policy which in turn give them new opportunities to exert influence?

As is evident from discussion of Robinson's work on roads policy, earlier in the book, policy changes may be dependent on a number of factors which include:

- The salience of the issue to the electorate.
- The political outlook of the government in office.
- Expert 'scientific' opinion on the subject.
- The balance of pressure group activity.

Despite its importance, Whiteley and Winyard (1987, p.111) note that 'the question of interest group effectiveness is probably the least adequately researched aspect of the study of pressure groups'. This is because such an analysis can raise as many questions as it answers, although that of itself can be worthwhile. The underlying problem is the difficulties that arise in the analysis of two concepts which are at the centre of the study of politics: power and influence. Indeed, the existence of two distinct terms – power and influence – itself hints at some of the problems. Without going into a complex conceptual debate, power may be said to refer to the exercise of authority ('legitimate power') by government and the deployment of coercive power by a non-governmental authority (such as a trade union). Both senses embody in them the notion of 'command', of obedience because one party either ought to be obeyed or has the ability to force the other party to obey. Influence, on the other hand, rests on the power to persuade, and is the most usual way in which pressure groups are able to influence the decision-making process. Government makes concessions to a pressure group because of the validity of its arguments, for example, because the group is able to demonstrate that the proposed policy is unworkable or would damage the economy, or because its arguments have moral force. Government and Parliament may also be influenced by the state of public opinion on the particular issue, although it must be stressed that the majority of issues discussed between pressure groups and government are of such a technical character that there is no public opinion in relation to them.

Why Measuring Pressure Group Influence is Difficult

Even if the British political process were conducted in conditions of less secrecy, it would be difficult to estimate the effectiveness of a pressure group. The first problem arises from the objectives of the group itself. Some cause groups have relatively simple objectives, and it is possible to say whether or not they have been attained. For example, those who worked for handgun control in the Snowdrop campaign achieved their objective and the organization was dissolved. If all blood sports were banned, the role of organisations opposing them might be limited to helping to ensure that they did not take place illegally. Even most cause groups, however, have multiple objectives.

Matters become much more difficult when one considers sectional groups. Such groups invariably have multiple objectives. Some of these objectives may matter a great deal to them, others much less so. Indeed, the complex internal politics of such groups may lead to policies being developed which are intended to appease some faction or interest within the group, but which are not really supported by the leadership. Obviously, such policies will not be pressed very hard. Even supposing, however, that it were possible to attach weights to the various policies being advocated by a group, one would still be left with the problem of measuring the degree of success attained.

Occasionally, a sectional group gets all that it wants on a particular issue. For much of the time, however, it has to agree to a compromise. The compromise may be a bad one from the group's point of view, yet the group leadership may put a gloss on it to calm the membership. Equally, the compromise may be quite a favourable one, but the group may complain loudly about the harshness of its treatment, largely for the consumption of its membership. Even trying to trace the real impact of the compromise on the groups members may be very difficult, as much will depend on its implementation. There are many provisions on the statute book which are hardly ever used.

There are also problems in deciding what government's priorities really are. Sometimes government may toughen up a green paper or a white paper so that it has something to give away to pressure groups at a later stage without compromising its core position. In other cases, issuing a green paper may be interpreted as a sign that the Cabinet is internally divided, and that the government's commitment to any particular outcome is limited. Policy often emerges as a series of compromises produced on the basis of interdepartmental arguments, with each department frequently arguing for the client groups with which it is associated.

In any case, how does one compare a substantial impact on a policy which is basically unfavourable to a group with some small adjustments to a policy which is more in line with a group's thinking? This is not a purely academic issue. The CBI had much more influence on the policy of the Labour Government of 1974–9 than it did on the policies of the preceding and succeeding Conservative governments. However, the policy proposals of the Labour government were potentially more threatening to the CBI's interests than those of the Conservatives. The position is further complicated by the fact that members of the Labour Government were either opposed to particular policies such as substantial intervention in industry or unenthusiastic about them as in the case of industrial democracy. Hence, the CBI was a useful ally for the more moderate members of the Government in their internal policy struggles.

If one considers the interaction betwen pressure groups and government, it is relatively rare for only one group to be active on a particular issue. A number of groups will be taking a variety of positions, and using different strategies. In some cases, they may have allies in government departments. For example, Alarm UK, which co-ordinates 250 anti-road groups, claimed that the cut back in road building projects was partly due to a broad and growing opposition movement, but added, 'We can't take all the credit because and the Treasury and the Environment department are also applying pressure' (*The Independent*, 27 April 1994).

Whiteley and Winyard (1987, p.111) suggest that 'a second-best solution to observing the decision-making process directly' is to interview participants and obtain their perceptions of effectiveness. Much useful data can be obtained in this way, although large-scale studies of this kind such as have been carried out in the United States are expensive and would need to be repeated from time to time to capture changing perceptions. In the rest of this chapter, an attempt is made to isolate the more important factors which might bear on the effectiveness of a pressure group.

A Typology of Factors Affecting Pressure Group Effectiveness

The following typology draws on a number of sources in the pressure group literature. Among the most influential have been Presthus (1973, 1974); Schmitter and Streeck (1981), and the literature of the Organization of Business Interests project in general; Whiteley and Winyard (1987); and the work of the Aberdeen group (for example, Jordan 1994).

The typology is divided into three main categories which are then subdivided into subsidiary headings:

1.   Features of the proximate environment of groups, the domains they are seeking to organize. In particular:
     (i)   the characteristics of the potential membership being organized or represented;
     (ii)   competition between groups for members and influence.

2.   The resources available to groups:
     (i)   internal group structures such as decision-taking and conflict reduction mechanism;

   (ii)   marketing skills in terms of the attraction and retention of members;
  (iii)   membership mobilization capabilities;
  (iv)   financial resources;
   (v)   staffing resources;
  (vi)   sanctioning capability;
 (vii)   choices of strategy.

3. Features of the external economic and political environment:
   (i)   public opinion/attitudes;
  (ii)   the political party in office;
 (iii)   economic circumstances, especially in relation to public expenditure
 (iv)   sponsorship or support by a government department, and/ or opposition by other departments;
  (v)   delegated authority.

The rest of the chapter will be structured around a consideration of these various points.

Domain Organization

Schmitter and Streeck (1981, pp.146–7) observe:

> The most basic decision in the design of an interest association is to select from the variety of existing interests those which the association will represent, and to institutionalize a distinction between these and other interests whose representation is left to other associations. Interest associations define the interests they choose to internalize by formally demarcating an organizational domain.

In other words, pressure groups will decide whom it is they are seeking to represent, and this decision will be reflected in criteria of membership eligibility set out in their constitution. Of course, membership of some cause groups is open to the population at large. For all sectional groups, however, membership is limited in some way. Among cause groups, some may draw their members from a particular disadvantaged category, while others may be made up of concerned individuals seeking to remedy the problems of those in the disadvantaged category. Whiteley and Winyard (1987, p.27) formalize this distinction, considering promotional groups as those that 'speak on behalf of, or 'for' the poor, while representational groups are those whose membership is made up 'of the poor, or a particular category of claimant'. Interestingly, Whiteley and Winyard found that, if anything, the promotional groups were more effective than the representational groups. This appeared to be because the representational groups were not seen by civil servants as truly representative of their categories, or able to deliver their clienteles, while the promotional groups displayed more professional expertise in pressure group activity (pp.132–3). Another relevant factor appeared to be the 'attractiveness' of the client group in terms of its electoral influence and the degree to which it was seen as 'deserving'. It is easier to arouse public concern and the support of decision makers for the elderly than for, say, offenders or the low paid (p.131).

It is important for a group with a restricted eligible membership to organize as large a proportion of it as possible in order to be credible. One expert on trade associations commented wryly in interview that they would always claim to organize 80 per cent of the firms by turnover in whichever sector they were organizing, never more and never less. Indeed, Presthus (1974, p.111) argues that 'size and quality of membership are probably among the major political resources of interest groups'. Cause groups in Britain tend to attract a disproportionate number of well-educated, middle-class members. The Aberdeen group's data shows that 35.3 per cent of Friends of the Earth members have a first degree, 18.9 per cent held a postgraduate degree, and 10 per cent were still in higher education, making a total of 64 per cent of members with a high level of education (Jordan, 1994, Table 7). Such individuals tend to have high levels of self-confidence and to be articulate, good at drafting papers, knowledgeable about the political system and able to hold their own in meetings with officials.

In practice, there is considerable overlap between the domains of pressure groups. Sometimes, this overlap is accidental. For example, the structure of trade associations in Britain has grown on an *ad hoc* basis over a hundred years or so, and is consequently beset by a lack of coherence in the division of responsibilities. Competition for members and influence is not limited to sectional groups. Cause groups may be divided along such lines as the tactics to be used to further a shared objective, as, for example, with the anti-hunting lobby. In the disability field, 'There has been considerable rivalry between the Disablement Income Group, the Royal Association for Disability and Rehabilitation and the Disability Alliance' (Whiteley and Winyard 1987, p.134). As existing organizations concerned with the elderly moved towards greater consensus in the mid 1980s, they found themselves faced with a new wave of group formation, in part stimulated by the availability of funding from local councils. 'These fledgling groups were indicative of a grass roots upsurge, to which the more-established pensioner organizations now struggled to respond' (Pratt, 1993, p.143.)

If groups representing a potentially homogeneous category of interest are divided, then government has the option of using a 'divide and rule' strategy. In the dispute about new contracts in further education colleges in 1994, the National Association of Teachers in Further and Higher Education (NAFTHE), the main union, made use of the strike weapon, leading some members to leave and join the more moderate Association of Teachers and Lecturers (ATL) which emphasized negotiations. However, even leaving aside ideologically based disagreements about strategies and tactics, it is not necessarily easy for groups to get together and present a united front. A merger or joint action may be more in the interests of one group than another. Teaching unions have been particularly prone to competition for members and influence, but Coates makes it clear in his study of the teaching unions that the National Union of Teachers (NUT) had the most to gain from organizational unity:

> The impetus for the creation of a single teachers' organisation has come always from the largest association, the NUT ... Lack of unity, in the Union's view, dissipated the potential for influence that the teachers collectively possessed through the traditional forms of their pressure. And, of course, as the largest of the associations by far, the NUT had the most to gain from the creation of an organizational unit that it would inevitably dominate, and in which sectional voices would be muted.
>
> (Coates, 1972, p.47)

It is not surprising that, over twenty-five years later, the teaching unions remain divided with one new organization being added to the total, the anti-strike Professional Association of Teachers.

Resources: Internal Group Structures

Many trade associations use a variety of organizational devices to take account of the interests of different sections of their membership such as special committees or reserved seats on the main decision-making body for small-firm members who may otherwise feel excluded by larger members. Despite the usefulness of devices of this kind, there is a difficult trade-off between a widely based organization with a large membership but significant internal tensions, and an organization with a small but tightly knit membership.

It is sometimes said, for instance, that the CBI suffers from 'stifling breadth' because it attempts to represent small and large firms; manufacturers, financiers and retailers; nationalized industries and private sector firms; importers and exporters and the like.

It is clear that 'A central problem in the design of associational structures is the management of internal interest diversity' (Schmitter and Streeck, 1981, p.142). Highly publicized exits of members (as has happened in the CBI) and the formation of breakaway organizations (as has happened in the CBI and NFU) can be damaging to an organization's reputation. On the other hand, the price of preventing such splits may be a high one in terms of the quality of the policies produced and their impact on government.

Pressure groups have to develop decision-making structures that take account of the different interests and viewpoints of their members whilst being able to develop effective policies and to respond to changing events. In many sectional groups, a typical pattern is to have a large council that is the ultimate decision-making body but that only really takes decisions in situations where significant sections of the membership are offended by a policy proposal. An executive committee is often in effective charge of the overall strategy of the organization. Much of the real work, however, is done by a series of specialized committees dealing with particular problem areas. These may, in turn, spawn working parties to deal with a particular piece of legislation or EU directive. Co-ordinating the work of these various committees, and keeping the overall committee structure under review, is one of the tasks of the professional staffs of the associations.

Cause groups vary in their structures from being hierarchical and centralized to democratic and decentralized. In general, however, they have less elaborate organizational charts (if they have one at all) compared with the larger sectional groups. Many cause groups have a relatively decentralized structure, often for ideological reasons, although Greenpeace is a conspicuous exception. Such structures have their advantages and disadvantages. They involve members in local protest actions which are often seen by cause groups as an important part of their work. They can feed back information on how government policies are working in practice on the ground. Whiteley and Winyard's research shows that civil servants valued information from pressure groups on how the social security system was working in practice so that shortcomings could be identified and rectified (1987, pp.131–2). On the other hand, a decentralized structure may lead to local groups taking actions which contradict group policy or embarrass the group and make its relations with civil servants more difficult. In a decentralized organization, the centre may be starved of the financial resources it requires to function effectively.

This helps to explain why groups such as Greenpeace have opted for hierarchical structures with little democratic control over the direction of campaigns:

> Internally, Greenpeace has a strictly bureaucratic, if not authoritarian, structure. A small group of people has control over the organization both at the international level and within national chapters. Local action groups, which exist in some countries, are totally dependent on the central body, and the rank and file is excluded from all decisions.
>
> (Rucht, 1993, p.85)

The Aberdeen group's research raises the general issue of whether many cause groups are networks of financial supporters rather than memberships. By subscribing one engages in a cultural identification rather than any form of political participation. Mail order membership means that 'For a cost that is not seriously considered by the relatively affluent potential member, they can make a political statement of preference without engaging in "real" participation' (Jordan, 1994, p.27). Following through the logic of this argument, one might 'join' an environmental group in the same way that one sends a donation to a charity: as a declaration of support, but not in the expectation or hope of participating in a decision making process. This does not mean that democratic decision-making structures within groups are always well used where they exist.

Marketing Skills and Membership Mobilization

The development of a marketing perspective on pressure group activities by the Aberdeen group draws our attention to the extent to which, in order to succeed, a cause group has to go out and sell a 'product' to a potential membership. Sectional groups are often in a rather different position, because their members are either institutions which face a different calculus about the costs and benefits of membership, or, if they are individuals, membership may be required for professional reasons. Dunleavy's work shows that 'endogenous groups ... formed simply by the coming together of like-minded people' (1991, p.55) face a number of problems in constructing group identities:

* The identity set is diffuse 'unrelated to any specific social situation or clear target profile' (p.66).
* The potential members are often socially invisible because they are distinguished by non-observable private mental states.
* Unstable identity sets with high turnover because one can change one's views more easily than a social role (such as an occupation).

Dunleavy goes on to draw out a number of second order implications from these observations. In summary, endogenous groups have heterogeneous memberships in which the shared identity can be pursued by means other than collective action. Exit costs are low: they involve, at most, changing a preference (whereas leaving a professional group might involve leaving an occupation). There is likely to be group rivalry and high membership turnover, the latter prediction being confirmed by the Aberdeen group's data.

The Aberdeen group sees 'the size of group membership as linked to the marketing strategies and success of the groups' (Jordan, Maloney and McLaughlin, 1994b, p.549). Thus, the conspicuous success of the RSPB 'reflects the success of regular and high profile press advertising and increased sophistication in recruitment rather than just a change in public attitudes' (ibid.). What is clear from the Aberdeen group's data is that there is a subset of the population who are 'joiners' (a term which had some currency in earlier empirical American sociological literature, but has been rather lost from view). Thus, 73.5 per cent of the members of Amnesty belong to another organization, with the corresponding figure for members of Friends of the Earth being 65.8 per cent. Overlapping membership is particularly high between Amnesty and Friends of the Earth with 17 per cent of Amnesty members in Friends of the Earth, while 13 per cent of Friends of the Earth members are also in Amnesty (Jordan and Maloney, 1997, p.119).

In a society in which a significant proportion of the population is affluent, the cost of multiple group membership is relatively low. Becoming an activist, however, incurs much higher costs. For example, an individual who becomes a hunt saboteur runs the risk of physical assault and prosecution. However, the identification involved in such a choice is far stronger than the person who sends off a cheque to the World Wide Fund for Nature and displays a sticker in their car. A hunt saboteur may well be involved in other forms of direct action on behalf of animals and their social life may be constructed around a group of animal activists. Some groups depend more than others on their ability to mobilize their members. The CBI does not ask its members to take to the streets, but if a trade union makes a strike threat, it needs to be able to rely on the support of members in a postal ballot. Following Dunleavy (1991, p.20) the actions which members are asked to perform on behalf of the group may be ranked from low cost to high cost, ranging from lobbying elected representatives, through demonstrations to civil disobedience. Groups such as Amnesty International depend substantially on their individual members to engage in campaigns on behalf of individual prisoners who are 'adopted' by local branches.

Enthusiastic volunteer activists may, however, lack the detachment and balance of professional staff members, and create problems for a pressure group. Tensions may arise in organizations which have a small core of professional staff and a large number of volunteer activists. The activists may resent the fact that resources are being devoted to the payment of staff for activities which they undertake for free, while the staff may consider that the activists lack the professional approach that successful group activity requires.

Financial Resources, Staff Size and Sanctioning Capacity

Financial resources are important to a group in the sense that if it is going to engage in the detailed monitoring of legislation including EU directives, and attempt to influence the content of such legislation through the presentation of a detailed case to civil servants, it will require a large, relatively well-paid staff.

As Moran (1983, p.51) observes, 'The characteristic way in which powerful interests have influenced policy-making in modern Britain may be summarised in one word: they have done so *bureaucratically*.' Having interviewed many pressure group officials over the years, one of the most striking characteristics of most of them is their similarity to civil servants in terms of their official personalities, modes of operation, language, and perceptions of the political process. After all, they are civil servants, preparing policy papers for and generally servicing committees, and making presentations to their counterparts in government. Such skills have to be developed by cause groups, just as much as by sectional groups, if they want to be effective. 'Insider access, indeed legitimacy, is granted to Amnesty because it provides the government with good information which can be used as a lever in international negotiations' (Christiansen and Dowding, 1994, p.21).

Buksti and Johansen suggest on the basis of Danish research that the size of the secretariat or bureaucracy of an organization is an important determinant of group effectiveness. They characterize organizations with fewer than six people on their staff as 'weak insiders' (1979, pp.209–10). A rather similar view was taken by the Devlin Commission on Industrial Representation, which suggested that an effective association should have an executive staff of at least eight people.

This view does, however, need some qualification. For example, a product-level association which has to consider particular EU directives can operate quite effectively with a part-time executive officer shared with other similar associations and operating out of the offices of the sectoral association (a pattern adopted in the chemical and food-processing industries, for example). At the other end of the spectrum, there is a danger that a large association bureaucracy will develop objectives of its own which are at variance with those of the members. Indeed, one argument that has been put to me in an interview is that a small secretariat of a few very well-paid executives concentrating on major issues can work just as well as an association with large numbers of middle-ranking officials scrutinizing the details of policy, although in practice such details can be very significant.

For campaigning groups, the whole idea of professionalism may seem anathema with career structures getting in the way of commitment and campaigning zeal. Unfortunately, a person who is good at running a campaign or thinking up a media stunt may not have the management skills necessary to run an office:

> This was a fundamental dilemma with which Greenpeace is still grappling today. Do you rely on well-meaning, highly motivated people working for an ideal rather than for money? Or do you recognise that the outfit is, to all intents and purposes, a multi-national which needs professional skills at the highest level?
>
> (Wilkinson, 1994, p. 42)

204   *Pressure Groups and British Politics*

If one examines contemporary Greenpeace advertisements, then it would seem that they have decided to emphasize the second model of the committed but well paid professional. (See Box 10.1.)

Box 10.1   Extract from Greenpeace advert for staff

> Greenpeace International ... has vacancies for two Political Advisers. Within the framework of Greenpeace's international campaigns to protect the environment and promote peace, Political Advisers play a key role in providing strategic direction to campaigns and interface with high-level contacts in government, international secretariats and industry ... The successful candidates will have a strong academic background and significant experience in intergovernmental and/or business decision-making in the relevant fields. They will also have a strong strategic flair, with a proven ability to develop political strategies to translate public concerns into environmentally-sound laws, policies and practices by government and industry.

There are instances where a group's influence may depend more on its sanctioning capacity than the quality of its arguments. The most successful political strike in the postwar period was that co-ordinated by the Ulster Workers' Council which paralysed Northern Ireland for two weeks in May 1974, bringing down the 'power sharing' executive after only five months in office. Although it achieved its immediate objective, it did nothing to solve Northern Ireland's problems, and may well have made them worse. The Conservative governments after 1979 set out, with considerable success, to restrain the use of the strike weapon by trade unions. When the government used state power to crush a number of strikes, notably that of the miners in the 1980s, there was little reaction from the public at large, fed up with the inconvenience of the strikes of the 1970s. The unions devalued the strike weapon by its excessive and inappropriate use.

The City of London has considerable sanctioning capacity because it can engage in a 'gilt-edged strike' by refusing to buy government stock, or 'talk down' sterling because of unease about government policy. Because of the internationalization of foreign exchange markets, however, sterling is more likely to be influenced by, for example, statements by the Bundesbank about the trend in interest rates. Movements in share prices in London are, however, extensively reported by the media, and can be interpreted as a verdict on government performance. The sanctioning power of the financial services sector is not exerted through traditional pressure group channels, although financial institutions use those as well. Indeed, globalization of financial markets and the widespread acceptance of the supremacy of the market mechanism has created a situation in which the City no longer has to contemplate using its sanctioning power because its othodoxies form part of the common language of politics.

The Choice of Strategy

The choice of an appropriate stragey and tactics can be an important determinant of pressure group success, although there is a sense in which the adoption of unsophisticated strategies may be a reflection of ineffectiveness rather than its cause. Whiteley and Winyard (1987, p.136) conclude:

> A quiet insider strategy does not pay off any better than an open promotional strategy. Since the era of consensus politics described by Beer and Eckstein, policy making has become more conflictual, but also more fragmented.

Whiteley and Winyard's research shows that the responsible use of publicity by a group can reinforce the lobbying of government. It is also apparent that there are more opportunities for exerting influence through Parliament than was the case in the 1950s when the first empirical pressure group studies were undertaken. Even so, it is clear that much success in lobbying still depends on the careful research and analysis of a case, and its presentation to civil servants or Commission officials. In that sense, the lobbying process remains a highly bureaucratized one in which adequate resources are one of the keys to success.

As was discussed in Chapter 7, frustration at the lack of success of 'responsible' strategies has increasingly led activists opposed to animal experiments or new roads to resort to direct action. Direct action is a risky strategy because it may undermine attempts to influence public opinion and change public policy, although, as Garner goes on to point out, much depends on the form of direct action used:

> The media emphasis on the extreme forms of direct action, it is argued, discredits the whole of the movement since the more moderate groups are tarred with the same brush. In addition, attention is diverted away from the issues on

to the nature of the activities themselves – their threat to public safety and what can be done to stop them.

(Garner, 1993, p.225)

One of the most conspicuous examples of the apparent success of an outsider strategy which used direct action is the anti-poll tax movement. Considerable and successful use was made of non-payment as a tactic, developed into resisting bailiffs, while a demonstration at Trafalgar Square developed into a serious riot. Non-payment was a particularly effective tactic because 'It tapped into a … tradition of civil disobedience going back into British history. It had the rare advantage of combining strong moral anger with material self-interest' (Barr, 1992, p.145). Barr argues (p.145) that non-payment was 'the winning strategy', but one also has to take into account how far the decision to abandon the tax was taken simply because Conservative MPs in marginal constituencies were afraid of losing their seats. It is doubtful whether the Conservatives could have won the 1992 election without abandoning the poll tax, although under registration as a consequence of the tax may have helped them to win. Barr concludes (p.147) that 'The anti-poll tax movement has shown that outsider status and a total lack of interest in negotiation at the national level are not necessarily handicaps.' Certainly, it reminds us that outsider strategies can help to bring results, although refusals to pay tax have not usually been effective, and in this case were assisted by a widely shared sense that the poll tax was inherently unfair. Insider strategies are likely to be those pursued by the majority of pressure groups seeking to influence government policy.

External Environment

Public attitudes and opinions are an important feature of the external operating environment of groups. A pressure group will usually try and influence public opinion. Although such efforts may have some success, groups are more likely to benefit from a change in public views which they have not themselves brought about. One can distinguish here between 'attitudes' and 'opinions'. Attitudes may be taken to refer to more deeply held perceptions which structure the response of individuals to particular events. They generally change only either slowly or in response to some crisis situation. Opinions are more superficial; they may reflect more deeply held attitudes, but they may also be more

spontaneous responses to particular events.
As Richard Rose (1974, p.253) points out, 'The likelihood of any group gaining wide popular support for its demands depends upon the congruence between group demands and the values, beliefs and emotions widely diffused in the culture'. Rose (pp.254–5) develops a sixfold typology based on the level of congruence between a group's goals and wider cultural norms which is presented here with updated examples:

1. '*Harmony between pressure group demands and general cultural norms.*' Organizations opposing cruelty to children and to animals are clear examples.

2. '*A gradual increase in the acceptability of political values supporting pressure group demands.*' Anti-smoking groups were once regarded as marginal organizations, but their demands now occupy a central position in the political agenda, although more so in the United States than in Britain.

3. '*Bargaining with fluctuating support from cultural norms.*' An organization like the CPRE may be seen as drawing on essential values of 'Englishness', but its concern about intensive leisure uses of the countryside would win support from some segments of the population, but not from others.

4. '*Advocacy in the face of cultural indifference.*' Such a group lacks an audience either in government or outside it. The Pedestrians' Association has less than a thousand members compared with several million in the AA.

5. '*Advocacy in opposition to long-term cultural trends.*' The advocates of restricted shop opening on Sundays found it impossible to stem the combined effect of commercial pressures from retailers and apparent consumer preferences.

6. '*Conflict between cultural values and pressure group goals.*' Apart from the Campaign for the Abolition of Angling, animal protection groups 'have fought shy of criticising angling because it is an extremely popular pastime and also because it is much more difficult to establish that fish can suffer.'   (Garner, 1993, p.172)

The importance of public opinion in setting a context for pressure group activity can be seen by the way in which the environmental movement gained ground in the 1970s and 1980s, but then started to lose some ground in the early 1990s. A number of environmental groups had to cut staff because of falling income in the early 1990s. World Wide Fund for Nature lost £3 million in income between 1989 and 1992 and shed 20 jobs (10 per cent of its staff) in 1992, and another 5 jobs in 1993. Friends of the Earth made 24 of its 120 staff redundant in 1993. In part, the decline in income was a result of the recession, which also affected charitable giving, but it also reflected a growth of 'doom fatigue' among the public (*The Observer*, 27 June 1993).

Even before this fall off in support, which has been reversed to some extent in the case of the World Wide Fund for Nature, there was a risk associated with the increased issue salience of environmentalism. First, 'many campaigns of the environmental groups remain issue-specific, tending to fade away in true "issue-attention" style ... many groups still lack adequate resources to pursue and co-ordinate the campaigns they would like' (Robinson, 1992, p.98). Second, politicians may be tempted to jump on the bandwagon and make tokenistic commitments to the environmentalist cause.

Changes and Continuities: Parties and Departments

The party in office can make a considerable difference to the political influence exerted by a pressure group. It must be emphasized that two governments with the same party label can be very different in their approach to pressure group activity. The Heath Government tried to develop a close working relationship with the trade unions, while the Thatcher Government was keen to distance itself from them.

The TUC was the pressure group most adversely affected by the advent of the Thatcher Government. Using detailed data from TUC annual reports, Mitchell (1987) shows that the number of contacts at prime ministerial level fell off sharply after 1979, although ministerial contacts remained at the same level as under the Labour government of 1974–9. What changed even more dramatically was the effectiveness of contacts as perceived by the TUC. Between 1976 and 1979, the success rate in terms of government agreeing to take the action advocated by the TUC varied between 40.5 per cent and 47.0 per cent. In the years from 1979–1984, it ranges between 4.5 per cent and 22.5 per cent, a striking contrast with the earlier period. In 1992 it was announced that in the context of membership losses of 4 million from a 1979 figure of over 12 million, the TUC staff of 250 would have to be cut by up to a fifth (*Financial Times*, 24 February 1992).

The poverty lobby was also adversely affected by the political climate of the 1980s. 'In the Thatcherite era of conviction politics the influence of poverty groups has been reduced by the ideological beliefs of that administration, and by the deteriorating economic climate that monetarist policies have created' (Whiteley and Winyard 1987, p.138). A lobby of a very different kind, the British Medical Association, was singled out in both Mrs Thatcher's and Nigel Lawson's memoirs for campaigning against government policy. Smith (1993, p.183) brings out both the extent and the limits of the changes brought about in the nature of the health policy community:

> The government has attacked the consensus and ideology of the policy community by questioning clinical autonomy and removing the doctors' veto over both questions of implementation and wider policy. Consequently, conflict and new groups have ... undermined the closed policy community that previously existed . ... Doctors are still important to the process of making and implementing policy, and the structures of institutionalised access still exist.

In noting the changes brought about by the experience of Thatcherism, it is easy to ignore the continuities. Mrs Thatcher was reluctant to make changes in the structure of government (John Major created a new National Heritage department which became the Department of Culture, Media and Sport under Labour) and, if anything, the issue communities organized around government departments became more solidified in the 1980s and 1990s. One of the key and enduring features of the British political process is the symbiotic relationship between groups and departments. The groups need the department for access, status and information about policy developments; the departments need the groups for information about what is happening in their sphere of interest, for co-operation in the implementation of policy and, above all, as allies in the interdepartmental battles that are another key feature of the British political process.

Support from a particular government department may always be offset by opposition from another department with different priorities (for example Agriculture versus Health), or by interventions by Downing Street or the Treasury. Economic circumstances unavoidably have an impact on government's willingness to meet pressure group demands. Against a background of continued pressure on public expenditure, demands for increases in service provision, or other changes in policy requiring more expenditure, are unlikely to be met.

The Blair Government has been able to find extra money for education and health care, but cannot meet all the demands made by specialized pressure groups.

Delegating Implementation to Pressure Groups

Although this is less common in Britain than in countries such as Germany, government often shares its authority with pressure groups, delegating to them the responsibility for carrying out particular functions, or providing particular services. Although this reliance on private interest governments may seem to be a corporatist trait, its use tended to increase under the Thatcher Government as a result of the increasing reliance on 'contracting out' services which could not be completely abandoned. Examples include the provision of training funds through non-statutory training organizations (effectively employers' associations), which replaced the former statutory training boards in most sectors of the economy; the creation of self-regulatory organizations in the City of London with considerable disciplinary powers, including the ability to impose substantial fines; the involvement of the chambers of commerce in a number of government programmes; and the increased use of the voluntary sector for service delivery at the local level.

Some of the difficulties of voluntary organizations being used to implement policy is illustrated by the example of charities concerned with the Third World. Their position is further complicated by their charitable status which places limits on their political activities. Government financial support for their programmes through the Joint Funding Scheme is still only 10–15 per cent of the income of organizations such as Oxfam and Christian Aid, but after taking account of EU and other official grants, 'the proportion raised from voluntary contributions has been declining relative to official sources' (Robinson, 1991, p.166). The provision of government funds has the effect of emphasizing the role of the voluntary organizations as effective providers of assistance where and when it is needed and 'plays down their political role in challenging the structural causes of poverty' (p.176):

> Although it would be an exaggeration to claim that the government has deliberately sought to co-opt non-governmental organizations (NGOs) by offering them increased resources, it is nevertheless the case that voluntary agencies

have become more muted in their criticism of the Overseas Development Administration ... NGOs have also been put on the defensive by critical remarks about their work by government Ministers.

(p.175)

Bennett (1998) reviews the potential contribution of business associations to economic development in the absence of the public law status and compulsory membership of chambers that is found in countries such as Germany. He found that only just over 8 per cent of the associations surveyed provided a broad range of business services. 'This is at odds with the desires of the UK government that associations should extend their range of services to help develop the competitiveness of their members' (p.1383).

Bennett's analysis of the weaknesses of the associations 'suggest fundamental dilemmas for government policy concerning associations in the United Kingdom' (p.1385). His work shows that 'if government wants associations to play a different role, then this will not be possible by voluntary action alone' (p.1386). However, any form of closer government involvement or regulation would run counter to their self conception as voluntary associations whose autonomy is valued by their members. In a company state, buiness associations are likely to be resistant to entering into the kind of partnership relationships with government seen in developmental states such as Germany. Such a stance, although in line with the preferences of their members, may undermine their long run effectiveness.

Conclusions

An attempt has been made in this chapter to generalize about the factors affecting pressure group effectiveness. Although there are clearly some observable regularities in the ways in which successful groups operate, it must be emphasized that each pressure group faces a different situation, and has to develop and deploy a strategy to suit its particular circumstances.

The assessment of effectiveness thus remains a difficult task. It is probably easier to say which groups are ineffective, and to make general statements about apparent increases or declines in influence, than it is to estimate just how much influence a particular group has on policy outcomes. Even in relation to a single case study of a particular issue, the latter task is a difficult one, and one has to be very cautious about generalizing from a particular example. Even so, if we are interested in finding out who wins and who loses in the political process, and why they win and lose, the question of effectiveness cannot be ignored by pressure group analysts.

11

Conclusions: Pressure Groups and Democracy

This concluding chapter will not attempt to summarise all the arguments reviewed in the book, but will concentrate on the implications of the discussion for the democratic process. In what ways do pressure groups contribute to, or detract from, democracy? There has been a lively debate in Britain in the late 1980s and 1990s about the question of constitutional reform. The standard topics of discussion include: proportional representation; a bill of rights; freedom of information; reform of the House of Lords; legislative devolution for Scotland and Wales; and state funding of political parties. However, despite the decline in political party membership, and the rise of a whole generation of pressure groups, there has been little discussion of their future role in the political process.

Part of the blame for the inadequacy of the systematic discussion of pressure groups must rest with political scientists. The discussion of corporatism did at least try to provide a middle level theoretical perspective for understanding rather widespread developments in relations between producer groups and governments which occurred particularly in the 1970s. Yet in the end, the debate became enervating, absorbed with disputes about definition, and expending time and energy fighting off intellectual raids from pluralists affronted at the invasion of their territory. Policy networks and policy communities became established as the new orthodoxy. What is remarkable about this debate is that there has been little discussion of the normative implications of having policy made in what are often relatively closed policy communities.

The Contributions of Pressure Groups and Political Parties to Modern Democracy

Political parties and pressure groups are competitors: for resources, for members, for resources and for influence. 'The overall market for political activism has grown in terms of overall levels of participation, but the parties now take a smaller share of it' (Riddell, 1996, p.5). Richardson (1995) analyses their competition in terms of supply and demand factors. On the demand side, citizens are better educated, more sophisticated and more discerning in their choices of forms of political participation. On the supply side, there are entrepreneurs 'who see market opportunities for political participation' (Richardson, 1995, p.122). Hence, citizens are faced with a much wider range of choices of what appear to be exciting forms of political participation. Thus, in an anti-roads protest near Bath, 'Week End Crusties' arrived from the town. They became 'part-time Dongas for the day and got value from the protest not from its eventual success or failure, but from the experiences they felt along the way' (North, 1988, p.18). Meetings of the local Labour Party do not offer a chance to dress up in tribal warpaint. 'Parties may, therefore, be facing the classic situation of the old "product" which has been overtaken by innovation in the market-place ... their market share declines as new products attract new customers' (Richardson, 1995, p.124).

There has been a sharp and long-run decline in party membership in Britain:

> The evidence here is quite indisputable; individual membership of political parties in the UK has declined precipitously since the 1960s, even allowing for the vagaries of measuring party membership accurately. In 1964, 9.4 per cent of all registered electors were members of the main three British parties with nationwide organizations; by the time of the 1992 general election, just 2.0 per cent were (a 79 per cent decline in proportional terms).
>
> (Webb, 1995, p.306)

The Labour Party did enjoy something of a revival in membership as the 1997 general election approached, boosted by new recruitment techniques. Membership reached a peak of 405 000, but fell away again after the election to around 395 000, with a further net loss of 12 000 members anticipated by party officials in the twelve months from the autumn of 1998 (*The Guardian*, 14 August 1998). The situation in the Conservative Party, which has a rapidly ageing membership, has been even more serious. The available estimates suggest 'that the party has been losing, on average, about 64 000 members a year since 1960' (Whiteley, Seyd and Richardson, 1994, p.17).

Of course, there is not an either/or choice between political party and pressure group activity. Seyd and Whiteley's large-scale study of Labour Party members shows that 16 per cent of those surveyed were also members of Greenpeace, 8.2 per cent were members of Friends of the Earth and 6.8 per cent were members of Amnesty International (Seyd and Whiteley, 1992, p.92). Their complementary research on the Conservative Party showed quite high levels of membership in conservation organizations with the World Wide Fund for Nature heading the list with 12 per cent of party members surveyed in membership (even more were in membership of the National Trust, but that should not be regarded as a pressure group in the conventional sense) (Whiteley, Seyd and Richardson, 1994, p.186).

Although party members also join pressure groups, there is probably some causal connection between the decline of party membership and the rise of a new generation of pressure groups. As Porritt and Winner note (1988, p.69), 'it is precisely the inability of the Labour Party to dig itself out of its own fossilized form of in-fighting which understandably makes Greens doubt that they are likely to embrace green politics at anything more than the most superficial level'. For a young person, sitting in a tree to oppose a new by-pass is likely to seem both more exciting and more directly effective than getting a resolution on road building passed at the Labour Party branch meeting to be forwarded to the annual conference.

There is considerable evidence to support Richardson's argument (1995, p.136) 'that interest groups and social movements have come to present a major challenge to parties as channels of participation and for the resources which citizens are willing to donate'. While attempting to mount a defence of political parties, Webb admits (1995, p.316) that it is 'fairly clear that they do not fulfil the function of articulating and representing interests as efficiently as was once the case'. The growing importance of the media 'means that the agenda-setting capacity of political parties has most probably been reduced' (p.317). Nevertheless, he emphasizes that political parties 'remain vital for the functions of interest aggregation, political recruitment and decision making' (p.318).

Political parties have to aggregate a wide range of demands from citizens into coherent policy packages which can then be offered to the electorate. Pressure groups, by definition, cannot perform this function.

Political parties have to decide which of a range of demands coming from their constituencies can be met given budget constraints. Broadly based pressure groups do have to do this as well to some extent, but particular concern has been expressed about the role of single-issue pressure groups who are confined to articulating their particular demand. Some analysts see their influence as reflecting 'a general bias in the British political system in favour of higher public spending and more legislation and regulation. A particular case always sounds more deserving than general restraint' (Riddell, 1996, p.7).

The Case for Pressure Groups Reviewed

Des Wilson, well known in the past as a campaigner, has provided a list of key justifications for the existence of community/cause pressure groups. Of course, the population of pressure groups is also made up of sectional groups. Wilson has no time for 'vested interests, whose cause is usually maintenance of the status quo irrespective of the implications for the community' (Wilson, 1984, p.2). Such groups are seen by him as part of a pattern of failure 'by our institutions, failures rooted in a deep bias towards the status quo, and vested interest in power and wealth'. It is in these and other failures 'that we find the outstanding argument for pressure groups' (p.20). I am less sympathetic to the notion of 'cause groups good, sectional groups bad' which underpins much argument about pressure groups and the democratic process, a stance which ultimately reduces to a slightly more sophisticated way of saying one likes those pressure groups whose values one shares. Idealists, and those seeking to promote change, like Wilson, have a right to organize and be heard, but so do realists seeking to defend existing arrangements.

Wilson outlines seven key justifications for the existence of pressure groups, and the first three of these provide a good basis for reviewing many of the arguments about the contribution of pressure groups to democracy. The last four are less convincing and will be considered more briefly. The first is the argument that 'There is more to democracy than the occasional vote' (p.21). Wilson is an enthusiast for participatory democracy, and he regards pressure groups as one way in which participation could take place. The counter argument for representative democracy is that many people consider that there are more meaningful or enjoyable activities in life than politics, and are therefore prepared to have persons sharing their general political outlook acting on their behalf.

Wilson deals with the argument that opposition parties provide a means whereby people can exercise their democratic rights by maintaining that they 'are themselves part of the governing system ... Often specialist pressure groups are more effective than all-issue political parties in opposing "the system"' (p.21). What is clear from the discussion above is that the membership of cause groups has increased as the membership of political parties has declined. Many people are active in both political parties and cause groups, but it would seem that political parties have often seemed too unwelcoming, bureaucratic and preoccupied with questions of dogma to younger activists with a desire to bring about changes in society.

Wilson claims that pressure groups counterbalance two inherent weaknesses in democracy, the first being that democracy 'does *not* work for all people' and that 'Pressure groups offer a chance for minorities and disadvantaged groups to argue their case' (p.22). This goes to the heart of the problem about democracy which is that it is a majoritarian form of government which nevertheless aspires, in its defensible forms, to protect minority rights. The second inherent weakness identified by Wilson is that electioneering encourages a short-term perspective on issues.

The first weakness identified by Wilson raises such fundamental issues about the relationship between pressure groups and democracy that some space will have to be devoted to considering these problems before returning to Wilson's other arguments. The principal counter argument is that pressure group activity tends to reinforce existing biases within the political system rather than counteracting them. The idea that it is more difficult to organize general than particular interests recalls the discussion of Olson's theory of pressure groups in Chapter 3. What is evident from the discussion in the book as a whole is that business interests have tended to strengthen their privileged position in the 1980s and 1990s, especially at the EU level. There are a number of reasons for this trend: the existence of Conservative and Labour governments in Britain over this period which have been generally well disposed to business interests; the weakening of the principal countervailing force, organized labour, with environmental groups hardly an adequate substitute; and the growing sophistication of the political operations of firms. All governments want a successful economy, and this means that there has to be a dialogue with business whose views must be seriously considered. However, it may be that the balance has swung too far in the direction of business interests, and that the construction of the political agenda pays too much attention to what would serve the market economy, and not enough to the needs of less advantaged members of the population.

Another problem arises from what the Aberdeen group's data shows to be the overwhelmingly middle class, highly educated composition of the memberships of the cause groups they studied. It must be emphasized that not all highly educated members of the middle class join pressure groups: one is talking about a subset of a subset of the population. The evidence seems to suggest that those who join one group are likely to join others as well. This group of highly educated 'joiners' may have values that diverge quite substantially from those of the population at large, and yet be able to influence the political decision making process in a significant way through their campaigning activities so that popular opinion and government decisions increasingly diverge. That in turn could lead to a further decline in confidence in the institutions of government.

That is to put the position at its most pessimistic. It is important to distinguish between the social composition of a pressure group and the objectives for which it is fighting. This is a point that has been made particularly by supporters of the environmental movement. Porritt and Winner argue that Greens are concentrated in the 'caring' professions, and are usually committed to a non-materialist life style. Such individuals do not fit in 'too neatly with the role assigned to them in the Marxist demonology as oppressors of the working class' (1988, pp.182–3). That may be so, but what about those members of the population who do not have a university education and want to pursue a materialist lifestyle?

There is a danger of university educated activists assuming that their values ought to be shared by everyone else. It also has to be recognized that some amenity society activity is essentially concerned with protecting property values and preserving the exclusive social identity of particular locations.

Perhaps even a stronger counter argument is that the increased political activity of environmental groups has not led to major changes in policy outcomes (some activists would claim that more can be achieved by 'green consumerism') and that the underlying bias favours business interests:

> The environment lobby now has greater resources and a much higher profile than it had in the late 1970s. But it has a limited and erratic impact at the national level. Its influence has been great in spheres of policy like the countryside … But there are other areas in which business interests still predomi-

nate. On roads there may be isolated victories like withdrawal of the Oxleas
Wood and Hereford by-pass schemes. But the basic policy continues.

(Young, 1993, p.23)

Having digressed to consider the fundamental issues raised by Wilson's first point it is now possible to return to his other arguments. As
noted earlier, Wilson argues that a second inherent weakness in Parliamentary democracy is that the need to win elections leads to short-term
political considerations prevailing over the longer-term interests of the
country. I am less confident than he is that cause groups are able to take
a long-term perspective. Too often they are ensnared in the assumptions
of long-established policies, arguing for more resources to be devoted
to such policies, or for improvements to be made in them, rather than
for fundamental changes designed to meet long-term problems.

Wilson's third main argument is that 'Pressure groups improve surveillance of government' (1984, p.23). Pressure groups can help to expose
information which would otherwise remain secret. There have been important instances where pressure groups such as the Child Poverty Action
Group have influenced public policy by leaking Cabinet documents.
However, occasional exposures of this kind have to be set against a system of government which is still permeated by a preoccupation with
secrecy: promised freedom of information legislation is yet to be passed.
Because the desirability of greater freedom of information has become
a position shared by many academics and journalists commenting on
British government, it is worth noting that there is a counter view which
argues that open government would bring costs as well as benefits, particularly in relation to pressure group activity. Douglas Hurd has
commented that, if freedom of information 'simply means freedom for
pressure groups to extract from the system only those pieces of information which buttress their own cause, then conceivably the result might
be greater confusion and worse government' (Royal Institute of Public
Administration Report, 1986, p.1).

Wilson's other argument in favour of pressure groups as a means of
improving surveillance of government is a more conventional one. He
points out that they can bring to the attention of ministers and civil servants options and information of which they would not otherwise be aware.
This is an aspect of pressure group activity that is generally valued by
government.

Wilson's other four arguments are less impressive. The argument that
'Pressure groups combat other pressure groups' (1984, p.24), although

particularly directed at redressing the influence of sectional groups, is really a reflection of conventional pluralist wisdom about countervailing groups. The argument that pressure groups persist in fighting for causes in which the media takes only a short-term interest is a valid one, particularly in relation to the example Wilson gives of lead in petrol, but it is not a central argument in favour of pressure group activity. The argument that 'Community/cause groups offer people the weapons to fight on their own behalf' (p.25) reflects Wilson's belief in the value of political participation, and the way in which group activity can build up the skills required for effective collective action. His final argument, that 'Pressure groups relieve frustration' (p.25) is a double-edged one. No doubt they can act as a safety valve, and give people a sense of hope, but in doing so they may be serving more to promote political and social stability than to bring about real change.

Although some of his arguments are questionable, one may agree with Wilson's general conclusion that 'pressure groups are not a threat to a genuine democracy, but a real contributor' (p.25). This applies to 'vested interests' who have real knowledge and understanding of particular subjects and can enhance the quality of the policy debate, as well as the more popular cause groups.

The Limits to Pressure Group Power

If pressure groups were allowed to accumulate too much influence, then there would be a risk for democracy. As it is, pressure groups operate in a political system in which they are checked by other political forces. First, as has been pointed out a number of times, public opinion strongly influences the context in which pressure groups operate. Environmental policy has been given a high priority in part because of accumulating scientific evidence about the seriousness of environmental problems, but also because the public has become more concerned about environmental questions, and politicians of all parties have felt the need to make some response to this shifting climate of opinion. From the perspective of many environmentalists, the changes in public policy have been inadequate, but then environmental concerns have to be balanced against other considerations, particularly economic ones.

Pressure groups are also held in check by political parties, and by government ministers anxious to address a wider political audience than that of a sectional interest or cause group. Broadly based political parties have to appeal beyond the relatively narrow concerns of most pressure groups to win elections. Ministers wish to build their political and legislative reputations. Occasionally, an MP may build his or her reputation through the successful passage of a private member's bill, but, in general it is ministers who take important legislative initiatives. When the core executive makes a choice between conflicting priorities, the concerns of pressure groups may be taken into account, but they do not make the final decision.

Pressure group power is limited: it is based on the ability to persuade and to influence, rather than to take decisions or, with certain exceptions, to veto them. Groups which have enjoyed significant power at particular periods of time, such as the trade unions, have usually experienced a public reaction against them. Nevertheless, one should not be too complacent about the position of pressure groups in the political system. The cards are often stacked in favour of established insider groups. Policy communities are often too narrowly based, or too closed to new influences, producing policy solutions that represent incremental adjustments to existing policies.

The Emergence of the Political Class

One of the disturbing developments in modern British democracy is the emergence of what is referred to as a 'political class'. What this means is that it is possible to spend one's whole life in a series of political occupations, starting perhaps as an assistant to a MP or a lobbyist, and eventually entering the Commons and becoming a minister (Riddell, 1993). Not only does this mean that politicians have a rather narrow range of experience, it also means that they can network more effectively with each other, while those outside these networks become increasingly politically excluded.

As access channels become shut off, or are apparently only open to those with connections or the money to acquire them, ordinary citizens may become increasingly disillusioned with the political process. This may limit the extent to which pressure groups can 'perform a valuable role as a type of safety valve' (Secrett, 1996, p.15). They may come to rely increasingly on forms of direct action which have high disruption costs associated with them. Even if they get issues on to the political agenda, they do not offer an opportunity for the reasoned debate of complex problems or the identification of feasible solutions.

One of the classic defences of pressure groups is that they enhance opportunities for political participation:

> They help people stay informed, and get organized in order to realise their wider social, environmental or economic aspirations. Pressure groups enable individuals and communities, who would otherwise feel marginalised, to contribute usefully to society's pursuit of the common good through taking collective and personal action aimed at changing policy, behaviour and values.
>
> (Secrett, 1998, p.15)

There is certainly a substantial quantity of political participation through pressure groups. The quality of that participation is another matter. Jordan and Maloney argue (1997, p. 188) that 'public interest/ campaigning/protest group politics do not significantly extend participatory democracy.' Sending a donation to a 'mail order' pressure group does not involve any significant or sustained commitment of resources or effort. 'People now prefer to do very little in public interest groups as opposed to doing very little in political parties' (Jordan and Maloney, 1997, p.192).

Forms of Pluralism, Pressure Groups and Democracy

The view one takes of pressure groups is substantially influenced by the view one takes of democracy. It is pluralist interpretations of democracy that have given a particularly central and generally benevolent role to pressure groups. 'Whatever their differences, nearly all empirical democratic theorists defend an interpretation of democracy as a set of institutional arrangements that create a rich texture of interest-group politics and allow, through competition to influence and select political leaders, the rule of multiple minorities' (Held, 1996, p.206). What this vision of an active and diverse civil society in which the barriers to political participation are seen to be relatively low 'cannot in the end shed light on, or explain, [is] a world in which there may be systematic imbalances in the distribution of power, influence and resources' (p.208).

In terms of Held's alternative models of democracy, what one has in contemporary British and EU politics is something very similar to what he describes as neo-pluralism as distinct from classic pluralism. Among the relevant features of neo-pluralism which he identifies (1996, pp.217–8) are:

1. Multiple pressure groups, but political agenda biased towards corporate power.
2. The state, and its departments, forge their own sectional interests.
3. Poor resource base of many groups prevents political participation.
4. Distribution of socioeconomic power provides opportunities for and limits to political power.
5. Unequal involvement in politics: insufficiently open government.

If the political agenda is biased towards corporate power and if the political process is skewed in a way that leads to unequal involvement in politics, what are the feedback effects on the distribution of socioeconomic power? The 1990s has seen a growing political debate within Europe on the phenomenon of social exclusion which might be seen as a way of revisiting the debate on urban poverty. One view of social exclusion is that:

... structural processes affect the whole of society in a way which creates barriers which prevent particular groups from forming those kinds of social relationships with other groups which are essential to realising a full human potential. It is not that some groups 'exclude' other groups, but that processes affecting the whole of society mean that some groups experience social boundaries as barriers preventing their full participation in the economic, political and cultural life of the society within which they live.

(Allen, Cars and Madanipour, 1998, p.17)

While writing this book, the author was also working on a research project on social exclusion which involved visits to a council estate just one mile from the modern campus of the University of Warwick. One drove past a parade of partially shuttered shops and past a boarded up house into a road in which the between-the-wars council houses were barely adequate for modern living. The area was beset by problems of long-term unemployment and other indications of incipient social breakdown. There were community activists, and the city council was concerned about the problems they raised, but often lacked the resources to do anything effective about them. It was a long way from the world of Whitehall discussions between ministers and the Local Government Association.

Anyone concerned about empowerment or 'fuller participation by ... groups disadvantaged by societal change' (ibid. p.18) is unlikely to find answers in the pressure group literature, or at least not very comforting ones. Although class analysis is no longer popular, the pressure group world is inhabited largely by members of the middle class or at least the highly educated. As Schattschneider observed (1960, p.35), 'The flaw in the pluralist heaven is that the heavenly chorus sings with a strong upper-class accent' Perhaps the accent is estuarine English rather than upper class these days, but the voices are generally those of the included rather than the excluded.

It would, however, be unreasonable to blame the flaws of society or the deficiencies of democracy on pressure groups. They reflect and reinforce the existing distribution of power, rather than being the prime cause of it. For all their limitations as democratic organizations (which many of them do not claim to be), and taking account of the biases they reinforce in the political process, pressure groups do make a significant contribution to democracy. The extent and significance of that contribution can best be understood if we visualize a situation in which pressure groups were either banned or disregarded. Not only is the freedom to associate an important democratic principle, but pressure groups also offer an important mechanism through which the ruled can influence the rulers between elections. Most disinterested observers, for example, would regard the outcome of the Snowdrop campaign as a benign example of the electors successfully communicating the intensity of their concerns about an issue to decision makers.

Pressure groups are likely to remain at the heart of the political process in the opening decades of the twenty-first century. In particular, they are playing a key role in the emerging European polity whose final shape and form admittedly remains highly uncertain. What is disturbing is the extent to which this has developed as a rather elitist, technocratic project, driven by the interests of big business, in which the 'included' citizen is often marginalized while the 'excluded' citizen has no place at all.

New subnational forms of government as in Scotland may create forms of political debate which are closer to the citizen, but this is a limited consolation if the major decisions are being taken elsewhere. A complex, multi-level system of governance may actually be easier for established interests to manipulate. It is interesting that lobbying firms are already setting up branches in Edinburgh in anticipation of the establishment of the Parliament. There is understandable hope in Scotland that a modern and more consensual form of legislature is being created for the twenty-first century, and indeed devolution is at the heart of the Blairite project. Whether Holyrood will be accompanied by new forms of pressure group behaviour remains to be seen. In many respects, the Parliament is there to meet the aspirations of a new political class that has emerged in Scotland and one senses that the needs of the Scottish people can only truly be met by independence within the EU.

The conclusions of this volume on pressure groups are therefore somewhat more pessimistic than its predecessors, not so much because pressure groups have changed, but because the capacity of government to act on behalf of the least advantaged members of society appears to have been permanently weakened. Special interests have, if anything, become stronger but the more general interests once represented by political parties with a mass base have become weaker. As well as reinventing government, one may need to reinvent democracy.

Guide to Further Reading

Chapter 1

For a general survey of the social movement perspective, see Byrne (1997); for some criticisms of it, see Jordan (1998a). Jordan and Richardson (1987) have some interesting things to say about 'menus of definition'.

Chpter 2

The article by Maloney, Jordan and McLaughlin (1994) is a key critique of the insider-outsider typology. Dudley and Richardson (1998) raise some important issues about the 'new politics' and the continued validity of the insider-outsider typology. Ryan (1996) offers a good case study of an 'outsider' group.

Chapter 3

Sabatier (1993, 1998) makes a strong case for using 'belief systems' rather than 'interests' as the focus of an 'advocacy coalition' approach. Jordan (1990) reviews the pluralist case and Smith (1993) makes some telling criticisms. Olson's (1965) analysis remains a classic of the collective action literature. For the origins of the policy community model, return to Richardson and Jordan (1997). Important recent statements include Rhodes and Marsh (1992) and Marsh (1998), while an important critique is found in Dowding (1995). It is still worth returning to the work of Beer (1956, 1965, 1982), Finer (1958) and Eckstein (1960).

Chapter 4

Recent literature has emphasized the role of the 'core executive' at the heart of the policy-making process (Rhodes, 1995). Mitchell (1997) contains some interesting data on the perceptions of business associations and trade unions on the most effective ways of contacting the executive. Grant (1997) contains material on the intensification of food production which serves as useful background to the case study of the formation of the Food Standards Agency.

Chapter 5

There is a large and growing literature on this subject. The best places to start are Greenwood (1997) and Aspinwall and Greenwood (1998). Green Cowles (1997) is an excellent starting point for looking at business interests. On direct firm representation see Coen (1998). On trade unions it is still worth reading Visser and Ebinghaus (1992). For an analysis of the strengths of environmental groups see Mazey and Richardson (1992b).

Chapter 6

Coen (1997) conducted an interesting and innovative study of which channels of representation firms at the European level found most useful. Page (1997) contains some important material on the operations of the Commission. Hayes-Renshaw and Wallace (1997) have produced the most authoritative study of the Council of Ministers. Falkner (1998) has produced an important study of the functioning of social partnership.

Chapter 7

Anderson (1997) has provided a stimulating overview of the media and environmental issues. Solesbury's (1976) article is still worth reading for its insights on what happens once an issue starts being processed by the executive. Brass and Koziell (1997) have produced a sympathetic study of direct action. Some interesting case studies of particular uses of direct action are to be found in Griggs, Howarth and Jacobs (1998) and North (1998).

Chapter 8

Rush (1997) provides a useful overview of recent changes in the rules governing advocacy by Members of Parliament. Thomas (1983) and Garner (1993) discuss the difficulties of banning hunting through private members' legislation. Moloney (1996) provides a wide-ranging overview of role of paid lobbyists. Parry, Moyser and Day (1992) offer some useful data on participation at the local level.

Chapter 9

May, McHugh and Taylor (1998) is an important article for understanding recent developments in business representation. Tivey (1974) is still worth reading in terms of the difficulties of 'representing' consumers, and Young (1998) brings the story up to date. Horton (1997) offers an analysis of why football supporters may weaken their influence by defining themselves as consumers. Sinclair, Seifert and Ironside (1995) explore the weakening of teachers as a producer group. Giddens (1998) can be used to link some of the issues reviewed in the chapter to discussions of the Blair Government's 'Third Way'.

Chapter 10

Whiteley and Winyard (1987) have some interesting observations to make about pressure group effectiveness which are still relevant today. Jordan and Maloney (1997) present an innovative marketing perspective on pressure group activities. Bennett (1998) shows the limitations of business associations as a mechanism for implementing public policy in the British context compared with continental European countries.

Chapter 11

Richardson (1995) analyses the competition between pressure groups and political parties in terms of supply and demand factors. Webb (1995) reviews the question of whether British political parties are in decline. Secrett (1996) provides a statement of the case for pressure groups. Alternative models of democracy developed by Held (1996) provide a framework for analysing the role of pressure groups in contemporary politics.

References

Ainley, P. and Vickerstaff, S. (1994) 'Transitions from Corporatism: The Privatisation of Policy Failure', *Contemporary Record,* 7 (3) 541–56.

Allen, J., Cars, G. and Madanipour, A. (1998) 'Introduction' in A. Madanipour, G. Cars and J. Allen (eds), *Social Exclusion in European Cities* (London: Jessica Kingsley).

Amery, L.S. (1947) *Thoughts on the Constitution* (Oxford: Oxford University Press).

Anderson, A. (1997) *Media, Culture and the Environment* (London: UCL Press).

Arp, H.A. (1993) 'Technical Regulation and Politics: the Interplay between Economic Interests and Environmental Policy Goals in EC Car Emission Legislation' in J.D. Liefferink, P.D. Lowe and A.P.J. Nol (eds), *European Integration and Environmental Policy* (London: Belhaven).

Aspinwall, M. (1998) 'Collective Attraction – the New Political Game in Brussels', in J. Greenwood and M. Aspinwall (eds), *Collective Action in the European Union* (London: Routledge).

Aspinwall, M. and Greenwood, J. (1998) 'Conceptualising Collective Action in the European Union: an Introduction' in J.Greenwood and M.Aspinwall (eds), *Collective Action in the European Union* (London: Routledge).

Atkinson, M.M. and Coleman, W.D. (1985) 'Corporatism and Industrial Policy' in A. Cawson (ed.), *Organized Interests and the State* (London: Sage).

Baggott, R. (1995a) 'From Confrontation to Consultation: Pressure Group Relations from Thatcher to Major', *Parliamentary Affairs,* 48, 484–502.

Baggott, R. (1995b) *Pressure Groups Today* (Manchester: Manchester University Press).

Baldwin, N. (1990) 'The House of Lords' in M. Rush (ed.), *Parliament and Pressure Politics* (Oxford: Clarendon Press).

Barr, G. (1992) 'The Anti-Poll Tax Movement: an Insider's View of an Outsider Group', *Talking Politics,* 4 (3) 143–7.

Beer, S. (1956) 'Pressure Groups and Parties in Britain', *American Political Science Review,* 50 (1), 1–23.

Beer, S. (1965) *Modern British Politics* (London: Faber and Faber).

Beer, S. (1982) *Britain Against Itself* (London: Faber and Faber).

Bennett, R.J. (1997) 'The Impact of European Economic Integration on Business Associations: the UK Case', *West European Politics,* 20, 61–90.

Bennett, R.J. (1998) 'Business Associations and their Potential to Contribute to Economic Development: Reexploring an Interface between the State and Market' *Environment and Planning* A, 30, 1367–87.

Boléat, M. (1996) *Trade Association Strategy and Management* (London: Association of British Insurers).

231

Bomberg, E. (1998) *Green Parties and Politics in the European Union* (London: Routledge).

Bose, A. (1991) 'Aid and the Business Lobby' in A. Bose and P. Burnell (eds), *Overseas Aid since 1979* (Manchester: Manchester University Press).

Brass, E. and Koziell, S.P. (1997) *Gathering Force* (London: the Big Issue Writers).

Brittan, S. (1964) *Steering the Economy* (Harmondsworth: Penguin).

Brittan, S. (1975) 'The Economic Contradictions of Democracy', *British Journal of Political Science*, 5, 129–59.

Brittan, S. (1987a) '"The Economic Contradictions of Democracy" Revisited', *Political Quarterly*, 60 (2) 190–203.

Brittan, S. (1987b) *The Role and Limits of Government* (Aldershot: Wildwood House).

Brittan, S. (1989) 'The Thatcher Government's Economic Policy', Esmée Fairbairn Lecture, University of Lancaster Economics Department.

Brooke, R. (1989) *Managing the Enabling Authority* (Harlow: Longman).

Browning, A. (1997) 'Opening Address' in B.J. Marshall and F.A.Miller (eds), *Management of Regulation in the Food Chain - Balancing Costs, Benefits and Effects* (Reading: Centre for Agricultural Strategy).

Bruce-Gardyne, J. (1986) *Ministers and Mandarins* (London: Sidgwick and Jackson).

Buksti, J.A. and Johansen, L.N. (1979) 'Variations in Organizational Participation in Government: the Case of Denmark', *Scandinavian Political Studies*, 2 (new series) (3) 197–220.

Burnell, P. (1997) *Foreign Aid in a Changing World* (Buckingham: Open University Press).

Burson-Marsteller (1991) 'Lobbying the EC. The Views of the Policy-Makers', Brussels: Burson-Marsteller.

Butler, D. A. Adonis and T. Travers (1994) *Failure in British Government: the Politics of the Poll Tax* (Oxford: Oxford University Press).

Byrne, P. (1997) *Social Movements in Britain* (London: Routledge)

Caldwell, N. and Morgan, C. (1997) *Lessons from the Sea Empress* (Cardiff: Institute of Welsh Affairs).

Campbell, J.I.Jr (1993) 'Couriers and the European Postal Monopolies' in R.H.Pedler and M.P.C.M. van Schendelen (eds), *Lobbying the European Union* (Aldershot: Dartmouth).

Cawson, A. (1997) 'Big Firms as Political Actors: Corporate Power and the Governance of the European Consumer Electronics Industry' in H.Wallace and A.R.Young (eds), *Participation and Policy-Making in the European Union* (Oxford: Clarendon).

Christiansen, L. and Dowding, K. (1994) 'Pluralism or State Autonomy? The Case of Amnesty International (British Section): the Insider/Outsider Group', *Political Studies*, 42 (1) 15-24.

Churchill, W. (1930) 'Parliamentary Government and the Economic Problem', Romanes Lecture, Oxford.

Cm.3830 (1998) *The Food Standards Agency: a Force for Change* (London: HMSO).

Coates, David (1972) *Teachers Unions and Interest Group Politics* (London: Cambridge University Press).

Coates, Dudley (1984) 'Food Law: Brussels, Whitehall and Town Hall' in D. Lewis and H. Wallace (eds), *Policies into Practice* (London: Heinemann).

Coen, D. (1997) 'The Evolution of the Large Firm as a Political Actor in the European Union', *Journal of European Public Policy*, 4, 91–108.

Coen, D. (1998) 'The European Business Interest and the Nation State'. Large-firm Lobbying in the European Union and the Member States', *Journal of Public Policy*, 18, 75–100.

Coffin, C. (1987) *Working with Whitehall* (London: Confederation of British Industry).

Collins, K. and Burns, C. (1998) 'Co-Decision and the Democratic Deficit' in European Parliamentary Labour Party, *A Democratic Europe* (London: EPLP).

Compass Partnership (1998) *Core Competences for the Senior Managers of Trade Associations* (London: Trade Association Forum).

Cram, L. (1998) 'The EU Institutions and Collective Action: Constructing a European Interest' in J. Greenwood and M. Aspinwall (eds), *Collective Action in the European Union* (London: Routledge).

Crouch, C. and Streeck, W. (1997) 'Introduction: the Future of Capitalist Diversity' in C. Crouch and W. Streeck (eds), *Political Economy of Modern Capitalism* (London: Sage).

Curtice, J. and Steed, M. (1997) 'The Results Analysed' in D. Butler and D. Kavanagh (principal authors), *The British General Election of 1997* (London: Macmillan).

Daugbjerg, C. (1998a) *Policy Networks under Pressure* (Aldershot: Ashgate).

Daugbjerg, C. (1998b) 'Similar Problems, Different Policies: Policy Networks and Environmental Policy in Danish and Swedish Agriculture', in D. Marsh (ed.), *Comparing Policy Networks*, (Buckingham: Open University Press).

Daugbjerg, C. and Marsh, D. (1998) 'Explaining Policy Outcomes: Integrating the Policy Network Approach with Macro-Level and Micro-Level Analysis' in D.Marsh (ed.), *Comparing Policy Networks*, (Buckingham: Open University Press).

Davies, M. (1985) *Politics of Pressure* (London: BBC Publications).

Day, M. (1998) *Environmental Action: a Citizen's Guide* (London: Pluto Press).

Devlin Commission (1972) *Report of the Commission of Inquiry into Industrial and Commercial Representation* (London: Association of British Chambers of Commerce/Confederation of British Industry).

Dowding, K. (1994) 'Rational Mobilisation' in P. Dunleavy and J. Stanyer (eds), *Contemporary Political Studies, Volume 1* (Belfast: Political Studies Association).

Dowding, K. (1995) 'Model or Metaphor? A Critical Review of the Policy Network Approach', *Political Studies*, 43, 136–58.

Dowse, R.E. and Hughes, J. (1977) 'Sporadic Interventionists', *Political Studies*, 25 (1) 84–92.

Dryzek, J.S. (1998) 'Strategies of Ecological Democratization' in W.M. Lafferty and J. Meadowcroft (eds), *Democracy and the Environment: Problems and Prospects* (Cheltenham: Edward Elgar).

Dudley, G. (1983) 'The Road Lobby: a Declining Force' in D. Marsh (ed.), *Pressure Politics* (London: Junction Books).

Dudley, G. and Richardson, J. (1998) 'Arenas without Rules and the Policy Change Process: Outsider Groups and British Roads Policy', *Political Studies*, 46,727–47.

Dunleavy, P. (1988) 'Group Identities and Individual Influence: Reconstructing the Theory of Interest Groups', *British Journal of Political Science*, 18 (1), 21–49.

Dunleavy, P. (1991) *Democracy, Bureaucracy and Public Choice* (Hemel Hempstead: Harvester Wheatsheaf).

Eberlie, R. (1993) 'The Confederation of British Industry and Policy-Making in the

European Community' in Mazey, S. and Richardson, J. (eds), *Lobbying in the European Community* (Oxford: Oxford University Press).

Eckstein, H. (1960) *Pressure Group Politics: The Case of the British Medical Association* (London: Allen and Unwin).

Eden, S. (1996) *Environmental Issues and Business* (Chichester: John Wiley.

Edwards, R. (1988) 'Spirit of Outrage' *New Statesman and Society* 29 July, 16 and 18.

Elbaum, B. and Lazonick, W. (eds) (1986) *The Decline of the British Economy* (Oxford: Clarendon Press).

Elliott, B., Bechhofer, F., McCrone, D. and Black, S. (1982) 'Bourgeois Social Movements in Britain: Repertoires and Responses', *Sociological Review,* 30 (1) 71–94.

Everitt, R. (1991) *Battle for the Valley* (London: Voice of the Valley).

Everitt, R. (1997) 'Charlton Fans Take Their Marx', *Greenwich Mercury*, 4 September 1997.

Falkner, G. (1998) *EU Social Policy in the 1990s* (London: Routledge).

Field, F. (1982) *Poverty and Politics* (London: Heinemann).

Finer, S.E. (1958) *Anonymous Empire* (London: Pall Mall).

Fischler, F. (1998) 'Keynote Address', Agra Europe conference on the reform of the Common Agricultural Policy, Sheraton Hotel, Brussels.

Fisher, C. (1994) 'The Lobby to Stop Testing Cosmetics on Animals' in R.H.Pedler and M.P.C.M. van Schendelen (eds), *Lobbying the European Union* (Aldershot: Dartmouth).

Franklin, M. (1994) 'Food Policy Formation in the UK/EC' in S. Henson and S. Gregory (eds), *The Politics of Food* (Reading: Department of Agricultural Economics and Management, University of Reading).

Gardner, B. (1996) *European Agriculture* (London: Routledge).

Gardner, J.N. (1991) *Effective Lobbying in the European Community* (Deventer: Kluwer).

Garner, R. (1993) *Animals, Politics and Morality* (Manchester: Manchester University Press).

Garner, R. (1996) *Environmental Politics* (Hemel Hempstead: Harvester Wheatsheaf).

Garner, R. (1998) *Political Animals: Animal Protection Policies in Britain and the United States* (London: Macmillan).

Giddens, A. (1998) *The Third Way* (Cambridge: Polity).

Gilmour, I. (1978) *Inside Right* (London: Quartet).

Gilmour, I. (1983) *Britain Can Work* (Oxford: Martin Robertson).

Grant, W. (1977) *Independent Local Politics in England and Wales* (Farnborough: Saxon House).

Grant, W. (1978) 'Insider Groups, Outsider Groups and Interest Group Strategies in Britain', University of Warwick Department of Politics Working Paper No. 19.

Grant, W. (1993a) *Business and Politics in Britain,* 2nd edn (London: Macmillan).

Grant, W. (1993b) *The Politics of Economic Policy* (Hemel Hempstead: Harvester Wheatsheaf).

Grant, W. (1995a) *Pressure Groups, Politics and Democracy in Britain* (Hemel Hempstead: Harvester Wheatsheaf).

Grant, W. (1995b) *Autos, Smog and Pollution Control* (Aldershot: Edward Elgar).

Grant, W. (1996) 'Direct Democracy in California: Example or Warning'?, *Democratization*, 3, 133–49.

Grant, W. (1997) 'BSE and the Politics of Food', in P. Dunleavy, A. Gamble, I.

Holliday and G. Peele (eds), *Developments in British Politics 5* (London: Macmillan).

Grant, W. and Marsh, D. (1977) *The CBI* (London: Hodder and Stoughton).

Grant, W., Nekkers, J. and van Waarden, F. (eds) (1991) *Organizing Business for War* (Oxford: Berg).

Grant, W., Paterson, W.E. and Whitston, C. (1988) *Government and the Chemical Industry* (Oxford: Clarendon Press).

Grant, W. and Streeck, W. (1985) 'Large Firms and the Representation of Business Interests in the UK and West German Construction Industry' in A. Cawson (ed.), *Organized Interests and the State* (London: Sage).

Grantham, C. and Seymour-Ure, C. (eds) 'Political Consultants' in M. Rush (ed.), *Parliament and Pressure Politics* (Oxford: Clarendon Press).

Graziano, G. (1998) 'Lobbying and Interest Representation in Brussels', paper presented at the 1998 Annual Meeting of the American Political Science Association, Boston.

Green, M.L. (1993) 'The Politics of Big Business in the Single Market Program', paper presented for the European Community Studies Association conference, Washington DC.

Green Cowles, M. (1995) 'Setting the Agenda for a New Europe: The ERT and EC 1992', *Journal of Common Market Studies*, 33, 501–26.

Green Cowles, M. (1996) 'The EU Committee of AmCham: the Powerful Voice of American Firms in Brussels', *Journal of European Public Policy*, 3, 339–58.

Green Cowles, M. (1997) 'Organizing Industrial Coalitions: a Challenge for the Future?', in H.Wallace and A.R.Young (eds), *Participation and Policy-Making in the European Union* (Oxford: Clarendon).

Green Cowles, M. (1998) 'The Changing Architecture of Big Business' in J.Greenwood and M.Aspinwall (eds), *Collective Action in the European Union* (London: Routledge).

Greenwood, J. (1997) *Representing Interests in the European Union* (London: Macmillan).

Greenwood, J., Grote, J.R., and Ronit, K. (1992) 'Introduction: Organized Interests and the Transnational Dimension' in J. Greenwood, J. R. Grote and K. Ronit (eds), *Organized Interests and the European Community* (London: Sage).

Greenwood, J. and Jordan, G. (1993) 'The United Kingdom: a Changing Kaleidoscope' in M.P.C.M. van Schendelen (ed.), *National Public and Private EC Lobbying* (Aldershot: Dartmouth).

Griggs, S., Howarth, D. and Jacobs, B. (1998) 'Second Runway at Manchester', *Parliamentary Affairs*, 51, 358–69.

Gronbech, E.M. (1998) 'The Emergence of Professional Lobbyists in Britain', M.Litt in Politics thesis, University of Oxford.

Grote, J.R. (1992) 'Small Firms in the European Community: Modes of Production, Governance and Territorial Interest Representation in Italy and Germany', in J.Greenwood, J.R.Grote and K.Ronit (eds), *Organized Interests and the European Community* (London: Sage).

Hall, P. (1986) *Governing the Economy* (Cambridge: Polity Press).

Hall, P. (1989) 'Conclusion: the Politics of Keynesian Ideas' in P.Hall (ed.), *The Political Power of Economic Ideas* (Princeton: Princeton University Press).

Hall, P. (1998) 'Social Capital in Britain', paper presented to the Annual Meeting of the American Political Science Association, Boston.

Hayes-Renshaw, F. and Wallace, H. (1997) *The Council of Ministers* (London:

Macmillan).

Held, D. (1996) *Models of Democracy,* 2nd edn (Cambridge: Polity).

Heller, A. and Féher, F. (1988) *The Postmodern Political Condition* (Cambridge: Polity).

Hirsch, F. (1977) *Social Limits to Growth* (London: Routledge and Kegan Paul).

Hodge, M. (1998) 'Fewer Teachers, Please, Not More', *New Statesman,* 22 May 1998, 10–11.

Holbeche, B. (1986) 'Policy and Influence: MAFF and the NFU', *Public Policy and Administration* 1, 40–7.

Horton, E. (1997) *Moving the Goalposts: Football's Exploitation* (Edinburgh: Mainstream).

House of Commons (1985) *First Report from the Select Committee on Members' Interests, 1984/85* (London: HMSO).

Hull, R. (1993) 'Lobbying Brussels: a View from Within' in S. Mazey and J. Richardson (eds), *Lobbying in the European Community* (Oxford: Oxford University Press).

James, P. (1997) 'Food Standards Agency: an Interim Proposal', typescript.

Jordan, A.G. and Richardson, J. (1987) *Government and Pressure Groups in Britain* (Oxford: Clarendon Press).

Jordan, G. (1990) 'The Pluralism of Pluralism: an Anti-theory?', *Political Studies* 38 (2) pp. 286–301.

Jordan, G. (1994) 'Why Bumble Bees Fly: Accounting for Public Interest Participation', paper presented at ECPR Joint Sessions, Madrid.

Jordan, G. (1998a) 'Politics without Parties', *Parliamentary Affairs,* 51, 314–28.

Jordan, G. (1998b) 'Indirect Causes and Effects in Policy Change: Shell, Greenpeace and the Brent Spar', paper presented at the Annual Meeting of the American Political Science Association, Boston.

Jordan, G. and Maloney, W. (1997) *The Protest Business?* (Manchester: Manchester University Press).

Jordan, G., Maloney A., and McLaughlin, A. (1992a) 'Insiders, Outsiders and Political Access', British Interest Group Project Working Paper No.3, University of Aberdeen.

Jordan, G., Maloney A., and McLaughlin, A. (1992b) 'Policy-Making in Agriculture: "Primary" Policy Community or Specialist Policy Communities', British Interest Group Project Working Paper No.5, University of Aberdeen.

Jordan, G., Maloney A., and McLaughlin, A. (1994a) 'Collective Action and the Public Interest Problem: Drawing a Line Under Olson' in P. Dunleavy and J. Stanyer (eds),*Contemporary Political Studies, Volume Two,* (Belfast: Political Studies Association).

Jordan, G., Maloney A., and McLaughlin, A. (1994b), 'Interest Groups: a Marketing Perspective on Membership' in P. Dunleavy and J. Stanyer (eds), *Contemporary Political Studies, Volume Two* (Belfast: Political Studies Association).

Jordan, G. and Richardson, J. (1987) *Government and Pressure Groups in Britain* (Oxford: Clarendon Press).

Judge, D. (1990a) 'Parliament and Interest Representation' in M. Rush (ed.), *Parliament and Pressure Politics* (Oxford: Clarendon Press).

Judge, D. (1990b) *Parliament and Industry* (Aldershot: Dartmouth).

Keynes, J.M. (1936) *The General Theory of Employment, Interest and Money* (London: Macmillan).

King, R. and Nugent, N. (1979) *Respectable Rebels: Middle Class Campaigns in Britain in the 1970s* (London: Hodder and Stoughton).

Kingdon, J.W. (1984) *Agendas, Alternatives and Public Policies* (New York: Harper-Collins).

Klandermans, B. (1997) *The Social Psychology of Protest* (Oxford: Blackwell).

Kogan, M. (1975) *Educational Policy-Making: a Study of Interest Groups and Parliament* (London: George Allen and Unwin).

Kohler-Koch, B. (1993) 'Germany: Fragmented but Strong Lobbying' in M.P.C.M. van Schendelen (ed.), *National Public and Private EC Lobbying* (Aldershot: Dartmouth).

Kohler-Koch, B. (1994) 'Changing Patterns of Interest Intermediation in the European Union', *Government and Opposition,* 29, 166–80.

Lang, T., Millstone E., Raven, H. and Rayner, M. (1996) *Modernising UK Food Policy: The Case for Reforming the Ministry of Agriculture, Fisheries and Food* (Thames Valley University: Centre for Food Policy).

Lawson, N. (1992) *The View From No.11: Memoirs of a Tory Radical* (London: Bantam).

Lawson, T. (1997) 'Adapting to Cyberspace – Who's Wired?', *Ecos,* 18 (3/4), 69–71.

Lindblom, C.E. (1977) *Politics and Markets* (New York: Basic Books).

Lively, J. (1975) *Democracy* (Oxford: Basil Blackwell).

Lowe, P. and Goyder, J. (1983) *Environmental Groups in Politics* (London: Allen and Unwin).

Lowe, P. and Ward, G. (1998) 'The Europeanisation of British Environmental Policy and Politics', Global Environmental Change Programme Briefings, No.20, June.

Lynn, L.H. and McKeown, T.J. (1988) *Organizing Business: Trade Associations in America and Japan* (Washington, DC: American Enterprise Institute).

McLaughlin, A. and Jordan, G. (1993) 'The Rationality of Lobbying in Europe: Why are Euro-Groups So Numerous and So Weak? Some Evidence from the Car Industry' in S. Mazey and J. Richardson (eds), *Lobbying in the European Community* (Oxford: Oxford University Press).

McLaughlin, A., Jordan, G. and Maloney, W.A. (1993) 'Corporate Lobbying in the European Community', *Journal of Common Market Studies,* 31, 191–212.

Maddox, B. (1994) 'Lobby groups left to carry the Green banner', *Financial Times,* 5–6 March 1994, p. 8.

Maloney, W. and Jordan, G. (1998) 'Group–Party Relations in Britain', paper presented at the Annual Meeting of the American Political Science Association, Boston.

Maloney, W., Jordan, G. and McLaughlin, A. (1994) 'Interest Groups and Public Policy: the Insider/Outsider Model Revisited', *Journal of Public Policy,* 14, 17–38.

Marsden, T. and Flynn, A. (1997) 'Constructing the Consumer Interest: Retailing, Regulation and Food Quality', ESRC End of Award Report L2095203101.

Marsh, D. (1998a) 'The Utility and Future of Policy Network Analysis', in D.Marsh (ed.), *Comparing Policy Networks* (Buckingham: Open University Press).

Marsh, D. (1998b) 'The Development of the Policy Network Approach', in D. Marsh (ed.), *Comparing Policy Networks* (Buckingham: Open University Press).

Marsh, D. and Chambers, J. (1981) *Abortion Politics* (London: Junction Books).

238   *References*

Marsh, D. and Read, M. (1988) *Private Members Bills* (London: Cambridge University Press).

Marsh, J.S. (1997) 'Making and Enforcing Food Chain Regulations – the Factors that Determine When, by Whom and How', in B.J. Marshall and F.A. Miller (eds), *Management of Regulation in the Food Chain - Balancing Costs, Benefits and Effects* (Reading: Centre for Agricultural Strategy).

May, T., McHugh, J. and Taylor, T. (1998) 'Business Representation in the UK since 1979: the Case of Trade Associations', *Political Studies*, 46, 260–75.

May, T. and Nugent, N. (1982) 'Insiders, Outsiders and Thresholders: Corporatism and Pressure Group Strategies in Britain', paper presented at Political Studies Association conference, University of Kent.

Mazey, S. (1998) 'The European Union and Women's Rights: from the Europeanization of national agendas to the nationalization of a European agenda?' *Journal of European Public Policy*, 5, 131–52.

Mazey, S. and Mitchell, J. (1993) 'Europe of the Regions? Territorial Interests and European Integration: the Scottish Experience' in S. Mazey and J. Richardson (eds), *Lobbying in the European Community* (Oxford: Oxford University Press).

Mazey, S. and Richardson, J. (1992a) 'British Pressure Groups in the European Community' *Parliamentary Affairs*, 45, 92–127.

Mazey, S. and Richardson, J. (1992b) 'Environmental Groups and the EC: Challenges and Opportunities *Environmental Politics*, 4, 109–28.

Mazey, S. and Richardson, J. (1993a) 'Introduction' in *Lobbying in the European Community*, S. Mazey and J. Richardson (eds), (Oxford: Oxford University Press).

Mazey, S. and Richardson, J. (1993b) 'Conclusion: a European Policy Style?' in S. Mazey and J. Richardson (eds), *Lobbying in the European Community*, (Oxford: Oxford University Press).

Mazey, S. and Richardson, J. (1993c) 'EC Policy Making: an Emerging Policy Style?' in J.D. Liefferink, P.D. Lowe and A.P.J. Mol (eds), *European Integration and Environmental Policy* (London: Belhaven).

Meat and Livestock Commission (1997) 'The Debate on the Need for New Thinking on How to Develop Control and Regulate Food Policy in the UK', typescript discussion paper.

Medhurst, K. and Moyser, G. (1988) *Church and Politics in a Secular Age* (Oxford: Clarendon Press).

Miller, C. (1990) *Lobbying* (Oxford: Basil Blackwell).

Mitchell, N.J. (1987) 'Changing Pressure-Group Politics: the Case of the Trades Union Congress, 1976/84', *British Journal of Political Science*, 17, 509–17.

Mitchell, N.J. (1997) *The Conspicuous Corporation* (Ann Arbor: University of Michigan Press).

Moe, T.M. (1980) *The Organization of Interests* (Chicago: Chicago University Press).

Moloney, K. (1996) *Lobbyists for Hire* (Aldershot: Dartmouth).

Moran, M. (1983) 'Power, Policy and the City of London, Capital and Politics' in R. King (ed.), *Capital and Politics* (London: Routledge and Kegan Paul).

Mulfinger, A. (1997) 'The European Commission's View' in R.J.Bennett (ed.), *Trade Associations in Britain and Germany: Responding to Internationalisation and the EU* (London: Anglo-German Foundation).

National Consumer Council (1997) *Government and Consumers* (London: National Consumer Council).

Nettl, J.P. (1965) 'Consensus or Elite Domination: the Case of Business', *'Political*

References 239

Studies, 8, 22–44.

Newby, H., Bell, C., Rose, D. and Saunders, P. (1978) *Property, Paternalism and Power: Class and Control in Rural England* (London: Hutchinson).

Newell, P. and Grant, W. (1998) 'Environmental NGOs and EU Environmental Law', paper presented at the conference on 'Flexible Environmental Regulation and the Internal Market', University of Warwick.

Newton, K. (1976) *Second City Politics* (Oxford: Oxford University Press).

North, P. (1998) '"Save our Solsbury!"': The Anatomy of an Anti-Roads Protest', *Environmental Politics*, 7, 1-25.

Norton, P. (1990) 'Public Legislation' in M. Rush (ed.) *Parliament and Pressure Politics* (Oxford: Clarendon Press).

O'Neill, M. (1995) 'How Shell Poured Oil on the Troubled Waters of Greenpeace', *European Brief*, 2 (8), 82–4.

Offe, C. and Wiesenthal, H. (1985) 'Two Logics of Collective Action' in C. Offe (principal author), *Disorganised Capitalism* (Cambridge: Cambridge University Press).

Olson, M. (1965) *The Logic of Collective Action* (Cambridge, Mass.: Harvard University Press).

Olson, M. (1982) *The Rise and Decline of Nations* (New Haven: Yale University Press).

Page, E.C. (1997) *People Who Run Europe* (Oxford: Clarendon).

Page, E.C. (1998) 'Consultation on Public Policy: Who is Left Out?' unpublished paper.

Parminter, K. (1996) 'Working For and Against Government' in Social Market Foundation (ed.), *Pressure Group Politics in Modern Britain* (London: Social Market Foundation).

Parry, G., Moyser, G. and Day, N. (1992) *Political Participation and Democracy in Britain* (Cambridge: Cambridge University Press).

Phillips, P.W.B. (1990) *Wheat, Europe and the GATT* (London: Pinter).

Pijnenburg, B. (1998) 'EU Lobbying by Ad Hoc Coalitions: an Exploratory Case Study', *Journal of European Public Policy*, 5, 303–21.

Plowden, W. (1985) 'The Culture of Whitehall' in D. Englefield (ed.), *Understanding the Civil Service* (Harlow: Longman).

Plowden, W. (1994) *Ministers and Mandarins* (London: Institute for Public Policy Research).

Pollack, M.A. (1997) 'Representing Diffuse Interests in EC Policy- Making', *Journal of European Public Policy*, 4, 572–90.

Porritt, J. and Winner, D. (1988) *The Coming of the Greens* (London: Fontana).

Porter, M. (1998) 'Intergroups and Interest Representation in the EP' ELIR (newsletter of the ECPR Standing Group on European Level Interest Representation), 4 (1), pp. 4-5.

Pratt, H.J. (1993) *Gray Agendas: Interest Groups and Public Pensions in Canada, Britain, and the United States* (Ann Arbor: University of Michigan Press).

Presthus, R. (1964) *Men at the Top* (New York: Oxford University Press.

Presthus, R. (1973) *Elite Accommodation in Canadian Politics* (London: Cambridge University Press).

Presthus, R. (1974) *Elites in the Policy Process* (London: Cambridge University Press).

Pretty, J. (1998) *The Living Land* (London: Earthscan).

Pross, A.P, (1986) *Group Politics and Public Policy* New York: (Oxford University

240   *References*

Press).

Public Policy Consultants (1987) 'The Government Report' (London: Public Policy Consultants).

Rallings, C., Temple, M. and Thrasher, M. (1994) *Community Identity and Participation in Local Democracy* (London: Commission for Local Democracy).

Rhodes, R.A.W. (1986) *The National World of Local Government* (London: Allen and Unwin).

Rhodes, R.A.W. and Marsh, D. (1992) 'Policy Networks in British Politics: a Critique of Existing Approaches' in D. Marsh and R.A.W. Rhodes (eds), *Policy Networks in British Government* (Oxford: Clarendon Press).

Rhodes, R. A. W. (1995) 'From Prime Ministerial Power to Core Executive', in R. A. W. Rhodes and P. Dunleavy (eds), *Prime Minister, Cabinet and Core Executive* (London: McMillan).

Richardson, J. (1993) 'Interest Group Behaviour in Britain: Continuity and Change' in J. Richardson (ed.), *Pressure Groups* (Oxford: Oxford University Press).

Richardson, J. (1995) 'The Market for Political Activism: Interest Groups as a Challenge to Political Parties', *West European Politics,* 18, 116–39.

Richardson, J. (1998) 'The EU as an Alternative Venue for Interest Groups', paper presented at the Annual Meeting of the American Political Science Association, Boston.

Richardson, J. and Jordan, G. (1979) *Governing under Pressure* (Oxford: Martin Robertson).

Richardson, K. (1997) 'Introductory Foreword', in H.Wallace and A.R. Young (eds), *Participation and Policy-Making in the European Union* (Oxford: Clarendon).

Riddell, P. (1993) *Honest Opportunism: the Rise of the Career Politician* (London: Hamish Hamilton).

Riddell, P. (1996) 'Introduction: Pressure Groups, Media and Government' in Social Market Foundation (ed.) *Pressure Group Politics in Modern Britain* (London, Social Market Foundation).

Roberts, E. (1966) *Consumers* (London: C.A. Watts).

Robinson, M. (1991) 'An Uncertain Partnership: the Overseas Development Administration and the Voluntary Sector in the 1980s' in A. Bose and P. Burnell (eds), *Britain's Overseas Aid since 1979* (Manchester: Manchester University Press).

Robinson, M. (1992) *The Greening of British Party Politics* (Manchester: Manchester University Press).

Robinson, N. (1998) 'Major Government, Minor Change: the Politics of Transport 1990–97', Ph.D. thesis, University of Warwick.

Rose, R. (1974) *Politics in England Today* (London: Faber and Faber).

Royal Institute of Public Administration Report (1986), newsletter of the Royal Institute of Public Administration, Vol.7, No.4.

Rucht, D. (1993) '"Think Globally, Act Locally?" Needs, Forms and Problems of Cross-National Cooperation among Environmental Groups' in J.D. Liefferink, P. D. Lowe and A.P.J. Mol (eds), *European Integration and Environmental Policy* (London: Belhaven).

Rush, M. (1990) 'Select Committees' in M. Rush (ed.), *Parliament and Pressure Politics* (Oxford: Clarendon).

Rush, M. (1997) 'Damming the Sleaze: The New Code of Conduct and the Outside Interests of MPs in the British House of Commons', *Journal of Legislative Studies,* 3, 10–28.

Ryan, M. (1996) *Lobbying from Below* (London: UCL Press).

Sabatier, P.A. (1993) 'Policy Change over a Decade or More' in P.A.C. Sabatier and H.C. Jenkins-Smith (eds), *Policy Change and Learning: an Advocacy Coalition Approach* (Boulder: Westview).

Sabatier, P.A. (1998) 'The Advocacy Coalition Framework: Revisions and Relevance for Europe', *Journal of European Public Policy*, 5, 98–130.

Salisbury, R.H. (1984) 'Interest Representation: the Dominance of Institutions', *American Political Science Review*, 78, 64–76.

Sargent, J. A. (1993) 'The Corporate Benefits of Lobbying: the British Case and its Relevance to the European Community' in S. Mazey and J. Richardson (eds), *Lobbying in the European Community* (Oxford: Oxford University Press).

Schattschneider, E.E. (1960) *The Semisovereign People* (New York: Holt, Rinehart and Winston).

Schmitter, P.C. and Grote, J.R. (1997) 'The Corporatist Sisyphus: Past, Present and Future', EUI Working Papers 97/4, European University Institute, Florence.

Schmitter, P.C. and Streeck, W. (1981) 'The Organisation of Business Interests: a Research Design to Study the Associative Action of Business in the Advanced Industrial Societies of Western Europe', International Institute of Management labour market policy discussion paper.

Secrett, C. (1996) 'Why Society Needs Pressure Groups' in Social Market Foundation (ed.), *Pressure Group Politics in Modern Britain* (London: Social Market Foundation).

Self, P. and Storing, H.J. (1962) *The State and the Farmer* (London: Allen and Unwin).

Seyd, P. and Whiteley, P. (1992) *Labour's Grass Roots: the Politics of Party Membership* (Oxford: Clarendon Press).

Sinclair, J., Seifert, R. and Ironside, M. (1995) 'Market-driven Reforms in Education: Performance, Quality and Industrial Relations in Schools' in S. Kirkpatrick and M.M. Lucio (eds), *The Politics of Quality in the Public Sector* (London: Routledge).

Skjaerseth, J.B. (1994) 'The Climate Policy of the EC: Too Hot to Handle?', *Journal of Common Market Studies*, 32, 25–45.

Smith, M.J. (1988) 'Consumers and British Agricultural Policy: a Case of Long-Term Exclusion', Essex Papers in Politics and Government No. 48, Department of Government, University of Essex.

Smith, M.J. (1990a) 'Pluralism, Reformed Pluralism and Neo-Pluralism: The Role of Pressure Groups in Policy-Making' *Political Studies,* 38, 302–22.

Smith, M.J. (1990b) *The Politics of Agricultural Support in Britain* (Aldershot: Dartmouth).

Smith, M.J. (1991) 'From Policy Community to Issue Network: Salmonella in Eggs and the New Politics of Food', *Public Administration,* 69, 235–55.

Smith, M.J. (1993) *Pressure, Power and Policy* (Hemel Hempstead: Harvester Wheatsheaf).

Solesbury, W. (1976) 'The Environmental Agenda', *Public Administration*, 54, 379–97.

Somsen, H. (1994) 'State Discretion in European Community Environmental Law: The Case of the Bathing Water Directive', State Autonomy in the European Community research seminar, Christ Church, Oxford.

Souza, C. (1998) *So You Want To Be a Lobbyist?* (London: Politico's).

Spence, D. (1993) 'The Role of the National Civil Service in European Lobbying:

242   *References*

the British Case' in S. Mazey and J. Richardson (eds), *Lobbying in the European Community* (Oxford: Oxford University Press).

Stedward, G. (1987) 'Entry to the System: a Case Study of Women's Aid in Scotland' in A.G. Jordan and J. Richardson (principal authors), *Government and Pressure Groups in Britain* (Oxford: Clarendon Press).

Stewart, J.D. (1958) *British Pressure Groups* (Oxford: Oxford University Press).

Stewart, M. (1984) 'Talking to Local Business: the Involvement of Chambers of Commerce in Local Affairs', Working Paper No. 38, School for Advanced Urban Studies, University of Bristol.

Stocker, T. (1983) 'Pressures on Policy Formation' in J. Burns, J. McInerney and A. Swinbank (eds), *The Food Industry: Economics and Politics* (London: Heinemann).

Stoker, G. (1991) *The Politics of Local Government* 2nd edn (London: Macmillan).

Stone, D. (1996) *Capturing the Political Imagination: Think Tanks and the Policy Process* (London: Frank Cass).

Streeck, W. (1983) 'Beyond Pluralism and Corporatism: German Business Associations and the State', *Journal of Public Policy*, 3, 265–84.

Streeck, W. and Schmitter, P.C. (1991) 'From National Corporatism to Transnational Pluralism: Organized Interests in the Single European Market', *Politics and Society*, 19, 133–65.

Stringer, J. and Richardson, J. (1982) 'Policy Stability and Policy Change: Industrial Training 1964/82', *Public Administration Bulletin* no.39, 22–39.

Taylor, E. (1979) *The House of Commons at Work*, 9th edn (London: Macmillan).

Thairs, E. (1998) 'Business Lobbying on the Environment: the Perspective of the Water Sector' in P. Lowe and S. Ward (eds), *British Environmental Policy in Europe* (London: Routledge).

Theakston, K. (1987) *Junior Ministers in British Government* (Oxford: Basil Blackwell).

Thomas, R.H. (1983) *The Politics of Hunting* (Aldershot: Gower).

Thomas, C.S. and Hrebenar, R.J. (1995) 'The Interest Group-Party Connection: Towards a Systematic Understanding', paper presented at the Annual Meeting of the American Political Science Association, Chicago.

Thomson, S., Stancich, L. and Dickson, L. (1998) 'Gun Control and Snowdrop', *Parliamentary Affairs*, 51, 329–44.

Tivey, L. (1974) 'The Politics of the Consumer' in R.Kimber and J.J. Richardson (eds), *Pressure Groups in Britain* (London: Dent).

Toke, D. (1997) 'Power and Environmental Pressure Groups', *Talking Politics*, 9 (2), 107–15.

Trade Association Forum (1998) *Directory* (London: Trade Association Forum).

Truman, D. (1951) *The Governmental Process* (New York: Alfred A. Knopf).

Verwey, W. (1994) 'HDTV and Phillips: Stepping Stone or Snake Pit?' in R.H.Pedler and M.P.C.M. van Schendelen (eds), *Lobbying the European Union* (Aldershot: Dartmouth).

Visser, J. and Ebbinghaus, B. (1992) 'Making the Most of Diversity? European Integration and Transnational Organization of Labour' in J. Greenwood, J.R. Grote and K. Ronit (eds), *Organised Interests in the European Community* (London: Sage).

van Waarden, F. (1991) 'Wartime Economic Mobilisation and State–Business Relations: A Comparison of Nine Countries' in W. Grant, J. Nekkers and F. van Waarden (eds), *Organising Business for War* (Oxford: Berg).

Walker, J.L. (1991) *Mobilizing Interest Groups in America* (Ann Arbor: University of Michigan Press).

Ward, S. (1993) 'Thinking Global, Acting Local? British Local Authorities and Their Environmental Plans', *Environmental Politics*, 2, 453–78.

Weale, A. (1992) *The New Politics of Pollution* (Manchester: Manchester University Press).

Webb, P.D. (1995) 'Are British Political Parties in Decline?' *Party Politics*, 1, 299–322.

Webster, R. (1998) 'Environmental Collective Action: Stable Patterns of Cooperation and Issue Alliances at the European Level' in J. Greenwood and M. Aspinwall (eds), *Collective Action in the European Union* (London: Routledge).

Wendon, B. (1994) 'British Trade Union Responses to European Integration', *Journal of European Public Policy*, 1, 243–61.

Wessels, W. (1997) 'The Growth and Differentiation of Multi-Level Networks: a Corporatist Mega-Bureaucracy or an Open City' in H. Wallace and A.R. Young (eds), *Participation and Policy-Making in the European Union* (Oxford: Clarendon).

Westergaard, J. and Resler, H. (1976) *Class in a Captialist Society* (Harmondsworth: Penguin).

White, D. (1997) 'Dealing with Trade Associations: a Two-Way Process' in R.J.Bennett (ed.), *Trade Associations in Britain and Germany: Responding to Internationalisation and the EU* (London: Anglo-German Foundation).

Whiteley, P., Seyd, P. and Richardson, J. (1994) *True Blues: the Politics of Conservative Party Membership* (Oxford: Clarendon).

Whiteley, P.F. and Winyard, S.J. (1987) *Pressure for the Poor* (London: Methuen).

Wilkinson, D. (1998) 'The Day I Fell Out of Love with Blair', *New Statesman*, 7 August 1998, 9–10.

Wilkinson, P. with Schofield, J. (1994) *Warrior: One Man's Environmental Crusade* (Cambridge: Lutterworth).

Wilson, D. (1984) *Pressure: The A to Z of Campaigning in Britain* (London: Heinemann).

Wilson, H. (1974) *The First Labour Government 1964–70* (Harmondsworth: Penguin).

World Bank (1990) *How the World Bank Works with Non-Governmental Organizations*, Washington DC: World Bank.

Young, A.R. (1998) 'European Consumer Groups: Multiple Levels of Governance and Multiple Logics of Collective Action' in J. Greenwood and M. Aspinwall (eds), *Collective Action in the European Union* (London: Routledge).

Young, S.C. (1993) *The Politics of the Environment* (Manchester: Baseline).

Index

250

Index